Marvin E. Wolfgang

May 18, 1988

From Boy to Man,
from Delinquency to Crime

From Boy to Man,
from Delinquency to Crime

Marvin E. Wolfgang

Terence P. Thornberry

Robert M. Figlio

The University of Chicago Press   Chicago and London

MARVIN E. WOLFGANG is professor of criminology and of law and director of the Sellin Center for Studies in Criminology and Criminal Law at the University of Pennsylvania. TERENCE P. THORNBERRY is dean and professor in the School of Criminal Justice at the State University of New York, Albany. ROBERT M. FIGLIO is associate professor of legal studies and criminology and associate director of the Sellin Center for Studies in Criminology and Criminal Law at the University of Pennsylvania.

THE UNIVERSITY OF CHICAGO PRESS, CHICAGO 60637
THE UNIVERSITY OF CHICAGO PRESS, LTD., LONDON

© 1987 by The University of Chicago
All rights reserved. Published 1987
Printed in the United States of America

96 95 94 93 92 91 90 89 88 87   54321

Library of Congress Cataloging in Publication Data

From boy to man, from delinquency to crime.

  (Studies in crime and justice)
  Bibliography: p.
  Includes index.
    1. Juvenile delinquents—United States—Longitudin.ıl
studies.   2. Crime and criminals—United States—
Longitudinal studies.   I. Wolfgang, Marvin E.,
1924–   .   II. Thornberry, Terence P.   III. Figlio,
Robert M.   IV. Series.
HV9104.F76   1987   364.3'6'0973   87-10776
ISBN 0-226-90555-1

Juvenile delinquency

Contents

Figures

Tables

Matrices

Preface

Thorsten Sellin, our mentor, first suggested we follow into adulthood a sample of males born in 1945, to trace the link between delinquency and criminality. In 1963 Saleem Shah, chief of the Section on Crime and Delinquency of the National Institutes of Health, encouraged our proposal, and his peer review committee recommended support of this research, which was financed by National Institute of Mental Health grant #5 RO1 MH13664-05-06 and resulted in the publication of *Delinquency in a Birth Cohort* in 1972.

The files of the original 9,945 members of this cohort were destroyed in a huge fire on 8 January 1968. But Albert Cardarelli, now a professor at the University of Massachusetts at Boston, then a Ph.D. candidate at the University of Pennsylvania, had already selected a random, stratified sample of 975 subjects for a postjuvenile study. That sampling by Cardarelli made possible this follow-up study, for his computer file of names and cases was not burned. It was, fortunately, in the back of his car.

At that time the University of Pennsylvania was insured by the Insurance Company of North America (INA), which had participated in the insurance claims of the *Titanic*. INA informed us that they had never before faced the difficulty of compensating for research losses. On the recommendation of Lloyd Ohlin, who evaluated the loss, INA compensated the Center for Studies in Criminology and Criminal Law for all we requested, and the Center has been most grateful to them.

Years went by as we slowly located a subset of the sample, supervised the interview process, and, with the generous cooperation of the Federal Bureau of Investigation, checked the criminal records of the sample of 975 up to their attaining age 30.

As social science researchers know, tracking specific individuals over time is a difficult task, especially if the last known address is at age 18 and one tries to locate them when they are 25. Former delinquents were much harder to find than nondelinquents. Perhaps one of the virtues of our society is one's capacity to remain anonymous, to escape detection. In any case, the 567 persons we located were cooperative and were willing to undergo nearly two hours of interviewing.

We believe this study is among the first to have the three following ingredients on the same subjects: official police arrest data; unofficial, self-report offense data; and victimization data. Moreover, all three data sets are temporally based so we can trace the progression of criminal involvement over time.

The chapters that have no names attached were written by the three of us, who conducted the study and supervised dissertations. The chapters bearing specific names were written by graduate students and are generally abbreviated versions of their doctoral dissertations.

Beyond these attributions, we wish to acknowledge the very important contributions made to this study by Elaine Silverman and Rhoda Piltch, former administrative officers of the Sellin Center for Studies in Criminology and Criminal Law, and to Selma Pastor, editor and librarian of the Center's Lipman Criminology Library, for her enormous, prodigious, and exquisitely careful work. Mark Keintz, Erica Ginsburg, and Robyn Mace also assisted at various stages.

In any large-scale research like this there are computer programmers, such as Frank C. Praeger, whose acumen and expertise went far beyond technical assistance. And a large group of former graduate students, in addition to the named contributors, made major commitments to the work: Christopher Armstrong, Joel P. Eigen, Gila Hayim, Joseph E. Jacoby, Susan Katzenelson, Satyanshu K. Mukherjee, Sheila O'Malley, Giannina Rikoski, Tania Sapko, Robert A. Silverman, Neil A. Weiner, Charles Wellford, Jocelyn Young, Beatrix Siman Zakhari, and the late Frank J. Cannavale, Jr. We are grateful to all of them.

Longitudinal research makes special demands on a staff. It requires long-term involvement in order to maintain continuity of task and attention to the problems of detail. The research reported here has been blessed with such commitment. Any group that undertakes longitudinal research—especially birth cohort research—must be aware of this need and deserves rewards for loyalty. We hereby acknowledge the dedication of all those who contributed.

Delinquency in a Birth Cohort was published by the University of Chicago Press in 1972. We are thankful to the staff of the Press for shepherding this manuscript through editing and production. We appreciate the endorsement that Franklin Zimring, current editor of the Studies in Crime and Justice series, gave to the study.

We are convinced that longitudinal studies in criminology and criminal justice, like some major medical research, constitute the best means available for obtaining data that permit causal inferences about past and future behavior. The debt owed, not only by this study but by future criminological work, to Thorsten Sellin is incalculable.

1   Introduction

Delinquency in a Birth Cohort (Wolfgang, Figlio, and Sellin 1972) described and analyzed the official delinquent careers of the Philadelphia birth cohort of 1945 as those careers unfolded across the maturational process. From the vantage point of a longitudinal design, the study examined the correlates of delinquency as well as such dynamic issues as the age of onset of delinquency, the age distribution of delinquent events, the probability that young males would become delinquent, and changes in the type and seriousness of delinquent acts committed across the offenders' adolescent years.

Delinquency in a Birth Cohort was the first American birth cohort study in the area of criminology and, along with a few European studies, one of the first of its kind. Many of its findings challenged traditional notions about delinquent careers based on cross-sectional research. Given the unique stance of that study in American research on juvenile delinquency, two subsequent studies continued these lines of research. The first study was a follow-up that traced a 10 percent sample of the original 1945 cohort through adulthood to age 30. The second study replicated the original cohort design and examined the Philadelphia birth cohort of 1958, extending the analysis to females as well. The present volume reports the findings of the follow-up study and investigates the delinquent and adult criminal careers of the sample drawn from the 1945 birth cohort.

The Original Study

We begin this investigation by summarizing the design and central findings of the parent study. The original study collected information on all males born in 1945 who were residents of the city of Philadelphia from at least their tenth to their eighteenth birthdays.[1] The information the analysis was based on came primarily from two sources: the records of the school systems of Philadelphia—including the public, parochial, and private schools—and those of the Juvenile Aid Division of the Philadelphia Police Department. Although the data gleaned from those records were adequate to define the cohort and to describe in detail the nature of their delinquent careers, their being officially recorded police contacts imposed certain interpretive limitations. However, the records provided basic sociodemographic information on each subject as well as information on

1. More detailed information on the definition of membership in this cohort is provided in chapter 2.

the sequence, nature, and types of police contacts and arrests.[2] The longitudinal design enhanced the analytic powers of the data and led to a variety of interesting findings.

The analysis was divided into two approaches: descriptive and inferential. In the descriptive section we examined the incidence and prevalence of delinquency, relating background variables available for analysis to various measures of delinquency. In the inferential section, we adopted a dynamic stance toward the data and examined the delinquent careers of the subjects across time, especially in relation to the probability of committing certain types of offenses.

Of the 9,945 boys who were members of the 1945 cohort, 3,475, or 35 percent, were officially recorded as delinquents; that is, they had been arrested or detained by the police once or more before their eighteenth birthdays. All told, the delinquent members of the cohort accounted for 10,214 arrests, or an average of 2.9 arrests per delinquent. A variety of school and social background variables were related to the variable of delinquent status (delinquent versus nondelinquent), and the sociodemographic variables of race and socioeconomic status (SES) were found to be related most strongly and consistently to delinquent involvement. For example, by age 18, 50 percent of the nonwhites and 45 percent of the lower SES subjects had been labeled delinquent, compared with the base rate of 35 percent for all the subjects. Although some of the school variables were strongly related to delinquent activity, none of them surpassed the variables of race and SES in accounting for the distributions observed.[3]

When boys defined as delinquent in the police records were examined in more detail, the distribution of their delinquent acts conformed closely to an inverted J curve. Of the 3,475 delinquents, 46 percent had been arrested only once before their eighteenth birthdays, and 54 percent could be classified as recidivists. Moreover, the recidivists could be broken down further into nonchronic and chronic offenders. The 1,235 nonchronic recidivists constituted 35.6 percent of the delinquents and 12.4 percent of the entire cohort. The 627 chronic recidivists, who were arrested five times or more, accounted for 18 percent of the delinquents and only 6 percent of the entire cohort.

The chronic offenders committed a far greater share of offenses than their distribution in the population would have suggested. Constituting only 6 percent of the entire cohort, they accounted for a total of 5,305 offenses, or 51.9 percent of all of the cohort's offenses. This finding was the first major discovery of the original cohort analysis. Although it had long been known that there was a relatively small group of serious, habitual offenders in the general population, it was not

2. In this chapter and in subsequent discussions of delinquency as defined by police records, we use police contact and arrest interchangeably as measures of delinquency.

3. Jensen (1976), in a secondary analysis of these data, claimed that academic achievement level was, in fact, more important than race for explaining delinquency outcomes. A reanalysis of the original data, however, suggested that the two variables were of approximately equal importance and that racial differences did not dissipate when achievement level was held constant. Moreover, Jensen failed to note that the variable of achievement level was available for only 3,849 of the 9,945 subjects, thereby limiting its utility in subsequent analyses vis-à-vis the variables of race and SES, which were available for all subjects.

known that the chronic offenders constituted such a small proportion while accounting for so much of the offensive behavior.

When we related the background variables to recidivism and to chronic offender status, the earlier results were replicated. That is, the nonwhites and lower SES subjects were more likely to be recidivists. Moreover, the two variables interacted such that the lower SES nonwhites had the highest rates of offensive behavior of any group within the cohort.

When the analysis shifted from the incidence of delinquent acts to their seriousness, findings were similar. Again, the overall distribution was J shaped such that most offenses were relatively trivial and proportionately fewer were very serious. For example, using the Sellin-Wolfgang seriousness scale, 30 percent of the offenses produced a score of 1, and 50 percent generated scores of less than 40. On the other hand, only 3 percent of the offenses had seriousness scores of 500 or more. Hence, most of the offenses for which these subjects were arrested were of relatively low seriousness. We should note, however, that a sizable minority of the offenses included within the study domain were very serious; for example, 2,728 of the arrests were for index offenses as defined by the *Uniform Crime Reports* (*UCR*).

The sociodemographic variables of race and SES were related to the seriousness of offenses in the expected direction. The mean seriousness score by race for all offenses committed was 92.9 for the whites and 130.8 for the nonwhites. Similarly, the mean seriousness score for the higher SES subjects was 93.3, compared with 121.2 for the lower SES subjects.

The descriptive analysis of the delinquent careers of the 1945 birth cohort had a number of intriguing outcomes. The first was that the simple rate of delinquency was considerably higher than previous estimates based on cross-sectional studies. Overall, 35 percent of the cohort members were official delinquents. This base rate escalated to 50 percent for the nonwhites, to 45 percent for the lower SES subjects, and to 53 percent for the nonwhite, lower SES subjects. The second major finding concerned the chronic offenders. Although constituting only a relatively small proportion of both the cohort population (6 percent) and the delinquent subset (18 percent), they accounted for over half of all the arrests recorded by age 18.

The longitudinal design of cohort studies provides an ideal setting for examining the relationship between age and dependent variables. In general, the age distribution for all the offenses was straightforward and conformed to expectations based on previous cross-sectional research. Very few offenses, only 5.7 percent, were committed when the subjects were age 10 or under. From age 11 to age 13 there was a steady increase in the proportion of offenses committed, and following that there was a sharp rise between ages 14 and 16. In fact, the modal age for offense commission in the cohort was 16, when 24.8 percent of all of the offenses were committed. At age 17, however, there was a sharp decrease; this age group accounted for only 16 percent of the offenses.

Although the age distribution at which offenses are committed is of interest, such distributions do not exhaust the analytic capacities of the cohort data. In-

3

deed, they could be generated from cross-sectional data as well. To exploit the longitudinal design more fully, we turned to an examination of the age of onset of delinquency and its relationship to other characteristics of delinquent careers, including the number of offenses committed and the seriousness of those offenses.

The distribution for the age of onset of delinquency tended to mirror the age distribution at which offenses were committed. That is, the probability of becoming a first offender increased gradually from age 7 through age 11, increased rapidly from age 12 through age 16, and dropped sharply at age 17. Overall, the probability of becoming an official delinquent increased exponentially, and a second-degree curve was found to fit the data more closely than a simple linear pattern. The mean age of onset was found to be 14.4 years, and the modal category was 16.

Age of onset was related to the length of the delinquent career. Cohort members who began their delinquent activity at younger ages accumulated a greater number of offenses than subjects who began their careers later. Although age of onset was related to the total number of offenses committed, it was not related strongly and consistently to their seriousness. On the average, subjects with earlier ages of onset did not commit more serious offenses than those who entered the delinquent category later.

After examining the age distributions of delinquency, the analysis in *Delinquency in a Birth Cohort* then considered the dynamic process of delinquent conduct. More specifically, it examined changes over time in the types and seriousness of delinquent acts committed by members of the cohort.

Five offense types were used: index offenses, which involved personal injury, theft, property destruction, and any combination of those elements, and nonindex offenses, which did not involve injury, theft, or property damage. The analysis investigated the pattern of offenses across time and followed the career of each delinquent from the first to the ninth offense committed, looking primarily at the stability of those offense transitions. Was the probability of committing a particular type of offense influenced by the number and type of previous offenses committed, or was this probability relatively constant and stable across the delinquent careers?

Although the analysis of these data was complex, the results can be summarized briefly. In general, the transition probabilities from the first to the ninth offense committed by members of the cohort were found to conform closely to the requirements of a first-order Markov process. That is, the probabilities were relatively constant across time, and the type of offense did not vary substantially by the number of offenses previously committed. As Wolfgang, Figlio, and Sellin stated: "We are also suggesting that the offense history up to the immediately previous offenses, or prior to the $k - 1$st offense, has no bearing on the observed probabilities of committing the kth offense. That is, knowledge of the number and type of offenses prior to the $k - 1$st gives no aid in predicting the type of the next offense" (1972, 206). To state the issue somewhat differently, the probability of committing a particular type of offense, say a nonindex offense, was approximately the same regardless of which of the subject's offenses, from the second to the ninth, was examined.

The conclusion that the data conformed to a first-order Markov process allowed us to estimate a parent or generating matrix. This matrix, which is the average of each of the observed matrices, reflected the underlying probabilistic process that led to the observed offense transitions. The probabilities contained in the matrix indicated that offenders were most likely to commit a nonindex offense, regardless of the type of $k - 1$st offense; were most likely to desist from further offenses; and then were likely to commit, in descending order, theft offenses, combination offenses, injury offenses, and finally, damage offenses.

In addition to examining the transition probabilities, the analysis also allowed us to investigate offense specialization (i.e., the tendency to repeat the same type of offense across time). In general, however, we found little evidence of such specialization. The probability of moving to a particular offense after committing the same type of offense was not substantially elevated above the comparison probabilities.

We also examined the increasing seriousness of offenses over time. This issue is complementary to that of specialization and suggests that delinquent offenses may become increasingly serious even though the type of offense does not change as delinquent careers unfold. The results of the analysis, however, again suggested that delinquent careers were relatively stable. Although each offense committed tended to be somewhat more serious than the previous one, the increase in seriousness scores was small. In general, with the exception of injury offenses, for which there was a tendency of increasing seriousness, the offenses these subjects committed did not become more serious as their delinquent careers developed.

Finally, *Delinquency in a Birth Cohort* examined the way the 10,214 police contacts were officially handled by the juvenile justice system. In both the original and subsequent analyses of these data (Thornberry 1973, 1979) the seriousness of the offenses committed and the number of previous offenses in each offender's career were found to be related most strongly to the severity of the penalty received. Nevertheless, the nonwhites and lower SES subjects received more severe penalties than the whites and higher SES subjects even when seriousness and prior record were held constant.

Although these findings were intriguing, there was a sense in which they were incomplete and told only part of the tale of the delinquent careers of this cohort. Given the decentralized record keeping in our country, the task of defining the cohort and collecting its members' entire official records placed severe limits on the extensiveness of the data available for analysis. Thus the findings reported in *Delinquency in a Birth Cohort* seemed to be as important for the questions they raised as for those they answered. Because of this situation the follow-up project was initiated to extend the analysis and to provide closure to the investigation of the criminal activity of the birth cohort of 1945.

The original analysis was limited in two ways—in time and in the types of data available. Temporally, the analysis ended at age 18, when offenders in Philadelphia become adult offenders rather than juvenile delinquents. Although this was a logical point at which to end the first study, we were aware that the selection of the eighteenth birthday as the end of the data collection period was arbitrary. Criminal behavior, like any other form of human behavior, is continuous and develops independent of legal boundaries such as the switch from juvenile to adult criminal status. Thus a number of questions were raised by the original analysis that could not be answered within that analysis.

For example, we have seen that the age distribution of both offenses and the age of onset of delinquency increased through the first sixteen years of the subjects' lives and then dropped rather substantially during their seventeenth year. What the original data could not determine, of course, was whether that drop would go on or whether the general upward trend observed from age 12 would continue through the early twenties. Similarly, the delinquent behavior of these subjects was shown to conform to a first-order Markov process in which the offense transitions were independent of time and there was little evidence of offense specialization. It is possible that such a pattern of behavior would obtain only during the more volatile juvenile years and that offense specialization would increase considerably and offense transitions would become more patterned for adult offenders. The juvenile data also indicated only slight increments in the severity of offenses committed across time, and relatively trivial offenses dominated both the earlier and the later stages of the delinquent careers. Again, the original study was unable to determine whether the uniformity of offense seriousness observed during the juvenile years would continue into adulthood. Because of these and similar questions, the follow-up study was designed to collect data on the cohort between ages 18 and 30 that were comparable to the data collected up to age 18.

The second area in which the original study was limited concerned the types and extensiveness of data available for analysis. Those data came entirely from official records and did not exhaust the range of information that is relevant for criminological investigation. Unofficial data that told the subjects' versions of their life stories were also important. There was no information on self-reported delinquency, nor did we know if the subjects had been victims of crime as well as offenders. Moreover, attitudinal data that would indicate the subjects' perceptions about family, education, occupational history, their contacts with juvenile and criminal justice systems, and the like were absent.

Because of these limitations in the original study, the follow-up design not only extended the analysis temporally but also extended the range and type of information available for analysis. Interviews were conducted with the subjects so that information on the topics raised above could be collected and incorporated into the analysis. The following chapters describe in detail the design and methodology of the follow-up study and display the results of its analysis.

2   Methodological Issues

The original study, upon which the present one is based, examined the delinquent careers of the Philadelphia birth cohort of 1945. The subjects of that study were all males born in 1945 who resided in the city of Philadelphia at least from their tenth to their eighteenth birthdays. The rationale for defining the cohort in this manner and the operational steps taken to determine membership in it have been described in detail elsewhere (Wolfgang, Figlio, and Sellin 1972, 27–38) and need only be summarized here.

In brief, we searched the files of the three school systems of Philadelphia (public, private, and parochial), the Philadelphia Police Department, and the Selective Service System for the names of all males born in 1945. From this master list of 14,313 potential subjects, we excluded the 4,368 who did not reside in the city for the entire criterion period, that is, from their tenth to their eighteenth birthdays. In the end, the cohort numbered 9,945 subjects, who were studied in *Delinquency in a Birth Cohort* and who constitute the universe from which we drew the sample under study here.

The Sample

This sample was originally selected for a study of middle-class delinquency (Cardarelli 1973), and as such it reflects that interest. But because of the careful and detailed way it was chosen, it in fact constitutes a 10 percent random sample of the entire cohort with no demonstrable biases.[1]

In selecting the sample Cardarelli began by stratifying the 9,945 members of the entire birth cohort into socioeconomic groupings. For reasons described by Wolfgang, Figlio, and Sellin (1972, 47), SES was measured by using appropriate data from the census tract where each subject lived. To create the strata necessary for drawing the sample, therefore, 337 census tracts[2] of Philadelphia were split into quartiles according to median family income. To refine the measure of SES, the educational level of the census tracts was also determined, and the tracts were again divided into quartiles, this time according to the median years of education completed for persons age 25 or older. Thus there were two quartile groupings of the 337 census tracts.

1. For a detailed discussion of the sampling design, see Cardarelli (1973, 27–48).
2. In actuality there were 370 census tracts, but for a variety of reasons 33 were excluded from the analysis. See Cardarelli (1973, 35) for a discussion of this point.

The next step combined the two quartile distributions to examine the overlap between the two measures of SES and to identify tracts that were inconsistent relative to these two variables. The results of this exercise demonstrated a striking consistency. Fifty-seven percent of the tracts were in the same quartile, and 93 percent were in the same or adjoining quartiles on the two measures. In general, therefore, the income and educational levels of the census tracts were highly consistent.

A detailed examination of the census tracts in which the two variables were discordant indicated that ten were, in fact, anomalies and not representative of the socioeconomic structure of the city as a whole. Because of this difference and because those tracts contained too few subjects to create separate strata, they were eliminated, "leaving a sampling frame composed of 327 tracts representing 1,930,672 inhabitants or 96.41 percent of the total population of Philadelphia" (Cardarelli 1973, 39).

The next step in the selection of the sample distributed the 9,945 cohort subjects into the strata created by the income and education groupings, using the last known address for each subject, which was the address on file as of the subject's eighteenth birthday. "Upon completion of this procedure, 9,780 subjects, or 98.34 percent of the total age cohort, fell into the 327 tracts making up our sampling frame" (43). Fifty-four percent of the subjects were in strata in which the traits were in the same quartile on income and education, and 97 percent were in strata in which the tracts were in the same or adjoining quartiles.

Once the subjects were distributed into the various strata, the final step was to take a 10 percent systematic random sample within each stratum. After randomly choosing a starting number in each of the strata, every tenth element was selected, yielding 978 subjects for the follow-up sample. These subjects were representative of the entire birth cohort, which is not surprising given the relatively large size of the sample. Although we will demonstrate the representativeness of the sample with respect to specific issues at a number of points in the analysis, it is worthwhile to compare the cohort and the follow-up sample at this juncture on a number of basic demographic characteristics and offense variables (see table 2.1).

The differences between the sample and the population it was drawn from were virtually nil for all these variables. For example, the whites constituted 70.8 percent of the cohort and 71.4 percent of the sample, and nonwhites constituted 29.2 percent and 28.6 percent, respectively. The similarity for the variable of SES was equally impressive. In terms of delinquency variables, the sample and the population were also nearly identical. The proportion of the subjects who could be classified as delinquents, as recidivists (two or more offenses), or as chronic offenders (five or more offenses) varied by only one percentage point for the two groups. Finally, we examined the mean number of offenses committed per offender and the average seriousness scores of the offenses committed. The cohort members had committed an average of 2.9 offenses by their eighteenth birthdays, while the sample offenders had committed an average of 3.1 offenses. The mean seriousness score of the offenses committed by the cohort offenders

TABLE 2.1 Comparison of Cohort Subjects and Sample Subjects for Selected Variables

Variables	Entire Cohort	10% Sample
Race		
% White	70.8	71.4
% Nonwhite	29.2	28.6
SES		
% Low	46.1	46.7
% High	53.9	53.3
Delinquency status		
% Delinquent	34.9	35.4
% Recidivist	18.7	19.3
% Chronic	6.3	7.5
Mean number of offenses per offender	2.9	3.1
Mean seriousness score per offense	114.2	110.9

was 114.2, compared with 110.9 for the sample offenders. Thus the representativeness of the sample with respect to these basic demographic and offense variables was evident.

Tables 2.2 and 2.3 compare the cohort offenders and the sample offenders with respect to two basic bivariate relationships. In table 2.2 we see that there was little difference in the relationship between race and delinquency status across the two groups. For both the cohort and the sample, whites were more likely to be one-time offenders; the two racial groups were equally likely to be recidivists; and nonwhites were more likely to be chronic offenders. Moreover, percentages within racial and offender status categories were of the same relative magnitude for the cohort and the sample.

Table 2.3 examines the relationship between SES and delinquency status, and the substantive conclusions that can be drawn from the data are the same for both the cohort and the sample. The low SES subjects were less likely to be one-time offenders and were far more likely to be chronic offenders. Again we note that the proportions were of the same relative magnitude.

Although this review is not a complete assessment of the representativeness of

TABLE 2.2 Comparison of Cohort Offenders and Sample Offenders for the Relationship between Race and Delinquency Status

Delinquency Status	Whites		Nonwhites	
	Cohort %	Sample %	Cohort %	Sample %
One-time	55.0	51.0	34.5	37.6
Recidivist (2–4)	34.6	35.3	36.8	30.5
Chronic (5+)	10.4	13.7	28.6	31.9
Total	100.0	100.0	100.0	100.0
(N)	(2,019)	(204)	(1,456)	(141)

TABLE 2.3   Comparison of Cohort Offenders and Sample Offenders for the Relationship between SES and Delinquency Status

Delinquency Status	Lower SES		Higher SES	
	Cohort %	Sample %	Cohort %	Sample %
One-time	39.0	41.3	57.2	51.8
Recidivist (2–4)	23.5	30.6	32.7	37.4
Chronic (5+)	37.5	28.1	10.1	10.8
Total	100.0	(100.0)	100.0	100.0
(N)	(2,056)	(206)	(1,419)	(139)

the 10 percent sample, a more detailed presentation of the data would not alter the conclusion. Moreover, comparisons of the sample and the entire cohort will continue in the data analysis sections of this work when we attempt to extend to age 30 the types of analyses conducted in the earlier work. As will be seen in later sections that examine more complex relationships such as the Markovian nature of delinquent careers, the representativeness of the sample was robust, even for multivariate purposes.

Data Collection

Once the sample had been selected for the follow-up study, the research agenda turned to collecting data on each of the subjects. This task was conducted at two stages—when the subjects were 26 years of age and again when they were 30. For age 26 both official arrest and interview data were collected, whereas for age 30 only official arrest data were collected. Because the procedure for collecting official data was essentially the same for both periods, we can discuss them together, after which we shall discuss the interviews.

For both age 26 and age 30 the project staff searched the records of the Philadelphia Police Department to collect all available information on the criminal histories of the follow-up subjects. Because we had detailed information on each of the subjects, including full name, date of birth, race, sex, and past addresses, it was relatively easy to determine whether the subjects had official records. For those who did, we transcribed information on each arrest so that the project had, for each subject, a complete history of all the arrests that had occurred in Philadelphia. In addition, for age 30 the name and identifying data for each subject were sent to the FBI to augment the information collected in Philadelphia. The FBI provided "rap sheets" for all the sample members who appeared in their files, and those offenses not already uncovered in Philadelphia were added to the subjects' criminal histories. Most offenses committed by the sample members— approximately 93 percent—occurred in Philadelphia; thus the bulk of the information collected on the follow-up sample came from the files of the Philadelphia Police Department. Our discussion concentrates on that information.

At this stage of the data collection the project had information about the number of subjects arrested and the number of times they had been arrested. We next collected detailed information about each arrest from the police investigation reports that are routinely completed after arrests are made. These reports, which note the character of the offense committed and the events surrounding the crime, constituted the major source of data on the criminal careers of the followup subjects. These data were coded in a manner that paralleled the coding scheme used in *Delinquency in a Birth Cohort* (Wolfgang, Figlio, and Sellin 1972). Thus the data in this project extended the observation period for the 10 percent sample so that the delinquent and criminal careers of the sample subjects who had been arrested could be examined from early adolescence to age 30.

For each arrest we coded the following information: type of offense; date, time, and location of the offense; offender's age; information on co-offenders; information on victims; elements of the offense, including the extent of injury, theft, and property damage; seriousness of the offense as measured by the Sellin-Wolfgang scale; legal dispositions of the offense; and information on incarceration.

The second major source of information on the delinquent and criminal careers of the sample members was personal interviews conducted with the subjects at age 26. These interviews provided additional and alternative perspectives, for the behavior of the subjects was seen not from the viewpoint of official agencies of the criminal justice system but through the eyes of the subjects themselves. We hope this dual perspective can produce a richer understanding of factors associated with criminal behavior. In the interviews we collected information on a variety of topics and life experiences; for the present we shall describe only the general topics that were included.[3] The measurement of the variables is discussed in the data analysis section of this book.

Although the interview covered a wide range of topics, two general principles guided construction of the items. We attempted, whenever possible, to avoid long-term retrospective questions, especially of an attitudinal sort. For example, we posed no questions about a subject's early family life and his satisfaction or dissatisfaction with it. The obvious methodological reasons for avoiding such questions were variations in recall and memory distortion. Nevertheless, there were some behavioral areas—for instance, victimization experiences—in which we asked for long-term recall. An assessment of the effects of recall on these data will be presented in chapter 13.

The second principle is related to the longitudinal form of cohort studies. Because we had information on the entire criminal careers of the sample subjects from adolescence to adulthood, including the time intervals between arrests, it was important that the data collected in the interviews also preserve temporal order. Thus, whenever possible, questions were posed so that we could determine *when* rather than if a certain event had occurred. For example, we were less concerned with the subject's marital status than with his marital history, including the dates of all marriages, separations, divorces, and remarriages.

With these two points in mind we can outline the types of data collected in the

---

3. A copy of the interview schedule is available upon request.

interviews. All interviewed subjects were asked questions in the following areas: marital history, both legal and common law, including the number of children fathered; educational history, including opinions about and satisfaction with their education; occupational history since leaving high school; gang membership; contacts with the police that did not result in arrest, including data on the events surrounding the first such contact; victimization experiences before age 12, between ages 12 and 18, and after age 18; and self-reported data on criminal behavior before and after age 18.

Another series of questions looked into the subjects' arrest histories. The first question screened the subjects by asking if they had ever been arrested. Those who said they had were asked about their first arrest and, if they had been arrested more than once, their last arrest. The other questions collected information on event characteristics such as the type of offense, its victims, location of the offense, data on co-offenders, extent to which the event was planned (see Erez 1979), information on where and when the arrest occurred and how the police treated the subject, extent to which the subject became involved in the judicial and correctional systems as a result of the offense, and extent to which the individual's self-image and public image changed as a consequence of the offense and the way he was treated. The questions varied somewhat for offenses that occurred before and after age 18, but the same basic issues were covered for both time periods.

The Interview Process

In many respects the interviewing was the most difficult stage of the entire project. We attempted to locate and interview 975 men 26 years old who had never been approached by the project before and whose last known addresses were those recorded in the files of the original study. These addesses were invariably the last addresses of the subjects' families as recorded in the school files. Thus at the outset we were confronted with two sources of mobility that occurred over an eight-year period: the mobility of the families either within or outside Philadelphia and the mobility of the subjects away from their parental families. For the ages at issue here, 18 to 26, such mobility is enormous, for during this period young men establish their independence from their parents, and mobility associated with military service, higher education, marriage, new employment, and so forth is at its greatest. The result, of course, was that the addresses on file for many subjects were outdated.

The first step was to update the files as much as possible. Unfortunately there was no central register, such as the school system, to turn to for addresses. Therefore we pieced together information from as many sources as possible before the interviewers were sent into the field. Among the sources examined were the files of the Selective Service System; the Social Service Registry of Philadelphia, which is a central repository of information on all clients seeking assistance from social service agencies; the Philadelphia Gas Company, whose billing addresses were searched for the family names of interest; motor vehicle registrations for driver's licenses; and the records of state and local prisons. In the end we were able to update addresses for many of our subjects and, for some, to locate the current addresses. For many others, however, we succeeded only in adding addresses to the subjects' files, each of which might be the correct one.

At this stage we had addresses for all the subjects but in most cases had little or no way of assessing their accuracy or deciding which were most recent. The project, therefore, sent a letter to each subject (some were sent more than one at different addresses) on the letterhead of a social agency—the Council for Urban Concern. One purpose of the letter was to sensitize the subjects to citizens' responsibility to do something about urban problems such as poverty and crime, even if that "something" consisted only of responding to questionnaires and interviews conducted by responsible researchers. The primary purpose, though, was to help update our address files. The mailing envelopes were marked "address correction requested." When letters bearing that phrase cannot be delivered, the United States Postal Service will provide, for a modest fee, any forwarding addresses they have in their records. These additional addresses were, of course, added to the files. When letters were returned with no forwarding addresses, the original addresses were moved to a "backup" category, and an interviewer was sent there only if other addresses for the subjects proved barren. When letters were not returned, those addresses were considered the most appropriate to start with.

Once the address files were as complete as possible, the project staff hired and trained full-time interviewers. The training consisted of orientation sessions and simulated interviews with colleagues, the research staff, and juvenile gang leaders involved in another project being conducted at the Criminology Center when the interviewing began. Once we were convinced that the interviewers could work accurately and reliably, they were sent into the field.

The anticipated problems with the accuracy of the addresses immediately became evident. Many of the addresses turned out to be current, and interviews were readily obtained; but many were not current. The "bad" addresses tended to fall into three major categories. Some were those of the men's families, but the subjects no longer resided there. Although these addresses provided leads for reaching the subjects, this was by no means an easy task. The families, usually the parents, were far more suspicious of the interviewers and protective of the subjects than were the men themselves. Thus we were often left with a situation in which the parents refused to provide their sons' addresses or even to relay a simple message explaining the purpose of the interviewers' visits and asking their sons to make contact with the project office at their convenience. In many cases all we could do was wait a respectable time and approach the parents again.

The second category of inaccurate addresses comprised cases in which neither the subjects nor their families still lived there. In such cases the interviewers could only ask the current residents or neighbors for forwarding addresses or even information on neighborhoods to which the subjects or their families had moved.

The third situation, even more dismal, was when houses had been abandoned or torn down and there were obviously no current residents to speak with. In those areas even neighbors were at a premium because the entire neighborhood was usually in an upheaval.

In these instances all we could do was restart the process either with the next addresses in the files or with addresses secured from neighbors. It seems best to describe this as principally detective work. The interviewers were given addresses for subjects that may or may not have been current, and they had to follow up any leads they could find, no matter how slim, until they had located the subjects or exhausted all leads. This was clearly a tedious and time-consuming process that stretched over the better part of a year. It was also not conducive to a high response rate. However, it was the reality we faced and dealt with.

Once we found a subject, the interview itself was a fairly straightforward procedure. After introducing himself and presenting his credentials, the interviewer read to the subject a standard statement describing the project in general terms and asking permission to conduct the interview. The interviewer was instructed to answer all the subject's questions as thoroughly as possible and to withhold no information.[4] Once the subject was comfortable with the situation and agreed to be interviewed, the formal interview began. The only additional request we made was that it be conducted privately, away from other family members, because there were some potentially sensitive questions.

The interview was highly structured. Once it began there was little variation from one case to another. Very few subjects discontinued an interview or refused to answer specific questions, even though they were told they could do so. At the close of the session the interviewer thanked each man for his cooperation and gave him the telephone number of the project office where he could get additional information about the survey.

Results of the Interviews

Although the project attempted to interview all 975 members of the sample, we were successful with only 567, for a completion rate of 58.2 percent. We made every effort to provide a more complete enumeration of the sample members, but problems in locating them thwarted us. Because of this situation, it is important to examine the reasons for the nonresponse rate and also to assess the bias that could result from so large a nonresponse rate.

Of the 408 subjects who were not interviewed, complete information on the factors associated with nonresponse was available for 364, or 89 percent. The most common reasons were linked to the difficulty in locating subjects. In 40.5 percent of the cases the man no longer resided at any of the addresses to which an interviewer was sent, and no forwarding address could be obtained for him or his family. In the typical case the subject and his family had moved so long ago that no current or recent address could be obtained from either the present resident or

4. One of the major purposes of the orientation session the interviewers attended was to train them in this area. In addition to providing the interviewers with general information on the project, we anticipated as many questions as we could and provided the interviewers with the information they needed to answer them.

neighbors. These efforts resulted in a dead end with no further leads. In addition to these situations, 46 houses (12.6 percent) had been razed or deserted, and no further leads were possible. These two reasons accounted for over half the cases (53.1 percent), and both were linked directly to our inability to secure current addresses at the outset.

In 66 cases (18.4 percent) the interviewer uncovered a forwarding address that showed the subject had moved away from the Philadelphia area. Although we conducted some interviews with subjects who lived within commuting distance of Philadelphia—for example, New York City—we did not try to interview most of those who had left the area.

Refusals accounted for approximately a quarter of those not interviewed and were divided between refusals by the subjects (13.7 percent) and by their families (10.5 percent). In most of the latter cases parents refused to provide their sons' current addresses.

Only 13.7 percent of the subjects refused to be interviewed. If these 50 cases are added to the 567 completed interviews, we see that the interviewers reached a total of 617 subjects, or 63.3 percent of the sample. Of the 617, 91.9 percent agreed to be interviewed. Given these data, it is clear that the nonresponse rate was due primarily to our inability to find subjects eight years after they had left high school.

Although these various reasons help explain the nonresponse rate, the paramount reason is still our inability to start with more current addresses. The interviewers thus had to spend far more time locating subjects than interviewing. The lack of central registries in this country, combined with the high mobility of urban males in their early twenties, effectively precluded a higher completion rate.

Although a substantial proportion of the subjects were not interviewed, we made every effort to find and interview the follow-up subjects. Table 2.4 presents the frequency distribution of the number of times an interviewer attempted to make contact with a noninterviewed subject. These contacts were not necessarily at the same address and, especially for the higher frequencies, probably represented attempts at a number of locations.

TABLE 2.4   Distribution of Number of Interviewer Calls for Noncompleted Interviews

Number of Interviewer Calls	Frequency	%	Cumulative %
1	111	30.5	30.5
2	60	16.5	47.0
3	44	12.1	59.1
4	51	14.0	73.1
5	32	8.8	81.9
6–9	53	14.5	96.4
10+	13	3.6	100.0
Total	364	100.0	

In 30.5 percent of the cases only one interviewer call was made because only one address was available, and it led to a dead end. For example, in 30 percent of the cases the interviewer discovered that the subject had moved away from the Philadelphia area, and no further callbacks were warranted.

With the exception of these one-call-only cases, the subjects received substantial attention. Over half were approached three or more times, and slightly more than a quarter were approached five or more times. In all, 1,635 calls were made in an effort to locate and interview these subjects, an average of 4.5 calls per subject. Eliminating the 111 subjects for whom only one call was made, the average was 6.5 calls per subject. Despite this effort, we were unsuccessful in obtaining interviews with these men.

Effects of Nonresponse

Of the 975 subjects selected for the follow-up sample, 567, or 58.2 percent, were interviewed. Given this response rate, it is important to examine the extent to which the interviewed group differed from the noninterviewed group and also how much the nonresponse rate could bias or distort the analysis. We begin by comparing the interviewed and noninterviewed groups with respect to variables that were collected in the original study and were available for both groups.

A comparison of interview status by race, table 2.5, reveals that the whites were significantly more representative than the nonwhites in the interviewed group. The response rates were 65 percent and 42 percent, respectively; and a chi-square test indicated that these differences were significant at the .001 level.

In table 2.6 we also observe a significant relationship between interview status and SES as measured by the median income of the census tract of residence. The response rate was 66 percent for those in the higher SES group and 49 percent in the lower group; the chi-square test was again significant at the .001 level.

To determine the relative strength of the relationship between these two variables and interview status, table 2.7 cross-tabulates interview status by both SES and race. When race was controlled the relationship between SES and interview status diminished considerably, although higher SES subjects were still more

TABLE 2.5 Interview Status by Race

Interview Status	Whites % (N)	Nonwhites % (N)	Total % (N)
Interviewed	65.0 (450)	42.0 (117)	58.0 (567)
Not interviewed	35.0 (246)	58.0 (162)	42.0 (408)
Total	100.0 (696)	100.0 (279)	100.0 (975)

$p < .001$.

TABLE 2.6   Interview Status by SES

Interview Status	Lower SES % (N)	Higher SES % (N)	Total % (N)
Interviewed	49.0 (222)	66.0 (345)	58.0 (567)
Not interviewed	51.0 (233)	34.0 (175)	42.0 (408)
Total	100.0 (455)	100.0 (520)	100.0 (975)

$\chi^2 = 30.3$; $p < .001$.

TABLE 2.7   Interview Status by SES and Race

Interview Status	Whites			Nonwhites		
	Lower SES % (N)	Higher SES % (N)	Total % (N)	Lower SES % (N)	Higher SES % (N)	Total % (N)
Interviewed	58.0 (121)	68.0 (329)	65.0 (450)	41.0 (101)	48.0 (16)	42.0 (117)
Not interviewed	42.0 (88)	32.0 (158)	35.0 (246)	59.0 (145)	52.0 (17)	58.0 (162)
Total	100.0 (209)	100.0 (487)	100.0 (696)	100.0 (246)	100.0 (33)	100.0 (279)

likely to be interviewed. Controlling for SES, however, we see that the strength of the relationship between race and interview status was maintained. Moreover, we note an interactive effect of these variables such that the lower SES nonwhites had the lowest interview rate and the higher SES whites had the highest.

In addition to race and SES, we examined the relationship between a number of other background variables and interview status. These analyses indicated that poor achievement and high residential mobility during high school were associated with low response rates, but the effects of these variables were not nearly as pronounced as the effects of race and SES. In general, social background variables other than race and SES did not appear to account for a significant proportion of the variation in the dependent variable of interview status.

In table 2.8 interview status is cross-tabulated by offender status, which was based on the official delinquency records collected in the original study and classified into three groups: nonoffender, single offender, and multiple offender. There was a direct and significant relationship between interview status and offender status: only 37 percent of the nonoffenders were not interviewed, compared with 56 percent of the multiple offenders.

When the control variable of SES was added to the analysis (table 2.9), the

TABLE 2.8   Interview Status by Offender Status

Interview Status	Nonoffender % (N)	Single Offender % (N)	Multiple Offender % (N)	Total % (N)
Interviewed	63.0 (402)	55.0 (84)	44.0 (81)	58.0 (567)
Not interviewed	37.0 (234)	45.0 (69)	56.0 (105)	42.0 (408)
Total	100.0 (636)	100.0 (153)	100.0 (186)	100.0 (975)

$\chi^2 = 23.6; p < .001.$

observed differences were maintained. Moreover, the relationship between offender status and interview status appeared to be stronger for those in the lower SES category. The nonresponse rate for the lower SES multiple offenders was 68 percent, compared with 30 percent for the higher SES nonoffenders.

Controlling for race, offender status again had a significant relationship with interview status, as illustrated in table 2.10. For the nonwhite offenders the response rate was 67 percent; for the whites it was 34 percent for the single offenders and 46 percent for the multiple offenders.

It should be evident from these data that we cannot assume the interviewed subjects were a representative subset of the sample. The nonwhites, lower SES subjects, and official delinquents were all underrepresented in the interviewed group. The question we must now address is whether corrective weights should be applied to counteract the effects of nonresponse.

After careful analysis we decided not to weight the interview data. The data collected in the interviews would not be used to make parametric estimates. Such estimates, when made, would be based solely on official data for all 975 subjects and, as we demonstrated earlier, the 10 percent sample was a solid representative sample of the entire cohort.

Summary

This chapter has presented a detailed description of the methodological issues that affected the follow-up study. In brief, official data were available for the entire 10 percent sample, up to age 30, and interview data were available for 58 percent of these subjects. The following chapters present the findings of our analyses of these data. We first concentrate on the official data and examine the extent to which the patterns observed in the original study were observed during the adult years as well. Following that, the analyses concentrate on the data collected in the interviews. The division between official and interview data is not rigorous, however, and in several chapters we will use data from both sources.

TABLE 2.9 Interview Status by Offender Status and SES

	Lower SES				Higher SES			
	Non-offender	Single Offender	Multiple Offender	Total	Non-offender	Single Offender	Multiple Offender	Total
Interview Status	% (N)	% (N)	% (N)	% (N)	% (N)	% (N)	% (N)	% (N)
Interviewed	54.0 (135)	52.0 (43)	37.0 (44)	49.0 (222)	70.0 (267)	59.0 (41)	56.0 (37)	66.0 (345)
Not interviewed	46.0 (117)	48.0 (40)	68.0 (76)	51.0 (233)	30.0 (117)	41.0 (29)	44.0 (29)	34.0 (175)
Total	100.0 (252)	100.0 (83)	100.0 (120)	100.0 (455)	100.0 (384)	100.0 (70)	100.0 (66)	100.0 (520)

$\chi^2 = 30.0$; $p < .001$.

TABLE 2.10 Interview Status by Offender Status and Race

	Whites				Nonwhites			
	Non-offender	Single Offender	Multiple Offender	Total	Non-offender	Single Offender	Multiple Offender	Total
Interview Status	% (N)	% (N)	% (N)	% (N)	% (N)	% (N)	% (N)	% (N)
Interviewed	67.0 (335)	66.0 (67)	54.0 (51)	65.0 (453)	51.0 (64)	33.0 (17)	33.0 (30)	42.0 (111)
Not interviewed	33.0 (164)	34.0 (35)	46.0 (44)	35.0 (243)	49.0 (61)	67.0 (34)	67.0 (61)	58.0 (156)
Total	100.0 (499)	100.0 (102)	100.0 (95)	100.0 (696)	100.0 (125)	100.0 (51)	100.0 (91)	100.0 (267)

3   Juvenile and Adult Criminal Careers

We begin the analysis of these data by describing the official juvenile and adult criminal careers of the sample subjects. In this chapter we describe socioeconomic correlates of official criminality, investigate structural similarities between delinquency and criminality, and finally, examine the effect of delinquent conduct on the frequency and types of adult offenses.

Of the 975 members of the follow-up sample, 459, or 47.1 percent, had an official recorded arrest for a nontraffic offense by age 30. As would be expected from the results of the previous studies, the offenders were more likely to be nonwhites and to be drawn from the lower SES subjects.[1] Table 3.1 presents these relationships; although the results are expected, the magnitude of the differences is striking.

TABLE 3.1   Offenders and Nonoffenders by Race and SES

| Offender Status | Race | | SES | | |
	Whites %	Nonwhites %	Lower %	Higher %	Total %
Offender	38.2	69.2	60.0	35.8	47.1
Nonoffender	61.8	30.8	40.0	64.2	52.9
Total	100.0	100.0	100.0	100.0	100.0
(N)	(696)	(279)	(455)	(520)	(975)

Overall, the probability of being arrested by age 30 was .47, a considerable increase over the .35 probability observed up to age 18. For the nonwhite subjects, however, the probability of ever being arrested between birth and age 30 was .69, compared with .38 for the white subjects. In other words, seven of every ten nonwhite males in the Philadelphia cohort would have an official record as either a delinquent or a criminal by age 30. The difference between the lower and higher SES subjects was also large, though not as large as the difference between the nonwhites and the whites. Among the lower SES males, 60 percent had an official record, compared with 35.8 percent of the higher SES males. Hence the variables of race and SES continued to play a major role in explaining the like-

---

1. Unless otherwise noted, the variable SES is measured in the same function as in the original study (Wolfgang, Figlio, and Sellin 1972, 47–52). In later chapters more detailed measures of social status position, based on the interview data, will be incorporated into the analysis.

lihood that individuals would become official offenders. Indeed, for the non-whites and to a somewhat lesser extent the lower SES subjects, official criminality is more the rule than the exception.

Although the simple comparison of offenders and nonoffenders is of interest, the variation that exists within the offender population is of greater importance to the present analysis. The rest of this chapter, therefore, will examine this internal variation.

Juvenile, Adult, and Persistent Offenders

Three groups of offenders can be identified: juvenile offenders, who committed offenses only during their juvenile years; adult offenders, who committed offenses only during adulthood; and persistent offenders, who committed offenses during both periods.[2] The analysis focuses on differences in the demographic backgrounds and in the nature of the offenses committed by these groups.

The three groups were approximately equal in size. Of the 459 offenders, 170 (37 percent) were juvenile delinquents only, 111 (24.2 percent) were adult offenders only, and 178 (38.8 percent) were persistent offenders. Although the total offender group was divided nearly evenly on this variable, this was not the case within various demographic subgroups of the sample.

Table 3.2 presents the relationship between race and offender status. The as-

TABLE 3.2   Offender Status by Race

Offender Status	Whites % (N)	Nonwhites % (N)	Total % (N)
Juvenile offenders only	47.37	22.80	37.04
	(126)	(44)	(170)
Adult offenders only	22.56	26.42	24.18
	(60)	(51)	(111)
Persistent offenders	30.08	50.78	38.78
	(80)	(98)	(178)
Total	100.00	100.00	100.00
	(266)	(193)	(459)

Likelihood ratio χ^2 = 32.15; d.f. = 2; $p < .0001$.

sociation is pronounced and, as indicated by the chi-square statistic of 32.15, is highly significant. Examining the percentages, we see that the major difference between the white and nonwhite subjects occurred in the distinction between the juvenile offender and the persistent offender groups. Of the white offenders, 47.4 percent were delinquent, having committed all their offenses before age 18, com-

2. In this section the three groups will be referred to as juvenile offenders, adult offenders, and persistent offenders. Bear in mind throughout this section that the juvenile offender group contains only offenders who committed all their offenses before age 18. Those who committed offenses both before and after age 18 are classified as members of the persistent group. The analogous situation, of course, obtains for the adult offender group.

pared with 22.8 percent of the nonwhite offenders. On the other hand, 30.1 percent of the white offenders were classified as persistent, compared with 50.8 percent of the nonwhite offenders. The two groups were very similar in terms of adult offenses: 22.6 percent of the whites and 26.4 percent of the nonwhites committed all their offenses during their adult years. In general, the offense careers of the nonwhite subjects were more likely to persist over both the juvenile and adult years, whereas the whites were more likely to be juvenile delinquents only.

The relationship between offender status and SES (table 3.3), though also significant, is not as pronounced as the relationship with race. Among the lower SES offenders 30.8 percent were classified as delinquents, compared with 46.2 percent of the higher SES offenders. At the other extreme, 45.4 percent of the lower SES offenders but only 29 percent of the higher SES offenders were persistent offenders. This situation is analogous to that found for the variable of race—the more socially disadvantaged group had a relatively high proportion of persistent offenders, while the more advantaged group had a higher proportion of only juvenile offenders.

TABLE 3.3   Offender Status by SES

Offender Status	Lower SES % (N)	Higher SES % (N)	Total % (N)
Juvenile offenders only	30.77	46.24	37.04
	(84)	(86)	(170)
Adult offenders only	23.81	24.73	24.18
	(65)	(46)	(111)
Persistent offenders	45.42	29.03	38.78
	(124)	(54)	(178)
Total	100.00	100.00	100.00
	(273)	(186)	(459)

Likelihood ratio $\chi^2 = 14.99$; d.f. $= 2$; $p < .0006$.

When race, SES, and offender status are examined jointly, however, we see that the original relationship is replicated for the variable of race but not for SES (table 3.4). The percentage differences between the whites and nonwhites were approximately the same for both the lower and higher SES offenders and tended to mirror the differences observed for the entire sample. The white offenders were most likely to be juvenile delinquents, while the nonwhite offenders were most likely to be persistent offenders, regardless of SES.

When we examine the relationship between SES and offender status, controlling for the effect of race, the situation is considerably different, however, as can be seen in table 3.4. Looking at the white offenders first, we see very little difference between the lower and higher SES groups; for example, of the lower SES offenders, 46.4 percent were delinquent and 35 percent were persistent offenders, while among the higher SES offenders 47.9 percent were delinquent and 27.2 percent were persistent offenders. For the nonwhite offenders the situation

TABLE 3.4   Offender Status by Race and SES

	Lower SES		Higher SES	
	Whites	Nonwhites	Whites	Nonwhites
	%	%	%	%
Offender Status	(N)	(N)	(N)	(N)
Juvenile offenders	46.39	22.16	47.93	29.41
only	(45)	(39)	(81)	(5)
Adult offenders only	18.56	26.70	24.85	23.53
	(18)	(47)	(42)	(4)
Persistent offenders	35.05	51.14	27.22	47.06
	(34)	(90)	(46)	(8)
Total	100.00	100.00	100.00	100.00
	(97)	(176)	(169)	(17)

is very similar. Of the lower SES offenders, 22.2 percent were delinquent and 51.1 percent were persistent offenders, while among the higher SES offenders 29.4 percent were delinquent and 47.1 percent were persistent offenders. These comparisons are substantially different from those observed when race was not held constant. In that situation the lower SES offenders were consistently more likely to be persistent offenders, and the higher SES offenders were more likely to be juvenile delinquents. Apparently that relationship was due primarily to the strong association between race and SES, for when race was held constant, the original relationship between SES and offender status almost vanished.

Table 3.5 compares these groups in terms of three central offender character-istics and shows substantial differences between them. In terms of the frequency of violations, the juvenile and adult offenders were very similar, with each group committing an average of slightly over 2 offenses. On the other hand, the per-sistent offenders committed far more offenses, an average of 8.9. This difference in frequency can also be seen in the proportion of subjects who were chronic offenders, a figure that increased from 9.4 percent for the juvenile offenders to

TABLE 3.5   Offense Characteristics of Juvenile, Adult, and Persistent Offenders

Offense Characteristics	Juvenile Offenders Only	Adult Offenders Only	Persistent Offenders
Offenses committed			
$\bar{X}$	2.11	2.28	8.93
SD	2.14	3.28	8.93
Chronic offenders			
%	9.41	17.12	70.22
Seriousness scores			
$\bar{X}$	94.36	368.38	281.08
SD	135.82	365.82	434.69

17.1 percent for the adult offenders and to 70.2 percent for the persistent offenders. With respect to the seriousness of offenses committed, however, the three groups were not ordered in the same fashion. The juvenile offenders produced the lowest mean seriousness score, 94.4, followed by the persistent offenders, 281.1, and the adult offenders, 368.4. Thus, although the persistent offenders committed the greatest number of offenses, the adult offenders committed the most serious offenses.

These results are somewhat confounded, however, by the fact that the persistent offenders committed offenses over the entire study period, while the other two groups did not. Thus, factors such as the systematic inclusion and exclusion of juvenile status offenses could distort the pattern of the relationships. To control for this effect, we compared the juvenile offenders with the juvenile portion of the persistent offenders' careers and the adult offenders with the adult portion of the persistent offenders' careers. The appropriate data are presented in table 3.6.

TABLE 3.6   Offense Characteristics and Offender Status by Time Period

Offense Characteristics	Juvenile Period		Adult Period	
	Juvenile Offenders Only	Persistent Offenders	Adult Offenders Only	Persistent Offenders
Offenses committed				
$\bar{X}$	2.11	4.01	2.28	4.92
SD	2.14		3.28	
Chronic offenders				
%	9.41	32.02	17.12	29.78
Seriousness scores				
$\bar{X}$	94.36	124.18	368.40	409.00
SD	135.82	191.57	365.58	526.10

When the data are arrayed in this fashion, it is clear that the persistent offenders exhibited the most prolonged and serious offense careers. Looking first at the juvenile period, we see that the juvenile delinquents who continued to adult offense careers had higher scores on all the offender variables. During this period the persistent offenders committed twice as many offenses, were three and one-half times as likely to become chronic offenders by age 18, and had a mean seriousness score of 124, compared with 94 for the juvenile offenders.

Comparisons during the adult years yield similar conclusions. The persistent offenders committed an average of 4.9 offenses after age 18, compared with the adult offenders' average of 2.3. Among the persistent offenders 30 percent were chronic offenders during adulthood, compared with 17 percent of the adult offenders. The result for the comparison of the seriousness of offenses reverses that observed earlier when the time period was not held constant. Here the persistent offenders committed the most serious offenses, with a mean of 409, compared with a mean of 368.4 for the adult offenders.

In general, these data are quite consistent with the results presented in *Delinquency in a Birth Cohort*. The social characteristics and offensive behavior of the persistent offenders differed markedly from those of the offenders whose careers did not extend over the entire time period. Compared with the juvenile offenders and adult offenders, the persistent offenders were more likely to be drawn from the more socially disadvantaged sections of society; that is, they were more likely to be nonwhite members of the lower SES group. They also exhibited more extensive and more serious offense careers. They committed more offenses, were more likely to be chronic offenders, and when the time period was controlled, were seen to commit more serious offenses. Thus, during their juvenile years the persistent offenders exhibited a more extensive involvement in delinquency than did the juvenile offenders, and similarly, during their adult years they exhibited a more extensive involvement in criminality than did the adult offenders.

Juvenile and Adult Offenses

The preceding discussion suggests that offenses committed by the sample after age 18, whether by adult offenders or by persistent offenders, differed in seriousness from offenses committed during the juvenile period. To examine this issue more directly, we focus on differences in the types and seriousness of offenses committed during these two time periods and examine changes over time.

We begin by analyzing the differences in the types of offenses committed by the subjects before age 18 and between ages 18 and 30. The data are presented in table 3.7 for the five offense types of nonindex, injury, theft, damage, and com-

TABLE 3.7   Offense Types during Juvenile, Adult, and Combined Periods

Offense Types	Juvenile Offenses		Adult Offenses		Combined Offenses	
	N	%	N	%	N	%
Nonindex	656	61.8	698	58.2	1,354	59.9
Injury	83	7.8	112	9.3	195	8.6
Theft	166	15.6	267	22.3	433	19.2
Damage	56	5.3	23	1.9	79	3.5
Combination	101	9.5	99	8.3	200	8.8
Total	1,062	100.0	1,199	100.0	2,261	100.0

Note: The data for these and the subsequent analyses were taken from different computer files, hence the slightly different *N*s in the categories from table to table.

bination.[3] As the percentages indicate, there were few differences between the patterns of offenses committed during the juvenile and adult years. In both periods nonindex offenses were the most common, constituting 62 percent of the juvenile offenses and 58 percent of the adult offenses. This difference is especially small when one considers that juvenile status offenses, which by definition are

---

3. Nonindex offenses are all those offenses that do not involve injury, theft, or damage components, while combination offenses involve at least two of these elements.

nonindex offenses, cannot lead to the arrest of an adult. Nevertheless, nonindex offenses appeared in almost equal proportions in the juvenile and adult periods.

Injury offenses and combination offenses were also equally distributed in the two time periods, each accounting for nearly 9 percent of the arrests. Theft offenses were more likely to occur during the adult years: 22 percent of the adult offenses involved theft, compared with 16 percent of the juvenile offenses. Damage offenses, on the other hand, were more likely to occur during the juvenile years (5.3 percent vs. 1.9 percent).

Despite these slight differences, the overwhelming conclusion to be drawn from the data presented in table 3.7 is that the distribution of offense types was almost identical for the two time periods. Regardless of age, the sample subjects were most likely to be arrested for a nonindex offense, followed in descending order by theft, injury, combination, and finally, damage offenses.

Although the types of offenses committed during the juvenile and adult years were similar, this does not mean that the quality of the offense careers was identical during the two periods. Offense careers can vary not only in terms of offense types but also in terms of seriousness, frequency, offense specialization, and other dimensions. We now turn to a consideration of these dimensions, beginning with offense seriousness.

Table 3.8 presents the mean seriousness scores for offenses committed during the juvenile, adult, and combined periods. In addition, mean scores are presented for each of the five offense types of nonindex, injury, theft, damage, and combination.

Examining the total offense row first, we see substantial differences between the three age groups. Offenses committed during the juvenile period were significantly less serious than those committed during adulthood. The average juvenile offense had a seriousness score of 111, while the average adult offense had a score of 387. The score for adult offenses was approximately three and one-half times as great as the score for juvenile offenses. As would be expected, the score for the combined period, 234, fell between these extremes.

When the five offense types are examined separately the general result is replicated. In every case the seriousness of the juvenile offenses is lower than the seriousness of the adult offenses, and the scores for the combined period fall between these extremes. The most notable difference between the juvenile and adult periods occurs for nonindex offenses. In this comparison adult offenses are, on the average, nine times more serious than juvenile offenses, the means being 278 and 32, respectively. This comparison is probably affected by the inclusion of status offenses during the juvenile period; but even so, the difference between the groups in relation to nonindex offenses is remarkable.

For the other four offense types, the adult scores are approximately two to three times greater than the juvenile scores. Juvenile and adult offenses involving injury were the most serious offenses committed, with scores of 338 and 868, respectively. Differences between juvenile and adult offenses for the other offense types are as follows: theft—adult offenses 2.2 times as serious, damage—

TABLE 3.8   Mean Seriousness Scores of Juvenile, Adult, and Combined Offenses

Offense	Juvenile	Adult	Combined
All offenses			
$\bar{X}$	110.9	387.0	233.6
SD	165.7	428.3	324.1
N	1,054	1,095	2,002
Nonindex			
$\bar{X}$	31.5	278.3	154.1
SD	63.6	338.9	267.2
N	655	682	1,313
Injury			
$\bar{X}$	338.4	868.1	642.7
SD	370.0	736.8	661.0
N	82	111	194
Theft			
$\bar{X}$	190.0	415.9	328.1
SD	114.0	304.9	268.0
N	165	258	429
Damage			
$\bar{X}$	158.1	279.7	193.5
SD	75.4	99.7	98.9
N	55	22	78
Combination			
$\bar{X}$	297.6	589.5	441.4
SD	149.4	375.0	315.4
N	100	97	198

adult offenses 1.8 times as serious, and combination—adult offenses 1.9 times as serious.

In general, the results of this analysis are quite clear. Offenses committed by adults were considerably more serious than those committed by juveniles. This assertion is true both for the entire set of offenses and for the five types of offenses analyzed. Moreover, the consistency of this finding for the offense types of injury, theft, damage, and combination demonstrates that the observed differences were not due to the exclusion of status offenses during the adult years.

We can also observe the rate of change in the seriousness of offenses committed during the criminal careers of the sample subjects. Here we are interested in determining whether offenses became more or less serious as the subjects accumulated arrests. Thus we are concerned not with the absolute value of the seriousness scores but with the rate at which offense gravity changes over time for juvenile offenders, for adult offenders, and finally, for the combined period up to age 30.

In the original study, when delinquent acts for the entire birth cohort were examined over the first fifteen offenses, the seriousness scores exhibited a slight

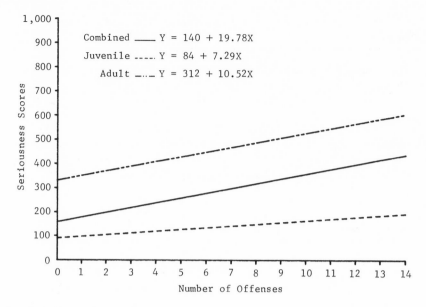

FIG. 3.1   Regression estimates of mean seriousness scores for first to fifteenth offense by juvenile, adult, and combined offenses.

but consistent upward trend (Wolfgang, Figlio, and Sellin 1972, 167). When all offense types were analyzed, the seriousness scores increased by an average of 4.3 points per offense, which, because the seriousness scores ranged from 1 to 2,600, was not substantial. Indeed, the average seriousness score for the first offense was found to be 105 and increased only to 165 by the fifteenth offense. When types of offenses were analyzed separately, the results were approximately the same. With the exception of injury offenses, the regression lines, representing the regression of seriousness on the rank number of the offense, were nearly flat, with regression coefficients ranging from -5.8 to $+6.9$. For injury offenses, however, the regression coefficient was 17.8, and seriousness scores increased from 331 for the first offense to 900 for the fifteenth.

Overall, however, the juvenile offense careers of the Philadelphia birth cohort were not marked by substantial increases in offense seriousness; with the exception of those offenses that involved injury, this seriousness was remarkably independent of the number of offenses already committed. Our task now is to see if this same conclusion is obtained when offense careers are examined up to the subjects' thirtieth birthdays.

Figure 3.1 presents the regression equations and least-squares regression lines for juvenile, adult, and total offenses when all offense types are considered. For all three groups the data indicate a positive trend such that the average seriousness score increased as the criminal careers developed. Although this general trend is evident, there are substantial differences across the three groups.

The most noticeable difference concerns the comparison between the juvenile and adult offenses, especially in relation to the point of entry. The first juvenile

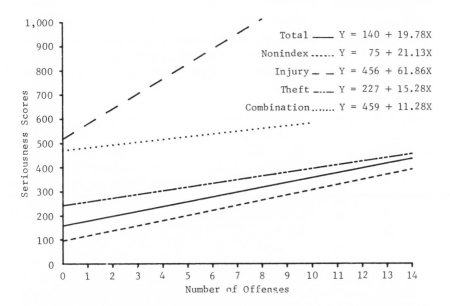

FIG. 3.2   Regression estimates of mean seriousness scores for combined juvenile and adult offenses by offense type.

offense had an average seriousness score of 92, while the first adult offense had an average score of 323. This difference is substantial and is indicative of the greater social harm inflicted on the community by adult offenders. Moreover, not only did adult offenses start at a substantially higher point, but they also increased at a higher rate, as demonstrated by the regression coefficients in table 3.9. The coefficient for the adult offenses, 10.5, is three points higher than that of the juvenile offenses committed by the follow-up subjects, 7.3. Thus every additional offense committed by an adult will be, on the average, 10.5 points more serious than the preceding one, while for juveniles the additional offense will be only 7.3 points more serious. By the fifteenth offense this difference can be seen clearly—at that point the average seriousness score for the juvenile offenses was 193, while for the adult offenses the score was 543 (see fig. 3.2).

TABLE 3.9   Correlation Coefficients and Standard Errors of the Regression Coefficient for Regression Estimates of Seriousness Scores

	Juvenile Offenses	Adult Offenses	Combined Offenses
Correlation coefficient[a]	.138	.089	.201
Regression coefficient[a]	7.29	10.52	19.78
Standard error of regression coefficient	1.61	3.83	2.15
Number of offenses	1,055	949	2,004

[a] All coefficients are significant at the .0001 level.

Examining the data for the combined juvenile and adult periods, we see an even steeper increase in the average seriousness over time. The offenses started at an average score of 160, reflecting the preponderance of juvenile offenses at the beginning of the careers; but by the fifteenth offense the average score was 438, reflecting the preponderance of adult offenses. The regression coefficient for this equation, 19.8, is the largest observed, indicating the rapid rate of increase in the seriousness of offenses over time.

These data, when all offense types are considered, demonstrate not only a uniform increase in the seriousness of offenses over time but also considerable variation within age groups. The unit change is lowest for juvenile offenses, at 7.3 seriousness points per offense; is considerably higher for adult offenses, at 10.5 points per offense; and is highest for combined offenses, at 19.8 points per offense. Thus, over the entire offense careers of the sample subjects, considering both juvenile and adult offenses, each offense was, on the average, about twenty points more serious than the preceding one.

Although the preceding data indicate that offenses increase in seriousness over time, the strength of this conclusion must be tempered somewhat, for there is considerable spread around these regression lines. Table 3.9 presents the correlation coefficients and the standard errors associated with these regression coefficients. As can be seen, the correlation coefficients are rather small, varying from .14 for the juvenile data to .20 for the combined data, indicating that the observed data are widely dispersed around the regression lines. Nevertheless, all the coefficients are significant, and the standard errors are not particularly large in relation to the regression coefficients. Thus we take the regression lines to be reasonably good estimates of the upward trend in seriousness but also point out that there is considerable spread in the observed data around these estimates.

Thus far we have examined changes in the seriousness of offenses over criminal careers without regard to the types of offenses committed. In the earlier study, however, considerable differences were found for the regression equations of the five offense types. Specifically, we found that the increase in seriousness scores was greatest for the injury offenses ($b = 17.8$), relatively modest for the combination offenses ($b = 6.9$), and approximately zero for the other three offense types. Thus the general positive relationship between the seriousness of the offense and the number of offenses committed was due primarily to the impact of injury and combination offenses. The question before us now concerns the stability of this finding when the data are extended to age 30.

Although it would be desirable to conduct this analysis for juvenile and adult offenses separately as well as in combination, the number of offenses committed by the 10 percent sample was not large enough, so analysis was performed on only the combined data set. Even within this data set, the small number of offenses in some categories will limit the analysis. First, the offense type of damage must be eliminated. Second, the analysis of injury and combination offenses can be conducted only to the ninth and eleventh offenses, respectively, because no subject committed more than nine injury or eleven combination offenses.

With these limitations in mind, figure 3.2 presents the regression lines and regression equations.

Unlike the situation for the juvenile data, the combined juvenile-adult data indicate substantial positive increases in seriousness scores for all offense types. The greatest rate of change is associated with injury offenses, with a regression coefficient of 61.9 and an intercept of 456. Injury offenses started at a much higher level than the other offenses and then increased more sharply. Combination offenses, which can involve an element of injury, had a regression coefficient of 11.3 and an intercept of 459, indicating a rather high entry level. Nonindex and theft offenses exhibited rates of change that were similar to that observed for total offenses ($b_{\text{nonindex}} = 21.1$ and $b_{\text{theft}} = 19.3$); the intercept for the nonindex offenses (75) is the only one that is lower than the intercept for total offenses (140).

Although these differences among offense types exist, the most notable conclusion to emerge from the data in figure 3.2 is that the coefficients are all positive and vary between 19.2 and 30.1. This situation is substantially different from that observed for the juvenile years of the entire birth cohort. Up to age 18 the coefficients varied from -5.8 to $+17.8$ and seemed to fall into two general groups—one for injury and combination offenses and the other for nonindex, theft, and damage offenses, with the regression equation for total offenses ($b = 4.32$) forming something of an average. (See Wolfgang, Figlio, and Sellin 1972, 165, for a discussion of these data.) For the combined data analyzed here, however, the groups are not at all evident. For all offense types the average seriousness scores increase with the rank number of the offense. The magnitude of the unit change varies somewhat, from 19.2 to 30.1, but the positive relationship between the seriousness of the offense and the number of offenses committed is universal.

As when all offenses were analyzed together, there is considerable spread around these regression lines, and the estimates presented in figure 3.2 must be qualified. The appropriate data are presented in table 3.10. Coefficients for the

TABLE 3.10 Correlation Coefficients and Standard Errors of the Regression Coefficient for Regression Estimates of Seriousness Scores by Offense Types

	Offense Types			
	Nonindex	Injury	Theft	Combination
Correlation coefficient	.249[a]	.128[a]	.149[a]	.028[b]
Regression coefficient	21.13[a]	61.86[a]	15.28[a]	11.28[b]
Standard error of regression coefficient	2.28	32.28	5.11	28.44
Number of offenses	1,313	224	392	200
Highest rank observed	15	9	15	11

[a]Significant at the .0001 level.
[b]Significant at the .04 level.

nonindex, theft, and combination offenses are all significant, but those associated with injury offenses are not. Moreover, the correlation coefficients are not substantial, varying from .03 for combination offenses to .25 for nonindex offenses. In general these coefficients indicate that the data are spread widely around the regression lines, especially for the injury offenses. Thus the regression coefficients can be considered only as rather rough estimates of the magnitude of the unit change in the seriousness of offenses committed over the criminal careers of the cohort subjects.

Nevertheless, the data do indicate that the offenses these subjects committed became more serious as the careers developed and that this trend was sharper for the entire careers of the subjects, up to age 30, than it was for the juvenile years alone. Although the data cannot estimate precisely the magnitude of the unit change, they can estimate the direction of the relationship, which is clearly positive for all the offense types analyzed.

Summary

This chapter has examined differences between the juvenile and adult portions of the criminal careers of the sample subjects. As was true in the original study, the variables of race and SES were found to be significantly related to the various measures of offender and offense status. Nonwhites and members of the lower SES group were more likely to be persistent offenders, that is, to have committed offenses during both their juvenile and their adult years.

In terms of the characteristics of offenses committed, we have seen that the juvenile-only and adult-only offenders committed approximately the same number of offenses, but that the persistent offenders committed far more. In terms of seriousness, though, the most harmful offenses were those committed by the adult group, followed in descending order by those committed by the persistent offenders and then the juvenile offenders.

When the analysis shifted from offender to offense status, we saw that the type of offenses did not differ markedly by age. For both the juvenile and adult periods, nonindex offenses were most likely to be committed, followed by theft offenses and then by injury, combination, and damage offenses. Although offense types did not vary by age, the seriousness of the offenses did. Offenses committed during the adult years were far more serious than the acts of delinquency, and they also tended to increase in seriousness at a more rapid rate. Thus the finding in the original study that offenses did not become more serious as delinquent careers developed was not repeated for adults. When the careers were extended to age 30, the data clearly indicate that, regardless of offense type, the offenses committed later in an individual's career were, on the average, much more serious than those he committed earlier.

4   The Link between Delinquency and Criminality

In the previous chapter we saw that the offenses the 10 percent random sample committed during the adult years differed in certain respects from those they committed during the juvenile years, but that the basic correlates of offensive behavior, race, and SES retained their importance for both the juvenile and adult periods. Here the analysis shifts to a somewhat more dynamic approach. Rather than simply contrasting the juvenile and adult periods, we will examine the effect of the juvenile careers on the frequency and seriousness of the adult careers of the sample members. Previous longitudinal studies, especially those of Shannon (1977, 1979), have suggested a strong link between juvenile and adult careers; that is, extensive and serious juvenile careers are associated with extensive and serious adult careers, and the most serious careers are continuous, extending from the juvenile through the early adult years.

Bivariate Relationships

Table 4.1, which cross-tabulates the number of adult arrests by the number of juvenile arrests, presents the most basic data for examining this relationship. As can be seen, there is a strong and consistent relationship between these variables. Of the subjects who were nonoffenders during their juvenile years, 81.9 percent were classified as nonoffenders during adulthood. Moreover, only 3 percent of the nondelinquents were arrested five or more times after age 18. Although the absence of delinquent behavior is not completely unrelated to adult offenses, it is clear that the absence of juvenile delinquency is a major correlate of continued absence from contact with the law.

At the other extreme, subjects who were classified as chronic offenders (five or more arrests) during their juvenile years were likely to continue in extensive patterns of offensive behavior. Among the juvenile chronic offenders, 45.2 percent were also classified as chronic offenders during their adult years, and an additional 5.5 percent were arrested four times. Overall, half of the chronic juvenile offenders had at least four adult arrests. Nevertheless, we should note that 21.9 percent of the chronic juvenile offenders were nonoffenders during their adult years, indicating a substantial level of desistance.

Aside from the extreme categories of nonoffenders and chronic offenders, the data in table 4.1 indicate a strong and consistent relationship between juvenile and adult careers. As the number of juvenile arrests increased, so too did the

TABLE 4.1 Number of Adult Arrests by Number of Juvenile Arrests

Adult Arrests	Non-offenders % (N)	Juvenile Arrests				
		1 % (N)	2 % (N)	3 % (N)	4 % (N)	5+ % (N)
Nonoffenders	81.9	62.4	55.0	45.4	31.8	21.9
	(516)	(98)	(33)	(15)	(7)	(16)
1	9.0	17.8	16.7	18.2	9.1	9.6
	(57)	(28)	(10)	(6)	(2)	(7)
2	4.0	6.4	10.0	9.1	9.1	8.2
	(25)	(10)	(6)	(3)	(2)	(6)
3	1.4	3.8	6.7	6.1	4.6	9.6
	(9)	(6)	(4)	(2)	(1)	(7)
4	0.6	3.2	3.3	0.0	13.6	5.5
	(4)	(5)	(2)	(0)	(3)	(4)
5+	3.0	6.4	8.3	21.2	31.8	45.2
	(19)	(10)	(5)	(7)	(7)	(33)
Total	100.0	100.0	100.0	100.0	100.0	100.0
	(630)	(157)	(60)	(33)	(22)	(73)

number of adult arrests. Moreover, the likelihood of being a nonoffender during the adult years declined monotonically as the number of juvenile arrests increased.

Although there was a strong positive relationship between juvenile and adult arrests, the data presented in table 4.1 also demonstrate a substantial drop in offensive behavior from the juvenile period to the adult period. For example, more than half of the one-time delinquents (62.4 percent) and the two-time delinquents (55 percent) were never arrested as adults. Moreover, 45.4 percent of the juveniles arrested three times and 31.8 percent of the juveniles arrested four times were nonoffenders during adulthood. Thus many subjects who were in police files as juvenile delinquents were apparently capable of altering their behavior as adults. Nevertheless, the dominant finding in table 4.1 is that nondelinquent careers were likely to be followed by noncriminal careers, and delinquent careers were likely to be followed by criminal careers.

To investigate issues other than the simple frequency of arrests, table 4.2 presents a correlation matrix for examining the relationship between the frequency, seriousness, and onset of juvenile careers on the one hand and the frequency and seriousness of adult careers on the other. Correlations above the diagonal are for all subjects, with nonoffenders having a score of zero on each of the variables, and correlations below the diagonal are for offenders only.

For all subjects, the correlation between juvenile and adult arrests is .44, which is to be expected given the data in table 4.1. In addition, there is a relatively strong association between the frequency of juvenile arrests and the seriousness of offenses committed as adults ($r = .45$).[1] The seriousness of juvenile

1. The seriousness variables in table 4.2 refer to the sum of the seriousness scores for all of the subjects' offenses during the juvenile and adult years.

TABLE 4.2   Correlation Matrix for Relationship between Juvenile and
Adult Careers

	Juvenile Arrests	Juvenile Seriousness	Juvenile Onset	Adult Arrests	Adult Seriousness
Juvenile arrests	—	.84	n.a.[a]	.44	.45
Juvenile seriousness	.83	—	n.a.[a]	.38	.41
Juvenile onset	−.47	−.37	—	n.a.[a]	n.a.[a]
Adult arrests	.33	.30	−.09	—	.92
Adult seriousness	.36	.34	−.16	.91	—

Note: All subjects above diagonal, offenders ony below diagonal.
[a] The variable age of onset cannot be calculated for nonoffenders and hence is not included in this section of the matrix.

careers is also related to the frequency of arrests and the seriousness of offenses committed during the adult years ($r = .38$ and $.41$, respectively). Overall, these coefficients are of the same relative magnitude and suggest a general relationship between juvenile and adult careers.

The data displayed below the diagonal in table 4.2 present the same relationships when the analysis is restricted to offenders. In general, the patterns and magnitude of the coefficients above and below the diagonal suggest that the results are not dependent on the subset of the sample that is analyzed. In addition to the frequency and seriousness of juvenile offenses, however, we can also examine the influence of the age of onset of juvenile careers on the characteristics of adult careers when the analysis is limited to offenders. The correlation coefficients suggest a relatively weak inverse relationship between these variables. Subjects whose delinquent careers began at an earlier age were likely to commit more serious offenses ($r = -.16$), but the relationships are not particularly strong.

In general, these data indicate that the frequency and seriousness of juvenile careers are consistently and strongly correlated with the frequency and seriousness of adult careers, a finding quite consistent with previous research. The age of onset of delinquent careers, however, is not strongly related to adult careers.

Multivariate Relationships

Both the original study and the results of the previous chapter suggest the importance of race and, to a lesser extent, SES. Thus, this section examines the relationship between juvenile and adult careers while simultaneously examining the influence of race and SES.

Table 4.3 regresses the frequency of adult arrests on the frequency of juvenile arrests, race, and SES.[2] Again, the analysis is conducted separately for all the subjects and for the offenders only. Both equations are significant, explaining

2. Race and SES are "dummy" coded, with nonwhites coded as 1 and higher SES coded as 1.

TABLE 4.3   Regression Analysis for Number and Seriousness of Adult Arrests
for All Subjects and for Offenders Only (Standardized Regression Coefficients)

Independent Variables	Number		Seriousness	
	All Subjects	Offenders Only	All Subjects	Offenders Only
Intercept	.39	1.04	178.6	411.3*
Juvenile arrests	.39*	.29*	.35*	.29*
Race	.13*	.19*	.19*	.19*
SES	−.03	−.04	−.03	−.04
R^2	.21*	.13*	.21*	.16*

*$p < .05$.

21 percent of the variance for all of the subjects and 13 percent for the offenders only.

In both equations it is clear that the number of juvenile arrests is the most important of the three independent variables in accounting for the number of adult arrests. The standardized regression coefficients for this variable are by far the largest in the equations and are statistically significant. Controlling for the effect of juvenile arrests, we see that race still exerts a strong influence on adult offensive behavior; nonwhites committed, on the average, more offenses than whites. The variable of SES, however, does not reach statistical significance in either of the models, and the standardized regression coefficient associated with this variable is small. In general, the variables of juvenile arrests and race appear to be the most important in accounting for the frequency of arrests as an adult.

The right-hand side of table 4.3 presents a similar analysis but replaces, at both the juvenile and adult levels, the number of arrests with the seriousness of arrests. Again the equations are significant and explain similar amounts of the variance—21 percent for all subjects and 16 percent for offenders only. The offense-related variable is seen as the most important. The standardized regression coefficient associated with the seriousness of juvenile offenses is the largest of the coefficients, followed by the coefficients for race and SES. Only the coefficients for seriousness and race are significant, however. In general, SES exerts a relatively small influence on adult careers once the character of juvenile careers and race are taken into account.

Summary

From the point of view of this chapter the most important conclusion to be drawn concerns the variables of frequency and seriousness of juvenile arrests. In the regression equations presented in table 4.3 it is clear that these are the most important variables in accounting for the number and seriousness of adult arrests. Even when the effects of race and SES are considered, subjects with long and serious juvenile careers are likely to have long and serious adult careers. This finding is consistent with previous longitudinal research and suggests the continuity of offensive careers across both the juvenile and adult years.

5 The Age Structure of Criminal Behavior

Analysis of juvenile careers among the cohort subjects demonstrated a distinct pattern in the age distribution of delinquent acts. Up to age 12 there was a gradual increase in both prevalence and incidence by age of onset of delinquency. After the twelfth year, however, there was a dramatic increase in both these rates until the peak of delinquent behavior was reached at age 16, following which there was a sharp drop during the seventeenth year. In this chapter we explore both the age of onset and the prevalence of criminal behavior when the age distribution is extended to age 30.

Age of Onset

We begin by examining the distributions of the ages of onset of delinquency and of criminal behavior. Age of onset refers to the age at which the first arrest occurred for each of the offenders in the sample. Figure 5.1 displays the basic data needed for this analysis.[1]

When the analysis is extended to age 30, the distribution of age of onset is remarkably similar to that observed for the juvenile years only. The peak age at which criminal careers began is still 16, with a steady upward progression from age 10 to that modal year. After age 16 there was a precipitous drop in the rate of new criminal careers. Whereas 16.6 percent of the offenders began their criminal activities during their sixteenth year, only 6.5 percent did so during their seventeenth year. Moreover, from ages 18 to 22 there is a fairly steady decline in new offenders, with a negligible number of subjects entering the criminal population after age 22. The characteristic of this distribution is evident in figure 5.1.

In addition to information on the age of onset, the data displayed in figure 5.1 also estimate the relationship between the age of onset and the average number of police charges the offender is likely to accumulate before his criminal career is over. The overall trend for this relationship is clear: the earlier an offender begins his criminal activity, the more offenses he will eventually commit. Offenders who began their careers at age 10 or earlier would be arrested, on the average, seven times. Those who began their careers at ages 11 or 12, however, would be arrested an average of ten times, the highest average number observed for any age-of-onset category. For those who began their criminal careers after age 13,

---

1. In this chapter we present the results in a series of graphs to demonstrate the temporal distribution of criminal involvement. Supporting tables are available upon request.

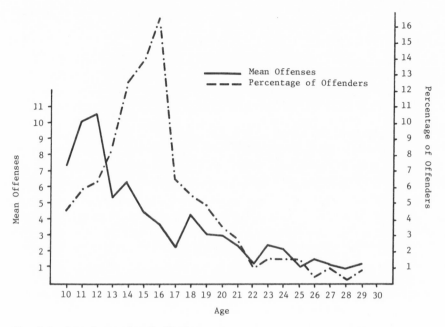

FIG. 5.1   Age of onset for all offenders.

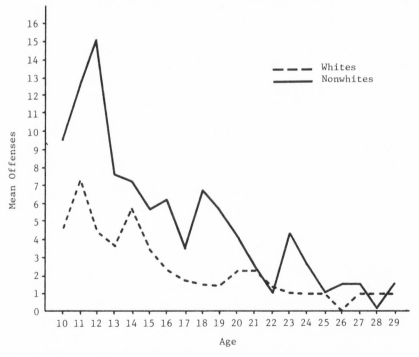

FIG. 5.2   Age of onset by race.

38

the average number of official offenses tended to decline nearly uniformly as the age of onset increased.

Figure 5.2 presents the same analysis when race is held constant; in general, the distributions are similar for the white and nonwhite subjects. For each group, the modal category for age of onset is again 16 years; 14.8 percent of the non-white offenders and 17.9 percent of the white offenders began their careers at this age. Again, there is a fairly steady increase in the onset of delinquent behavior from ages 10 through 16, followed by a sharp drop until the mid-twenties. After this point only a few subjects began criminal careers.

The relationship between age of onset and the number of offenses eventually committed is also invariant with respect to race. The younger the offenders when they began their careers, the greater the average number of offenses they committed. The largest means are associated with those who commenced their delinquent activities at ages 11 and 12.

In general, when the age-of-onset data are extended to age 30, the results are consistent with those observed during the juvenile period. Criminal careers were most likely to begin at age 16, then there was a sharp drop in the number of subjects entering the criminal population. Finally, the analysis suggests that offenders who began their careers earlier tended to accumulate a greater number of official offenses by the end of their careers.

Age Distribution of Offenses

The distribution of ages at which offenses were committed is presented in figure 5.3. The modal age at which offenses were committed was 16, which accounted for 12.9 percent of all of the sample's offenses. Only 1.3 percent of the offenses were committed before age 10. From age 11 (8 percent) until age 16 there was a steady and sharp increase in offenses. Following modal age 16 there was a steep decline to 8.1 percent at age 17 and 5.6 percent at age 18. Once the subjects entered adulthood there was a steady, albeit slow and fluctuating, decline; by the mid-twenties only 4 percent of the offenses were committed per year, and by age 30 it was less than 2 percent.

Thus the offenses accounted for by these sample subjects were committed predominantly during the mid to late teens. Overall, 42.6 percent of all of the offenses were committed between ages 15 and 19.

Figure 5.3 presents the age distributions of offenses for white and nonwhite offenders separately. Race appears to exert very little influence on the age distribution of offensive behavior.

For each group the modal age of offensive behavior was 16 (14.8 percent of the white offenses and 11.7 percent of the nonwhite offenses were committed at this age). Also, the rate of offending for both racial groups increased from ages 10 through 16, following which it declined in similar patterns.

The only discernible racial difference is a relatively minor one. Up to age 19 the proportion of offenses at each age tended to be somewhat lower for the nonwhite subjects; that is, proportionately fewer of the offenses by nonwhites were committed during the teenage years. Following the inflection point at age 19,

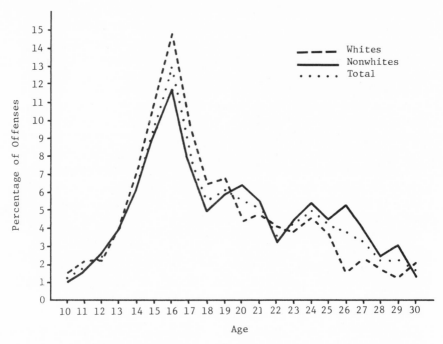

FIG. 5.3 Age distribution of offenses.

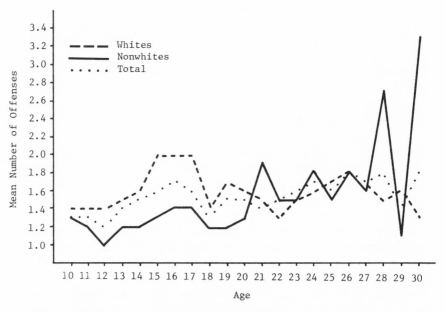

FIG. 5.4 Mean number of offenses per age group by race.

40

however, proportionately more of the nonwhites' offenses were committed; that is, the nonwhites were somewhat more likely to commit a larger share of their offenses during adulthood. Although evident, this trend is relatively minor compared with the overall similarity of the age distribution for both the white and nonwhite offenders.

Figure 5.4 presents information on the number of offenders who were active at each age, along with the number of offenses they committed at that age. The offender counts sum to more than the total number of offenders because the offenders were counted at each age when they committed an offense. Thus an offender who committed offenses at both age 15 and age 16 would be counted twice.

Although the age distribution of offenses is remarkably leptokurtic, peaking at age 16, the distribution of the average number of offenses committed per year is relatively flat. Beginning with total offenders, we see that the mean number of offenses committed at each age varied only from 1.2 to 1.8. This fact is well represented in figure 5.4, where the curve for the total group could be represented by a straight line with almost no slope. Thus, although most offenders were active at age 16 and most offenses were committed at that age, the average number of offenses committed by the active offenders was not particularly elevated at age 16 or at any other age. For example, the average number of offenses committed by 16-year-olds was only 1.7. In general, the distributions of offenses described in figure 5.4 are due primarily to the number of active offenders at each age and to the age-specific offense rate.

The same observation is also evident for both the white and nonwhite subjects. In figure 5.4 the curves for these two groups are relatively flat. The only exception to this is for the nonwhite subjects after age 27; but here the number of observations is so small that the mean values are too unstable to interpret. Thus the general observation holds for both the whites and nonwhites; *the average number of offenses committed at each age is relatively constant from ages 10 to 30.*

Age and the Seriousness of Offenses

The last issue we examine in this chapter is the seriousness of the offenses committed at each age. We are interested in determining whether offenders committed more serious offenses as they became older. Figure 5.5 presents, for both index and nonindex offenses, the mean seriousness scores of offenses committed at each age, from 10 to 30.

For the index offenses two rather distinct patterns are evident. During the juvenile years the average seriousness of offenses did not vary greatly. The means ranged from 162 at age 10 to 283 at age 16, and figure 5.5 demonstrates a moderate upward trend in seriousness. After age 17, however, there is a marked increase in the seriousness of the offenses committed. The scores peaked at age 20 with a mean of 709 and then declined somewhat until age 25, after which they tended to increase in a fluctuating pattern. Nevertheless, it is clear that the offenses committed during the adult years were considerably more serious than

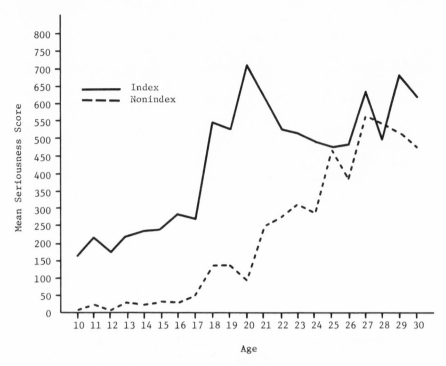

Fig. 5.5   Seriousness of offenses by age and offense type.

those committed during adolescence; index offenses tended to become more serious as the sample offenders grew older.

For the less serious nonindex offenses the same general pattern is evident. During the juvenile years the trend in seriousness was nearly flat; the means varied from 6 at age 10 to 49 at age 17. Following the juvenile period, however, the seriousness of the nonindex offenses increased sharply and uniformly, reaching its highest value at age 27 with a mean of 565.

Overall, these data suggest a fairly clear relationship between offender age and offense seriousness. As the cohort offenders aged, their offenses tended to become more serious. This trend is more evident for the nonindex offenses but holds for the index offenses as well.

Figures 5.6 and 5.7 present data on the same relationship for the white and nonwhite subjects. In general, the trends observed for all the subjects were replicated in the within-race analyses. Beginning with index offenses (fig. 5.6), we see that for both the whites and nonwhites there was very little increment in average seriousness during the juvenile period. Following age 17, however, there was a sharp increase for both groups. In general, index offenses committed by the nonwhite subjects tended to be more serious, especially during the adult period.

For the nonindex offenses (fig. 5.7) the general pattern displayed in figure 5.5 is replicated. Before age 17 there was very little increment in the average seriousness of the nonindex offenses from year to year, but after age 17 there was a

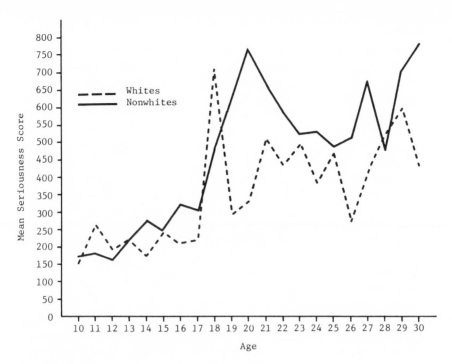

FIG. 5.6   Seriousness of index offenses by age and race.

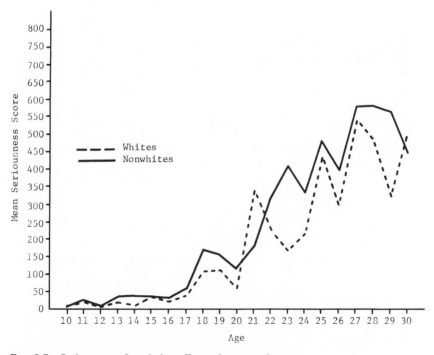

FIG. 5.7   Seriousness of nonindex offenses by age and race.

steady and uniform increase in the scores. Again we note that at most ages the seriousness of the offenses committed by the nonwhites tended to be somewhat more serious than those committed by the whites. Nevertheless, the strong age effects noted in these data are not greatly altered when race is held constant.

Summary

The analysis of age and delinquency in *Delinquency in a Birth Cohort* led to two important findings: the centrality of age 16—the modal age for both the onset and commission of offenses—to an understanding of delinquency and the sharp drop in offensive behavior from ages 16 to 17. The present chapter has continued the analysis of age and criminality by extending the observation period to age 30 in order to examine the stability of these findings. In general, the results are robust. We find that 16 remains the modal age of both onset and offense commission, and with few exceptions this finding holds when race and offense type are held constant. Moreover, the sharp drop in offensive behavior after age 16 continues into adulthood.

Although 16 is the modal age for onset and for offense commission, it is not the peak for the seriousness of offenses or for the average number of offenses committed. Indeed, offenses committed during adulthood tend to be considerably more serious than offenses committed during adolescence; for adult offenses there is a positive relationship between the seriousness of offenses and the offender's age. By and large, this relationship holds for both races and for both index and nonindex offenses.

However, the increment in seriousness scores is not matched by an increase in the average number of offenses committed by each age group. The average number of offenses committed by active offenders at each age is remarkably constant over the life span of the sample subjects, varying only from 1.2 to 1.8 offenses per year. Moreover, this result is observed for both the white and nonwhite subjects. Thus the sharp increase in the number of offenses committed at age 16, and more generally during the late teenage years, is due almost entirely to an increase in the number of active offenders and not to an increase in their annual "productivity." The policy implications of this finding, as well as a more detailed examination of these data, are presented in chapter 9.

6 Offense Transitions

The previous chapters have examined the adult arrest careers of the follow-up sample from a descriptive point of view. That is, the characteristics of a number of offender and offense groups were described and related to background characteristics, and the relationship between juvenile and adult offensive behavior was established. In this chapter the analysis models the criminal careers of the sample members as their careers developed over time. As in the original study, the dynamic analysis is concerned with offense specialization and permits us to examine the sequence of the offense types as offenders move from their first offense to their last. The central question is: Do offenders specialize in certain types of offenses as their careers unfold, or are the types of offenses committed similar at the beginning and at the end of their careers?

Juvenile Careers

To analyze the prevalence of offense specialization, we again divided offenses into five types: nonindex, injury, theft, damage, and combination. The original study began by examining the probabilities of committing these offense types, for each rank number of offense, regardless of the previous types of offenses committed. In other words, we examined the probability of offenders' committing a nonindex offense as the kth offense, an injury as the kth offense, and so on, regardless of the type of the $k - 1$st offense or $k - 2$d offense.[1] The data thus generated indicated that the probabilities changed very little by the rank number of the offense. The probability of committing a nonindex offense was about the same whether the offense was the subject's first, second, and so on, out to the fifteenth. Similarly, the probability of committing an injury offense was about the same for the first offense, the second, and so on; the same situation held for theft, damage, and combination offenses. (The appropriate data are displayed in table 10.3 in Wolfgang, Figlio, and Sellin 1972, 162.)

This finding was both intriguing and unexpected. It ran counter to a number of often-stated assumptions in the literature on delinquency; for example, that the seriousness of offenses increases as the offender commits a greater number and that offenders tend to specialize in certain types of offenses as their careers develop. The relatively invariant nature of the "static" probabilities just described do not support these assumptions. Moreover, the constancy of the static proba-

---

1. Read k minus first offense and k minus second offense.

bilities suggests that "the process which generates these offense-specific (by type) probability distributions operates essentially in the same manner at each offense number. This suggestion is an important one, for, if it is true, we are implying that the probability of being involved in a particular type of offensive behavior is independent of the number of offenses that a juvenile may have committed. We may state simply, as an example, that a boy is no more likely at, say, the eleventh offense to be involved in a violent act than he was at the fifth" (Wolfgang, Figlio, and Sellin 1972, 174–75).

To examine the likelihood that a generating probability process is operating, independent of the rank number of offenses, requires a shift from static to dynamic probabilities. In this case the type of previous offense must be examined along with the type of current offense. To do this the data are arrayed in transition matrices that allow the estimation of the probability $P_{ij}(k)$, where k refers to the kth offense in a series of offense ranks, i refers to the state the subject was in at the $k - 1$st offense, and j refers to the state he is in at the kth offense. Thus, $P_{ij}(k)$ refers to the probability that the subject's kth offense will be of type j when his $k - 1$st offense was type i and where the states, or offense types, are nonindex, injury, theft, damage, and combination. Once these transition matrices are estimated for each offense transition, the first to second, second to third, and so forth, the matrices are then compared to see if they are similar enough to warrant the conclusion that they are being generated by the same underlying probability model. This analysis poses two basic questions: "(a) Does the type of the offense that a cohort member committed at the $k - 1$st offense number have any bearing on the probability that he will commit a certain type of offense at the kth number? and (b) Does the same process operate at each offense level (1st, 2d, 3d, etc.) so that similar transition matrices will be generated when the offenses are classified by type? In short, are the transition configurations such that a homogeneous or number-independent Markov chain can be said to exist?" (Wolfgang, Figlio, and Sellin 1972, 175).

The results of the earlier cohort analysis for the first eight offense transitions indicated that the data could be typified by a one-step Markov chain. That is, the probabilities of moving from offense type i to offense type j were found to be independent of the rank number of the offense. Allowing for sampling fluctuations, the probability $P_{ij}(k)$ was the same whether the subject was moving from his first to second offense or from his seventh to eighth offense. Such a situation allows us to estimate a summary or generating matrix, reproduced here as matrix 6.1.

In addition to the five types of offenses already defined, this matrix also includes the category of desistance, which is an absorbing state. After committing an offense, the subject may not be arrested for another offense; hence the category of desisting has to be considered. This category appears in the last column of the matrix. (The desistance row is void with the exception of the desistance-to-desistance cell, which is 1.0, since by definition once an individual enters the state of desistance he cannot leave it, at least during the period of the study.)

MATRIX 6.1   Summary Transition Matrix: Original Cohort Data, First to
Eighth Transitions

$k - 1/k$	Nonindex	Injury	Theft	Damage	Combi-nation	Desist
Nonindex	.4473	.0685	.1054	.0228	.0492	.3068
Injury	.4090	.0920	.0854	.0222	.0600	.3314
Theft	.4051	.0530	.2130	.0235	.0928	.2126
Damage	.5013	.0882	.1463	.0529	.0343	.1770
Combination	.3922	.0703	.1378	.0169	.1350	.2478
Desist	.0000	.0000	.0000	.0000	.0000	1.0000

Source: Wolfgang, Figlio, and Sellin 1972, 183.

Matrix 6.1 indicates two major findings. (See Wolfgang, Figlio, and Sellin 1972, 183, for a more detailed discussion of these data.) The first concerns the type of offense likely to be committed. Regardless of the type of $k - 1$st offense, the subject's state at offense k is most likely to be nonindex, is next most likely to be desistance, and is least likely to be damage. Between these extremes the states are likely to be, in descending order, theft, injury, and combination. Moreover, the magnitudes of the probabilities within the columns of matrix 6.1 are very similar. For example, the probability of moving to a nonindex offense varies from .5013, when the prior offense was damage, to .3922, when the prior offense was a combination. Similarly, the probability of moving to an injury offense varies from .0920 to .0530, and the same tight clustering of probabilities can be observed in the other columns.

The second major finding concerns the lack of offense specialization. If the cohort subjects tended to specialize in certain types of offenses as their careers developed, the probabilities along the main diagonal would be considerably elevated vis-à-vis the probabilities in their respective columns. Such is not the case, however. For example, the probability of moving from one nonindex offense to another one, .4473, is in the middle of the distribution of its column. For the other four offense types the probabilities falling on the diagonal are the highest values observed. Nevertheless, their magnitudes are not substantially different from the other probabilities within the respective columns. The strongest evidence of specialization concerns theft offenses, for which the probability of moving from a theft to a theft is .2130, while the probability of moving from any other type of offense to a theft ranges from .0854 to .1463. With the slight exception of theft, therefore, there is little evidence of offense specialization among the *juvenile* offenses of the cohort subjects.

To summarize, we can repeat the conclusions presented in the earlier study: "To generalize the content of this matrix, then, it may be said that the typical offender is most likely to commit a *nonindex offense* next, *regardless* of what he did in the past. If he does not commit a nonindex type next, he is most likely to *desist from further delinquency.* If he were to commit an index offense next, it would most likely be the theft of property and least likely damage to property. With the exception of the moderate tendency to repeat the same type of offense, this pattern obtains *regardless* of the type of the previous offense" (Wolfgang, Figlio, and Sellin 1972, 189).

Juvenile Careers of the Sample Members

The data analyzed in *Delinquency in a Birth Cohort* referred only to the delinquent careers of the subjects. Offenses committed after age 18 were not included in the analysis; they were legally criminal acts and not acts of juvenile delinquency. The original study ended at the conclusion of the seventeenth year. The purpose of this chapter is to remove that boundary and continue the analysis of offense transitions up to each subject's thirtieth birthday by analyzing the criminal careers of the cohort follow-up sample.

Because we are dealing with a 10 percent sample of the cohort, the number of offenses available for analysis is considerably reduced; therefore, we shall analyze the first five offense transitions. We are concerned with the stability of the probability $P_{ij}(k)$ between the first-to-second and the fifth-to-sixth offense transitions.

We are interested in testing the hypothesis that the matrices of transition probabilities are constant over time. That is, the probabilities for the first-to-second offense transition are the same, taking into account sampling error, as those for the second-to-third transition and so on, out to the fifth-to-sixth offense transition. If the matrices are found to be constant, we can conclude that the probability of committing a particular type of offense is independent of the number of offenses committed. To predict the type of the kth offense, we need know only the type of $k - 1$st offense; knowledge of previous offenses is not required.

According to the model developed by Goodman (1962), the test of homogeneity is crucial for determining whether a one-step Markov chain exists. In this test the data contained in each transition matrix are arrayed in tables based on the individual's state at the $k - 1$st offense. The first row of this test table indicates the number of persons who moved from a nonindex first offense to each of the offense types on their second offense; the second row contains the number who moved from a nonindex second offense to each of the offense types on their third offense, and so on. If the transition probabilities are constant over time, the chi-square value for this table should not attain statistical significance. In other words, there should be no association between the rank number of the $k - 1$st offense and the type of kth offense committed. Such a finding would indicate that the probability of moving from a nonindex offense to each of the five types of offenses is the same, regardless of the number of offenses committed.

The chi-square values for the five tests of homogeneity, one for each type of $k - 1$st offense, are presented in table 6.1 along with the observed alpha levels. The decision to accept or reject the null hypothesis that the transition probabilities are the same will be made at the .05 level of significance.

The chi-square values range from 6.6 when the $k - 1$st offense is injury to 22.3 when it is combination. Because each of the tables has sixteen degrees of

TABLE 6.1   Homogeneity Tests for Juvenile Offense Transitions, First to
Fifth Transitions

Prior Offense	Number of Offenses	Chi-Square	Probability
Nonindex	315	17.08	.50
Injury	36	6.60	.80
Theft	87	14.16	.70
Damage	39	10.22	.95
Combination	59	22.28	.20

freedom, we see that none of the chi-square values approach significance. We
cannot reject the null hypothesis and therefore conclude that the probabilities are
constant over time. Moreover, because the sum of the chi-squares is also not significant, we can conclude that all the matrices in this test could have been
produced by the same generating process. This is the same conclusion reached
by Wolfgang, Figlio, and Sellin (1972, 182) for juveniles up to age 18 in the
universe of the original study.

The conclusion that the probabilities are independent of the number of the
offense allows us to estimate the generating matrix for this process (matrix 6.2).
The probability contained within each cell is the arithmetic mean of the probabilities contained in the corresponding cells for each of the five observed offense
transitions. If this summary matrix is the generating or parent matrix for the
entire process, then the observed values in each matrix should not differ significantly from the predicted values, based on the probabilities contained in the summary matrix. Again, a chi-square test can be used to assess this hypothesis, and
the results of this test are presented in table 6.2.

The chi-square values for the summary matrix versus the second to the fifth
data matrices are not significant, ranging in value from 9.9 to 20.2; but the statistic for the summary matrix versus the first data matrix, 34.6, is significant at the
.01 level. This suggests that the probabilities contained in the summary matrix
are close estimates of the transitions from the second offense on but that the
probabilities observed at the switch from the first to second offenses deviate
somewhat from those presented in matrix 6.2. Overall, however, the data are

MATRIX 6.2   Summary Transition Matrix: Juvenile Offenders, First to Fifth
Transitions

$k - 1/k$	Nonindex	Injury	Theft	Damage	Combi-nation	Desist
Nonindex	.4227	.0453	.1213	.0241	.0559	.3307
Injury	.2507	.1779	.1094	.0000	.0083	.4536
Theft	.4060	.0561	.1213	.0152	.1105	.2907
Damage	.6516	.0709	.0635	.0118	.0709	.1314
Combination	.4060	.0611	.2249	.0200	.1568	.1311
Desist	.0000	.0000	.0000	.0000	.0000	1.0000

TABLE 6.2   Matrix Tests and Chi-Square Values: Juvenile Offenses,
Summary Matrix, Excluding Desistance, versus First to Fifth Data Matrices

Summary Matrix vs.	Chi-Square	Probability
1st data matrix	34.6	.01
2d data matrix	19.9	.30
3d data matrix	9.9	.95
4th data matrix	20.2	.20
5th data matrix	13.2	.70

closely represented by a first-order Markov process. This conclusion is supported by the results of the homogeneity tests as well as by the pattern of results displayed in table 6.2.

Thus the probabilities contained in the summary matrix for the sample members lead to conclusions very similar to those based on the entire cohort. The major difference between matrices 6.1 and 6.2 is that the probabilities within each column are more tightly clustered when the analysis is based on the entire cohort. This finding is not surprising, for we should expect the estimates of the probabilities to become somewhat less stable as the number of observations decreases.

We also note the similarities between the two matrices. The most likely transition is still to a nonindex offense; the next most likely shift is to the absorbing state of desistance, followed by theft, injury, combination, and damage. Moreover, the probabilities indicate little support for the notion of offense specialization. Values along the main diagonal are not substantially greater than the probabilities of their respective columns. There is some indication of offense specialization in the injury-to-injury shift and in the combination-to-combination shift, but the area of specialization noted in matrix 6.1, theft-to-theft, is diminished here. In general there is little evidence of offense specialization for either these sample data or the entire cohort.

Although similarities between the findings based on a 10 percent sample up to age 30 and the original study up to age 18 demonstrate the representativeness of the sample, they do not address the major issue of this chapter—the extent to which the Markovian character of delinquent careers can be replicated when adult offenses are added to juvenile offenses.

Adult and Juvenile Careers

There are two major ways to determine the consistency of this finding for the adult years. The first is to examine the probabilities associated with offense switching for adult offenses only, and the second is to link together the juvenile and adult offenses of the subjects and examine their entire criminal careers. We have explored both processes.

The appropriate data for the adult portion of the subjects' careers are presented in table 6.3 and matrix 6.3. The number of cases in many of the cells is rather small, and by the fourth transition the number of offenses available for analysis diminishes considerably.

Despite this limitation the findings are, in general, consistent with those from the earlier data. The most important test results, of course, are those associated with the test of homogeneity (table 6.3). When the $k - 1$st offense is a nonindex offense the homogeneity test is significant ($\chi^2 = 34.7$, $p < .01$), indicating that transition probabilities are not independent of time. The other four homogeneity tests, however, are not significant, with chi-square values ranging from 6.3 to 20.4, allowing us to accept the null hypothesis for these tests.

The finding that the transitions are not independent of time when the prior offense is a nonindex offense was also observed in the original juvenile data (Wolfgang, Figlio, and Sellin 1972, 182) and was due primarily to the influence of shift from the first to the second offense, which differed from the higher-order offense transitions. The same situation obtains for the adult offenses, for when the analysis is limited to the second through fourth transitions, the homogeneity test is not significant ($\chi^2 = 18.21$, d.f. $= 12$, $p < .20$). Overall, then, the homogeneity tests presented in table 6.3 indicate that the adult offenses tend to conform to the requirements of a first-order Markov process, as did the juvenile offenses. This conclusion is clearest when the prior offense was injury, theft, damage, or combination; and for a prior nonindex offense the model holds after the switch from the first to the second offense. These results allow us to accept the null hypothesis and conclude for adult offenses, as we did for juvenile of-

TABLE 6.3   Homogeneity Tests for Adult Offense Transitions, First to Fifth Transitions

Prior Offense	Number of Offenses	Chi-Square	Probability
Nonindex	348	34.7	.01
Injury	54	11.7	.80
Theft	100	8.6	.90
Damage	10	6.3	.90
Combination	42	20.4	.20

MATRIX 6.3   Summary Transition Matrix: Adult Offenders, First to Fifth Transitions

$k - 1/k$	Nonindex	Injury	Theft	Damage	Combination	Desist
Nonindex	.4751	.0865	.1198	.0056	.0564	.2565
Injury	.3432	.1678	.1141	.0087	.0470	.3191
Theft	.3684	.0951	.2462	.0091	.0689	.2123
Damage	.2441	.1607	.0357	.0000	.3274	.2321
Combination	.4291	.0444	.1598	.0556	.1008	.2102

fenses, that the type of offense to be committed is independent of the number of offenses already committed.

For example, the likelihood of moving from a theft offense to an injury offense is approximately the same whether the shift is from the first to second offense or from the fourth to fifth offense. This is the same conclusion reached when only juvenile offenses were included in the analysis. On the basis of these data we conclude that the previous results were not produced by the fact that the analysis was limited to juvenile delinquency or ended at age 18 and that offense careers can be modeled by a one-step Markov chain for both the juvenile and adult years.

Because the data conform to this type of model, a summary or generating matrix can be estimated (matrix 6.3). Once again we can measure the goodness of fit between this summary model and each of the observed transitions. Given the results of the test of homogeneity, we would expect, at each of the offense transitions, that the observed transition probabilities would bear a close resemblance to the probabilities estimated by the model presented in matrix 6.3. With sixteen degrees of freedom, one of the test statistics reaches statistical significance, and it refers to the comparison of the summary matrix with the fifth data matrix. For the other four comparisons, however, the chi-square tests are not significant and, overall, the values in the summary matrix are similar to those in the observed matrices.

Probabilities contained in the summary matrix indicate that the most likely switch is to a nonindex offense regardless of the type of prior offense. The probabilities of moving to a nonindex offense vary from .2441, when the prior offense was damage, to .4751, when the prior offense was also nonindex. (The exceptionally low value associated with prior damage offenses relative to the other offense types is probably due to the very low frequency of damage offenses in the adult data file. In general, the probabilities associated with damage offenses appear unstable.) The next most likely move is to the state of desistance, with probabilities ranging from .2102 to .3191. These most likely switches are followed in order by moves to theft, injury, combination, and damage offenses. This is the same ordering observed in matrix 6.2, which is based on the juvenile data only. Moreover, the relative magnitudes of the corresponding probabilities for these two matrices are quite similar.

Finally, we examined offense specialization for the adult data. Recall that there was virtually no evidence of offense specialization for juvenile offenses. In general, the same conclusion is reached for adult offenses. The probabilities falling along the main diagonal are not substantially elevated above the probabilities for their respective columns. Nevertheless, one is most likely to move to a nonindex offense if the prior offense was nonindex, to an injury offense if the prior offense was an injury, and to a theft offense if the prior offense was a theft. Thus the evidence for offense specialization is somewhat stronger for adult offenses, especially for the offense of theft. Overall, however, the data presented in matrix 6.3 still argue against the conclusion that offenders become strongly specialized in their offense selections as their careers develop.

In general, the data for the sample's adult years are very similar to the data observed during the cohort's juvenile years. The offense transitions can still be typified as conforming to a one-step Markov chain in which the probability of committing a particular type of kth offense is dependent only on the type of $k -$ 1st offense and not on the prior offense history of the subject. In other words, the offense transition probabilities are independent of the number of offenses committed. Thus, even for adult offenses up to age 30 we can say that a subject is no more likely to commit an injury offense at the fifth offense than he is at the first offense. Moreover, although the adult data evidence a slightly greater tendency for offense specialization than the juvenile data, the probabilities in the summary matrix still indicate that there is no strong, consistent, statistically significant offense specialization. In general, the similarity of the data for the adult and juvenile years is remarkable. Our next task is to see if their entire careers, including *both* juvenile and adult offenses in the analysis, also conform to a one-step Markov model.

Juvenile and Adult Offenses Combined

As in the previous analysis, the crucial test is that of homogeneity. Are the probabilities of moving from offense types independent of the number of offenses committed when the juvenile and adult offenses are examined together? If we can accept the hypothesis of independence, we can conclude that the combined juvenile and adult careers can be typified as a Markov process.

The chi-square values (table 6.4) for the homogeneity tests indicate that we can indeed accept the hypothesis of independence. Values range from 10.0, when the $k -$ 1st offense is an injury, to 18.5, when it is a nonindex offense, and none of the values approach statistical significance. Thus the probability of moving from any type of $k -$ 1st offense to any type of kth offense can be said to be independent of time.

Given this conclusion, we can estimate a generating matrix (matrix 6.4) and test the "goodness of fit" between the observed transitions and those expected on the basis of the generating matrix. The test between the summary matrix and the first data matrix is significant, indicating that the probabilities contained in the summary matrix are not a close reflection of those observed for the transition from the first to the second offense. For comparisons of the summary matrix with

TABLE 6.4   Homogeneity Tests for Juvenile and Adult Offense Transitions, First to Fifth Transitions

Prior Offense	Number of Offenses	Chi-Square	Probability
Nonindex	586	18.5	.30
Injury	83	10.0	.90
Theft	160	12.9	.70
Damage	57	11.4	.70
Combination	86	17.7	.50

MATRIX 6.4   Summary Transition Matrix: Juvenile and Adult Offenders,
First to Fifth Transitions

$k - 1/k$	Nonindex	Injury	Theft	Damage	Combi-nation	Desist
Nonindex	.5083	.0588	.1164	.0199	.0468	.2514
Injury	.3616	.1951	.1139	.0083	.0358	.2853
Theft	.4241	.0915	.1929	.0187	.0831	.1897
Damage	.5706	.0668	.0574	.0108	.1472	.1472
Combination	.4696	.0618	.2029	.0318	.1521	.0819
Desist	.0000	.0000	.0000	.0000	.0000	1.0000

the second, third, and fourth matrices the chi-square tests are not significant. Finally, the chi-square associated with the comparison of the summary matrix and the fifth data matrix, 48.7, is again seen to be significant. One cell, however, which has extremely small expected and observed values, contributes 39.2 points to the total chi-square value of 48.72; if the contribution of that cell is eliminated the test is well below the .05 level of significance. In general, then, the results of both the homogeneity tests and these tests indicate that the probabilities contained in the summary matrix are reasonable estimates of the underlying process.

Matrix 6.4 presents the offense transition probabilities through the first five offense transitions. The major difference between this matrix and the one based on juvenile offenses only (matrix 6.2) is the diminution of probabilities associated with the absorbing state of desistance. For the juvenile data up to age 18 the probability of desisting after the kth offense is approximately .3000, while for the combined data it varies from .0819 to .2853. Although this is a considerable drop, it is not unexpected. The major impact of the addition of adult offenses between ages 18 and 30 is to extend the exposure period for the subjects and to dampen the biasing effect caused by truncating the earlier analysis at age 18. Because of this change we would expect the probability of desisting to be somewhat less when the adult data are included.

Aside from this major difference, the conclusions to be drawn from the probabilities in matrix 6.4 are similar to those based on the juvenile offenses only. Again we see that regardless of the type of $k - $ 1st offense committed, the kth offense will most likely be a nonindex offense. The probability of committing a nonindex offense varies from .3616, when the $k - $ 1st offense involves injury, to .5706, when the $k - $ 1st offense involves damage. The next most likely shift is to desistance, with probabilities ranging from .0819 to .2853, as we have just noted. After desistance the next most likely transition is to theft (.0574 to .2029), followed by injury (.0588 to .1951), combination (.0358 to .1521), and damage (.0083 to .0318). This is the same ordering observed for juvenile offenses only.

Finally, we note that there is little evidence of offense specialization. Probabilities along the main diagonal are not substantially greater than probabilities in their respective columns. The strongest evidence of offense specialization concerns injury offenses, for which the probability of moving from an injury to an injury is .1951, while the other probabilities in the injury column vary from .0588 to .0915. The probability of moving from a theft to a theft (.1929) is approximately the same as the probability of moving from a combination to a theft (.2029); and the probability of moving from a combination to a combination (.1521) is about the same as the probability of moving from a damage to a combination (.1472). Overall, the evidence for offense specialization is weak.

In general, the results for the juvenile and adult careers are very similar to those for the juvenile careers only. The stability of these results could be due, in part, to the inclusion of juvenile as well as adult offenses in the combined analysis. Two facts argue against this conclusion, however. The first is the similarity of the results based only on adult arrests; the second is that the combined analysis is based on 972 offenses, of which 436 are adult offenses. The combined analysis is not simply a replication of the juvenile analysis with a few adult offenses added. The number of adult offenses is sizable, and even with their inclusion, the earlier finding of the independence of offense type transitions and the number of offenses committed is replicated. Moreover, the earlier finding concerning the lack of offense specialization is also replicated.

The Effect of Juvenile Status Offenses

The foregoing analysis has indicated that transition probabilities based on adult offenses only and those based on combined juvenile and adult offenses can be said to conform to a one-step Markov chain. That is, the probability of moving to a particular type of offense is generally independent on the number of offenses already committed. Such a finding lends considerable support to the generalizability of the earlier conclusion (Wolfgang, Figlio, and Sellin 1972) when only juvenile offenses were available for analysis and suggests that the probabilistic model is not unique to the juvenile delinquency years. Nevertheless, the effect of one major difference between juvenile delinquency and adult criminality has yet to be controlled in this analysis: the effect of juvenile status offenses, which by definition cannot be lodged against an adult, has not been held constant.

The previous analyses were based on all offenses, including status offenses for which juveniles were arrested. As a result, there was an imbalance in the potential character of criminal activity during the juvenile and adult years for the sample subjects. In the present section all status offenses are eliminated from the data base and the offense transitions are reexamined for the juvenile and combined juvenile and adult categories. In this process criminal behaviors for which an individual could be arrested are held constant, and these data are directly comparable with the earlier data based on adult offenses only.

Because this analysis is concerned primarily with a methodological issue—the effect of status offenses on the results—our presentation is abbreviated and focuses on the results of the test of homogeneity and the probabilities found in the summary matrix. The data for juvenile offenders, eliminating status offenses, are presented in table 6.5 and matrix 6.5

TABLE 6.5   Homogeneity Tests for Juvenile Offense Transitions,
Excluding Status Offenses, First to Fifth Transitions

Prior Offense	Number of Offenses	Chi-Square	Probability
Nonindex	274	12.28	.70
Injury	36	13.07	.50
Theft	88	9.15	.90
Damage	38	10.38	.80
Combination	60	23.38	.10

MATRIX 6.5   Summary Transition Matrix: Juvenile Offenders, Excluding
Status Offenses, First to Fifth Transitions

$k - 1/k$	Nonindex	Injury	Theft	Damage	Combination	Desist
Nonindex	.3691	.0583	.1432	.0262	.0536	.3495
Injury	.2396	.1851	.1088	.0000	.0083	.4582
Theft	.3348	.0521	.1643	.0134	.1059	.3304
Damage	.6327	.0503	.0735	.0118	.0781	.1536
Combination	.3678	.0536	.2179	.0250	.1754	.1602
Desist	.0000	.0000	.0000	.0000	.0000	1.0000

With sixteen degrees of freedom, none of the chi-square tests for homogeneity reach statistical significance; only when the prior offense is classified as a combination offense does the test even approach significance at the conventional .05 level. Based on these test results, we cannot reject the null hypothesis and must conclude that the probabilities are, in fact, independent of time. At this level, then, the inclusion or exclusion of juvenile status offenses does not affect the results. Juvenile offense careers can be typified by a one-step Markov chain regardless of the presence or absence of juvenile status offenses in the offense counts.

The summary or generating matrix for these data is presented in matrix 6.5. The key issue with regard to these probabilities concerns their similarity to the probabilities contained in matrix 6.2, which includes status offenses. The two matrices are, in fact, almost identical. The only systematic difference between these and the previous probabilities is a slight decrease in the probabilities associated with moving to a nonindex offense. This finding is to be expected, however, because status offenses, which have been eliminated from matrix 6.5, are all classified as nonindex offenses. Aside from this expected difference the probabilities are remarkably stable.

Table 6.6 presents the results of the test for homogeneity for the combined juvenile and adult data, exclusive of juvenile status offenses. As with the data for juveniles only, none of the chi-square tests reach statistical significance. The test with the highest chi-square value is associated with prior combination of-

TABLE 6.6   Homogeneity Tests for Juvenile and Adult Offense Transitions, Excluding Status Offenses, First to Fifth Transitions

Prior Offense	Number of Offenses	Chi-Square	Probability
Nonindex	548	9.24	.90
Injury	84	11.04	.80
Theft	169	13.52	.50
Damage	49	18.72	.20
Combination	89	21.94	.10

MATRIX 6.6   Summary Transition Matrix: Juvenile and Adult Offenders, Excluding Status Offenses, First to Fifth Transitions

$k - 1/k$	Nonindex	Injury	Theft	Damage	Combi- nation	Desist
Nonindex	.4703	.0662	.1262	.0209	.0491	.2673
Injury	.3532	.1924	.1267	.0710	.0325	.2881
Theft	.4125	.0924	.2098	.0166	.0788	.1899
Damage	.4665	.1554	.0658	.0108	.1575	.1441
Combination	.4545	.0591	.1854	.0267	.1734	.1008
Desist	.0000	.0000	.0000	.0000	.0000	1.0000

fenses, but even here the probability level is less than .10. The null hypothesis of the independence of time and the probability of moving to a particular type of offense is not rejected.

The summary matrix for these data is presented in matrix 6.6. Again we are interested in the similarity of these probabilities and those obtained when status offenses were included in the data set; the latter were presented in matrix 6.4. The overall similarities of the probabilities contained in the two matrices are readily apparent. The systematic decrease in the probability of moving to a nonindex offense is again observable and expected. Aside from this one difference, the two matrices are identical.

Thus, eliminating juvenile status offenses from the data base does not seriously alter the results. The earlier findings are replicated, and the consistency of the results is remarkable. Whether one is examining the juvenile, adult, or combined careers of the sample subjects and whether one includes or excludes juvenile status offenses, the results of the analysis are almost identical.

Summary

This chapter has examined the Markovian character of the criminal careers of the 10 percent sample of the 1945 birth cohort. The original analysis, which was based on offenses up to age 18, indicated that the data were well represented by a first-order Markov process and that the type of offense committed was independent of the number of previous offenses. The probability of committing a particular type of offense was found to be dependent upon the type of $k - 1$st offense committed and not on the type of offenses committed before the $k - 1$st offense.

When the analysis is extended to age 30, the pattern of these results is unchanged. For both adult offenses and combined juvenile-adult offenses the results indicate that the data can be summarized by a one-step Markov process: the probability of committing a certain type of offense is found to be dependent only upon the type of $k - 1$st offense committed. Moreover, probabilities associated with shifts to various offense types are ordered in the same fashion for both the juvenile and the adult data. Regardless of the type of $k - 1$st offense, the sample offenders were most likely to move to a nonindex offense and were then most likely to move to the state of desistance, followed in order by theft, injury, combination, and damage. Finally, we note that even during the adult years there is little evidence of offense specialization. In general this analysis suggests that the findings presented in the original study are not unique to the juvenile years. The Markovian character of the criminal careers of the sample is evident for the juvenile period, for the adult period, and for the combined juvenile-adult period.

7   The Measurement of Time Intervals between Arrests

S. Bernard Raskin

This chapter is concerned with measuring the time span between offense transitions. This predictive study seeks to estimate the time between arrests for the first six offense transitions of the cohort sample. The measurement of time intervals between arrests is conceptually similar to an engineer's interest in the durability of a mechanical or an electronic component. In the same way, biostatisticians often must measure the effects of treatment regimens on the survival times of seriously ill patients. The technique they use, known as survival analysis, is thus most appropriate for estimating the length of an arrest-free period.

Survival analysis is especially applicable in that it minimizes the truncation effect related to censored observations. In this research an observation is censored when an individual was not apprehended for his next offense before the end of the thirtieth year of the sample. For example, an individual may have been arrested for his first offense in his twenty-sixth year and then arrested for a second offense two years later. This offender is therefore known to have desisted for exactly two years after his initial arrest. A second individual might have been apprehended for the first time at age 29 and then have desisted for one year until the observation period for the cohort was terminated at age 30. Although this offender is known to have desisted for at least one year after his first arrest, conventional techniques would either discard the information on him or treat him as a definite desister, even though an extension of the study period may well have shown recidivism. Unlike conventional techniques, survival analysis makes use of all the data by assuming that the same model applies to all individuals in the cohort regardless of the observations that may be truncated (Tuma and Hannan 1979, 213). Thus the life-table method assumes that those censored at the closing date of the study would have been exposed to the same hazard of recidivating as the noncensored cohort members who were exposed to risk for a longer time.

Survival or desistance times form a distribution that may be characterized by three mathematically equivalent functions in the sense that, if one of them is given, the other two may be derived (Gehan 1975, 629). Since two of the functions are used frequently in this report, a brief description of all three is given below.

1. The survivorship function (survival function) $S(t)$ can be defined as the probability that an individual desists longer than t. In practice, the survivorship function is estimated as the proportion of offenders desisting longer than t:

$$\hat{S}(t) = \frac{\text{number of individuals desisting longer than } t}{\text{total number of individuals}}.$$

$S(t)$ is also known as the cumulative proportion desisting at the end of the interval and is represented graphically by a survival curve.

2. The probability density function $F(t)$ is commonly estimated by:

$$\hat{F}(t) = \frac{\text{number of individuals recidivating in the interval beginning at time } t}{(\text{total number of individuals}) \, (\text{interval width})}.$$

3. The hazard function $H(t)$ is a conditional failure rate and can be defined as:

$$H(t) = \frac{\displaystyle\lim_{\Delta t \to 0} \quad P[\text{an individual of age } t \text{ recidivates in the time interval } (t, t = \Delta t)]}{\Delta t}.$$

The actuarial average hazard rate that yields a more conservative estimate is used in this study. It is obtained by:

$$H(t) = \frac{\text{number of individuals recidivating per unit time in the interval}}{(\text{number of individuals desisting at time } t) \\ - \frac{1}{2} \, (\text{number of recidivists in the interval})}.$$

The hazard function describes the aging process of the population and is represented graphically by a hazard plot. A related measure, the conditional proportion recidivating $q(t)$, is a single proportion and is thus conceptualized more readily than the less familiar hazard function. Nevertheless, like the hazard rate, it describes the proportion recidivating at time t, given that the individual has desisted up to time t. It is defined as:

$$q(t) = \frac{\text{number of recidivists in the interval}}{\text{number of desisters at the beginning of the interval}}.$$

Analysis

The sample data allow for the analysis of six successive offense transitions: first through sixth. The study of later transitions is not feasible owing to progressively smaller sample sizes. The survival experience of the sample can be summarized by examining the median time between offenses for the six transitions. The median is the preferred measure of central tendency, since the presence of offenders who did not recidivate by the end of the study renders the mean indeterminable, and it is also recommended when distributions are skewed to the right. The median is the point in time at which the value of the cumulative proportion desisting is 0.5; it is obtained through linear interpolation.

The longest median survival time, 36.28 months, was experienced between the first and second offenses. The second transition had a median desistance time of 18.86 months, representing a drop of 17.96 months from the first transition. Subsequent transitions ranged from 11.32 months, between the third and fourth offenses, to 8.31 months, between the fifth and sixth offenses. This range of only

3.01 months for the four transitions (third through sixth) suggests a uniformity of survival experiences for these transitions. This will be buttressed by other statistics presented in this chapter.

The life table provides an informative description of the status of the offenders at various time intervals subsequent to the prior offense. Table 7.1 describes the cumulative proportion of offenders who desisted until the end of the interval.

TABLE 7.1 Cumulative Proportion Recidivating at the End of the Interval for All Offenders

Months	Offense Transitions					
	1−2	2−3	3−4	4−5	5−6	6−7
0	.8299	.6905	.6313	.5920	.6211	.6230
6	.7337	.5933	.4880	.4591	.4283	.4672
12	.6503	.5090	.4226	.3708	.3141	.3680
18	.5820	.4346	.3428	.3110	.2636	.3262
24	.5377	.4072	.3099	.2991	.2485	.2676
30	.5044	.3831	.2958	.2870	.2327	.2174
36	.4394	.3343	.2301	.2184	.2082	.2174
48	.4188	.3165	.2053	.1985	.1648	.2082
60	.3882	.3015	.2053	.1776	.1551	.1777
72	.3785	.2852	.1927	.1776	.1551	.1666
84	.3612	.2766	.1927	.1598	.1437	.1551
96	.3484	.2721	.1853	.1385	.1175	.1551
108	.3404	.2624	.1853	.1385	.1175	.1396
120	.3289	.2570	.1853	.1385	.1175	.1396
132	.3258	.2570	.1853	.1385	.1175	.1396
144	.3258	.2484	.1853	.1385	.1175	.1396
156	.3210	.2484	.1853	.1385	.1175	.1396
168	.3089	.2484	.1853	.1385	.1175	—

The first row, at the zero interval, illustrates how the proportions surviving the first six months differed across offense transitions. The highest proportion surviving the first six months was obtained for the first transition (.8299), while the lowest proportion was obtained for the fourth offense transition (.5920). After the initial drop in the first two transitions, the third, fourth, fifth, and sixth transitions stabilized between .5920 (fourth transition) and .6230 (sixth transition). At the end of the next interval (6), the first transition again had the highest proportion surviving (.7337), while the fifth transition had the lowest proportion (.4283), which yielded a range of .3054. Table 7.2 describes the percentages of offenders who recidivated by the close of the first, second, third, and final years of the study. These percentages were obtained by subtracting from one the relevant proportions in table 7.1. The percentage recidivating by the end of the study was obtained from the final interval, which was 168 months for the first five transitions and 156 months for the sixth transition. At each interval there was an increase in the percentage recidivating from the first through third transitions.

TABLE 7.2   Percentage Recidivating by the End of the Interval

	Intervals					
Months	1st	2d	3d	4th	5th	6th
6 (1 year)	26.63	40.67	51.20	54.09	57.17	53.28
18 (2 years)	41.80	56.54	65.72	68.90	73.64	67.38
30 (3 years)	49.56	61.69	70.42	71.30	76.73	78.26
End of study	69.11	75.16	81.47	86.15	88.25	86.04

The third through sixth transitions displayed similar percentages recidivating. Thus the transition level was of greater importance up to the third transition, while later transitions were remarkably similar.

The cumulative proportion desisting, or the survival function as it is otherwise known, can also be illustrated graphically by a survival plot. The most striking contrast in survival functions was obtained when the first transition was compared with the fourth. This discrepancy in survival experience is reflected in figure 7.1, which is a plot of the cumulative proportions desisting for these two offense transitions. The steeper survival curve of the fourth transition represents a lower survival rate and therefore a shorter survival time. The more gradual and somewhat flatter survival curve of the first-to-second offense group reflects a higher survival rate and a longer survival time.

The survival curve may also be used to highlight the similarities between two or more populations. Figure 7.2 provides a graphic representation of the cumula-

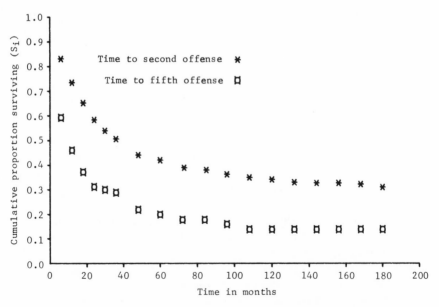

FIG. 7.1   Graph of survival function: first to second offense, fourth to fifth offense.

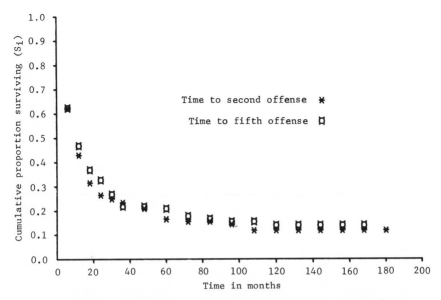

FIG. 7.2   Graph of survival function: fifth to sixth offense, sixth to seventh offense.

tive proportion desisting at both the fifth and sixth transitions. It is evident from this plot that the survival experiences of the two groups produced vividly similar curves. These graphic representations are, of course, in keeping with the numerical results reported earlier.

We have stated that the hazard rate $H(t)$ is a conditional failure rate, and it therefore indicates the hazard of recidivating for those who survive through time. A decreasing hazard rate suggests that the chances of continuing to desist improve with successive intervals. Similarly, an increasing hazard rate demonstrates increasing risks for desisters, while a stable hazard rate suggests a constant risk of recidivating across time.

Table 7.3 contains the hazard rates for the first six transitions. The first column reflects the hazards of those who survived until the beginning of the various intervals between the first and second offenses. Survivors were at the greatest risk of recidivating during the first six months, when the hazard rate was .0310. The lowest hazard rate (.0000) was found in the interval that began at the 144th month. During this period, none of those who survived to the beginning of the interval recidivated.

The general trend revealed from this column is one of decreasing hazards with time. The longer an individual is able to survive without committing his next offense, the better his chances of desisting from crime. This is a pattern that repeated itself throughout the analysis of this sample. In demography this is comparable to a population with a high infant mortality rate and improved life chances in later years. The crucial period for the delinquent is the initial months following an arrest, since the chances of recidivating at any one instant usually decrease over time.

TABLE 7.3   Hazard Rates for All Offenders for the First Six Transitions

	Offense Transitions					
Months	1–2	2–3	3–4	4–5	5–6	6–7
0	.0310	.0610	.0753	.0854	.0779	.0476
6	.0205	.0252	.0427	.0421	.0612	.0396
12	.0201	.0255	.0239	.0355	.0513	.0201
18	.0185	.0263	.0348	.0292	.0292	.0329
24	.0132	.0108	.0168	.0065	.0098	.0345
30	.0107	.0102	.0078	.0069	.0109	.0000
36	.0115	.0113	.0208	.0226	.0093	.0036
48	.0040	.0046	.0095	.0079	.0194	.0132
60	.0063	.0041	.0000	.0093	.0051	.0054
72	.0021	.0046	.0053	.0000	.0000	.0060
84	.0039	.0025	.0000	.0088	.0064	.0000
96	.0030	.0014	.0033	.0119	.0167	.0088
108	.0019	.0030	.0000	.0000	.0000	.0000
120	.0029	.0017	.0000	.0000	.0000	.0000
132	.0008	.0000	.0000	.0000	.0000	.0000
144	.0000	.0028	.0000	.0000	.0000	.0000
156	.0012	.0000	.0000	.0000	.0000	—
168	—	—	—	—	—	—

An additional measure described earlier that has greater currency in demographic analysis is the conditional proportion recidivating $q(t)$. The first column of table 7.4 describes the conditional proportion recidivating $q(t)$ at the various intervals for the first transition. Thus, .1701, or 17.01 percent, terminated in the first six-month interval; .1159, or 11.59 percent, of those who survived to the beginning of the next interval terminated within the second six-month period; and so on. Once again, the conditional proportion recidivating revealed a higher percentage of survivors committing their next offense in the earlier intervals. This is in keeping with the conclusion reached from the first column of table 7.3, in that the passage of time leads to reduced hazards.

In addition to the change in hazards as the individual moves further in time from the previous offense, there are also differences across the first six offense transitions. In the first six-month period, 17.01 percent of the first-time offenders would be rearrested. The next transition shows that 30.95 percent of the second-time offenders would be rearrested within six months. The remaining transitions ranged between 36.87 percent recidivating at the third transition and 40.8 percent recidivating at the first six months after a fourth arrest.

A general pattern has been noted in which the hazards increased from the first to the second transition and then stabilized at a higher level for the remaining transitions. This trend was apparently reversed at the later intervals, when most of the later transitions yielded a zero hazard rate (tables 7.3 and 7.4). A rate of zero means that none of the individuals recidivated within the interval. On the other hand, the first transition had only one interval with a zero hazard rate (144

TABLE 7.4   Conditional Proportion Recidivating for All Offenders for the First Six Transitions

| Months | Offense Transitions | | | | | |
	1-2	2-3	3-4	4-5	5-6	6-7
0	.1701	.3095	.3687	.4080	.3789	.3770
6	.1159	.1408	.2271	.2244	.3103	.2500
12	.1136	.1420	.1340	.1923	.2667	.2124
18	.1051	.1462	.1889	.1613	.1604	.1136
24	.0760	.0630	.0959	.0385	.0571	.1195
30	.0620	.0593	.0455	.0804	.0635	.1875
36	.1289	.1273	.2222	.2391	.1053	.0000
48	.0468	.0532	.1075	.0909	.2083	.0426
60	.0730	.0476	.0000	.1053	.0588	.1463
72	.0250	.0541	.0615	.0000	.0000	.0625
84	.0459	.0302	.0000	.1000	.0741	.0690
96	.0353	.0163	.0385	.1333	.1818	.0000
108	.0229	.0357	.0000	.0000	.0000	.1000
120	.0338	.0206	.0000	.0000	.0000	.0000
132	.0095	.0000	.0000	.0000	.0000	.0000
144	.0000	.0333	.0000	.0000	.0000	.0000
156	.0147	.0000	.0000	.0000	.0000	.0000
168	.0377	.0000	.0000	.0000	.0000	—

months), while the second transition yielded only three zero hazard intervals (132, 156, and 168 months). Thus, even though the first and second transitions revealed lower hazards during the initial intervals, they also produced nonzero hazard rates through most of the study period. This suggests more rapid and less protracted "burnout" periods for the third through sixth transitions, whereas the earlier transitions experienced slower and longer survival times.

Summary and Conclusions

This chapter has analyzed the survival experience of the sample offenders through the first six offense transitions. The longest median time between arrests, 36.82 months, was obtained for the first transition; the shortest, 8.31 months, was obtained for the fifth transition. The median survival time of the last four transitions yielded a range of only 3.01 months, thus suggesting a uniformity of survival experiences for these transitions. The cumulative proportion desisting, or the survival function $S(t)$, also demonstrated a decrease from the first to the second transition. Once again, the third through sixth transitions displayed similar percentages desisting and recidivating. This finding suggests a general principle in which the transition level is of greater importance up to the third transition, while later transitions are remarkably similar. This conclusion complements the analysis made by Wolfgang, Figlio, and Sellin in the original report on the cohort data. At that time they recommended that intervention programs would prove most profitable if instituted after the third offense:

The most relevant question, then, is at what point in a delinquent boy's career an intervention program should act. One answer would be that the best time is that point beyond which the natural loss rate, or probability of desistance, begins to level off. Because 46 percent of the delinquents stop after the first offense, a major and expensive treatment program at this point would appear to be wasteful. We could even suggest that intervention be held in abeyance until the commission of the third offense, for an additional 35 percent of the second-time offenders desist from then on. Thus we could reduce the number of boys requiring attention in this cohort from 3,475 after the first offense, to 1,862 after the second offense, to 1,212 after the third offense, rather than concentrating on all 9,945 or some other large subgroup (such as nonwhites or lower SES boys) under a blanket community action program. Beyond the third offense, the desistance probabilities level off. (1972, 254)

It is also evident from this analysis that the survival pattern leveled off after the third offense and that these latter offenders recidivated sooner than the first- and second-time recidivists. There was subsequently more room to stretch the survival time of those going through the third through sixth transitions, while the first and second transitions were already experiencing survival times that were relatively higher.

The hazard rates, the conditional proportion recidivating, and the cumulative proportions desisting all suggest that intervention programs, in addition to being directed at selected transitions, should be focused on the first six months after a prior arrest, for it is in this period that the heaviest concentration of delinquency exists. The second through sixth transitions all show that at least 30 percent of the offenders were rearrested during this initial interval. At the fourth transition as many as 41 percent committed their fifth known offense within six months of their fourth offense. Subsequent hazard rates in the later intervals of the six transitions describe a hazard function that decreased with time. An individual who survived through the initial intervals without recidivating would have been exposed in the later intervals to improved chances of desisting. Mobilization of incapacitative and rehabilitative efforts during the especially hazardous time soon after a prior arrest should have at least some effect in lengthening the crime-free period and thus the median time between offenses. The same effort invested at a later date would have a limited ability to reduce recidivism, since the risk of committing a next offense in the later intervals was already substantively lower. Thus a more rational distribution of criminal justice efforts could curtail recidivism or at least postpone the next offense.

There is a general pattern in which the first two transitions yielded nonzero hazards in almost all the intervals, while the third through sixth transitions produced mainly zero hazards in the later intervals. Thus, in the third through sixth transitions there was a combination of initially high hazards followed by a zero chance of recidivating in the closing intervals. It was suggested that this hazard pattern described a more rapid and less protracted "burnout" period for the third through sixth transitions, whereas the earlier transitions experienced a slower and therefore longer survival time. This finding buttresses the combined notions that intervention efforts should concentrate on the period immediately after the prior offense for the third through sixth transitions.

The findings reported in this chapter are of course tentative, but they nevertheless suggest possible policy decisions. There are additional questions that policymakers would need answered: What effect did intervention programs have on desistance trends? Are there specific variables that allow better prediction of survival trends? The first of these questions is more difficult to address with the current data, for detailed information is required about the kind of official reaction to the crime and the duration of that reaction; however, survival analysis appears to be a promising means of addressing this issue. The second question is currently under investigation using a more detailed analysis of the cohort broken down by various variables. Preliminary results indicate that there are variables that provide additional information about time intervals between arrests. Moreover, a multivariate proportional hazards technique that allows for the simultaneous consideration of a number of variables might be employed in future analyses.

8 The Disposition of Adult Arrests: Legal and Extralegal Determinants of Outcomes
James J. Collins

Thus far we have examined the official criminal careers of the sample members by types and patterns of offenses. In this chapter our attention shifts from the character of offenses to the official reactions to those offenses. The analysis describes the types and severity of sentences the subjects received as well as the legal and extralegal correlates.

The analysis relies on the extensive dispositional data base that was collected during the last phase of the cohort follow-up, that is, when the subjects were 30 years of age. A major aspect of the project was to assess the performance of the criminal justice system with respect to the policy of incapacitation.[1] As a result, instead of simply recording the final sentence for each arrest—probation or incarceration—we attempted to trace each case through the criminal justice process. The data analyzed in this chapter and the next reflect the interests of that portion of the follow-up project.

We secured conviction and incarceration data from a number of sources: Philadelphia police, court, and prison records; FBI criminal histories; state and local correctional institutions; and the Federal Bureau of Prisons. We used these sources in a complementary manner so that we could reconstruct the history of an offense from arrest through release from prison. In the most straightforward case, an arrest found in the police records was followed through the adjudication process, and the prison records were used to compute the amount of time served. In other cases, however, the progress of an arrest through the criminal justice system had to be pieced together from a variety of the data sources listed above.

For the most part, though, the sample members committed their offenses in Philadelphia; about 93 percent of their arrests were in the city. Thus we collected the bulk of our dispositional data from the Philadelphia courts and prisons. Overall, we gathered information on 94 percent of all the adult offenses.

The following sections describe the dispositions of the adult arrests of the cohort sample between ages 18 and 30. These outcomes depend on a variety of factors: offense type and seriousness, the quality of the evidence available, and the arrest history of the individual. The data also suggest that nonlegal factors, such as race and age, influence dispositional outcomes.

1. This portion of the follow-up study was conducted under an additional National Institute of Justice grant entitled Offender Careers and Restraint: Probabilities and Policy Implications.

Race and Disposition

Thornberry (1973, 1979) has shown that race influenced the sentencing of the cohort members during their juvenile period. The nonwhites received more severe dispositions, even after the effects of offense seriousness, prior record, and SES were controlled. Examination of the dispositional data for the cohort sample indicates that race was again a factor in sentence severity during the adult years.

In table 8.1 the results of three criminal justice system outcomes are summarized by race. Racial comparisons are presented separately for index and nonindex offenses[2] and for individuals with two or fewer and three or more previous arrests. Past research has shown that offense seriousness and prior record are the two primary determinants of the severity of sentencing and hence should be controlled in the present analysis.

The first row of table 8.1 presents the percentages of arrests that were *not* dismissed at or before the first court hearing. These percentages indicate that offenders committing the more serious index offenses and those with longer prior records were more likely to be held for court. They also indicate that the nonwhites were less likely to have arrest charges dismissed and were thus more likely to be held for court. In three of the four racial comparisons the difference is statistically significant: nonwhites arrested for index offenses regardless of their prior records, nonwhites arrested for nonindex offenses who had three or more prior arrests, and nonwhites arrested for nonindex offenses who had two or fewer previous arrests were more likely than the whites to be held for court, but this difference does not reach the .05 level of significance.

The second row of table 8.1 does not reveal significant racial differences in the percentages of individuals found guilty at the court stage. Three of the four racial comparisons indicate that the nonwhites were more likely to be found guilty, but the differences are not statistically significant.

There is strong evidence, however, that the nonwhites were more likely to be incarcerated.[3] They were disproportionately overrepresented in three of the four racial comparisons (beyond the .01 probability level). The nonwhites who committed index offenses and had two or fewer previous arrests were more likely to be incarcerated than comparable whites, but the difference is not significant.

It is clear from table 8.1 that offense seriousness and prior record are important determinants of criminal justice system outcomes. The findings of this table indicate that at the early disposition stage and in decisions to incarcerate, the nonwhites were treated more severely than the whites. The findings are consistent with a hypothesis that racial bias characterized criminal justice system operations during the adjudication and sentencing of the follow-up offenders.

---

2. In this chapter index offenses are criminal homicide, forcible rape, aggravated assault, robbery, burglary, larceny, and auto theft. Nonindex offenses are all others.

3. All incarcerations beyond three days' duration are included. Many of these incarcerations were served in a detention (preconviction) status.

TABLE 8.1 Disposition of Adult Arrests by Race, Offense Type, and Previous Arrest Record

	Previous Arrests							
	Index Offenses				Nonindex Offenses			
	0–2		3+		0–2		3+	
	Whites	Nonwhites	Whites	Nonwhites	Whites	Nonwhites	Whites	Nonwhites
	%	%	%	%	%	%	%	%
Disposition	(N)	(N)	(N)	(N)	(N)	(N)	(N)	(N)
Held for court	37.5[a]	76.7[a]	74.1[a]	87.2[a]	22.1	31.9	43.0[a]	59.2[a]
	(3)	(33)	(40)	(163)	(19)	(23)	(49)	(125)
Guilty at court stage	66.7	67.4	58.3	65.4	67.6	52.2	58.9	68.1
	(10)	(31)	(35)	(142)	(23)	(12)	(43)	(109)
Incarcerated	42.1	49.1	47.2[a]	64.2[a]	3.2[a]	21.5[a]	21.5[a]	40.7[a]
	(8)	(27)	(34)	(158)	(3)	(17)	(31)	(111)

Note: Owing to missing data the number of cases in each dispositional category may seem anomalous. For example, according to the table more whites arrested for index offenses who had zero to two previous arrests were found guilty at the court stage than were held for court (ten versus three). In actuality this was not the case. We did not code dispositional data for outcomes unless we explicitly found the appropriate record data, and the missing data are unevenly distributed over categories. However, we did not find evidence of systematic racial variation in the missing data.

[a] Chi-square test significant at less than .05.

There is no evidence, however, that racial bias affected the determination of guilt at the court stage. Thus the findings for the criminal justice system disposition of adult arrests for the 1945 Philadelphia cohort sample are consistent with Thornberry's findings for the arrests of juveniles in the cohort.

However, the consistency of racial bias for the sample is not in agreement with preponderant findings from other research, which, as Thornberry (1979) and others have pointed out, has tended to find little evidence of racial discrimination in sentencing when offense seriousness and prior record are controlled. Some research showed, however, that the racial factor is selectively significant. Pope (1976) found similar sentencing levels for nonwhites and whites in urban areas in California, but in rural areas nonwhites were sentenced more severely. Hagan's (1974) assessment of the effects of "extralegal attributes" in criminal sentencing for previously reported research supported the interpretation that race is selectively significant.

The findings of this chapter, supported by Thornberry's earlier analysis, suggest that the Philadelphia criminal justice system, during the period when the 1945 cohort members were exposed to it, was not color-blind. Race was not a primary determinant of dispositional severity, but it was a significant factor.[4]

The findings of table 8.1 also suggest an interpretation of certain criminal justice system characteristics that may permit or promote racial bias. As indicated in table 8.1, there was little evidence of discrimination at the stage of adjudication when operations are more formalized, rule bound, and visible. In general, less discretion was available to the system actors at the court stage than at the early stages or at sentencing. Before formal charges are filed by a prosecutor and after a formal determination of guilt, the decision makers in the criminal justice system are freer to act on the basis of personal evaluation. It appears that individual decision-making criteria are more likely than formalized rules and processes to include discriminatory components.

Age and Disposition

Interpreting age-related differences in the dispositions of arrests is complicated by the existence of separate juvenile and adult justice systems and by the systematic relationships that exist between age, offense seriousness, and prior record. Both offense seriousness and prior record are directly related to age, and because these two factors are the primary determinants of dispositional severity, they should be controlled in the estimation of age effects. But because the number of arrested sample cohort offenders at any given age, especially after age 16, is not large, the simultaneous control of age, offense seriousness, and prior record is not possible. For this reason we discuss the disposition of arrests by age for index offenses only, thereby partially controlling for offense seriousness.

4. The finding of apparent racial bias applies to the period of roughly 1955–75, for during these years the arrests of the cohort members were processed by the Philadelphia criminal justice system. The vast majority of cases that have determined the results reported here were processed before 1970. For this reason no judgment is possible about the existence of racial bias in Philadelphia's criminal justice system for the period since 1975.

TABLE 8.2   Probabilities of Conviction and Incarceration for Index Offense Arrests by Age Categories

Age at Arrest	Number of Index Offense Arrests	Probability of Conviction[a] (N)	Probability of Incarceration (N)	Probability of Conviction and Incarceration
< 18	290	.40 (116)	.43 (50)	.17
18–21	165	.61 (100)	.57 (57)	.35
22–25	165	.41 (71)	.58 (41)	.24
26–29	118	.46 (54)	.57 (31)	.26
Total	738	.46 (341)	.52 (179)	.24

[a]For the juvenile years, conviction refers to a formal adjudication of delinquency by the juvenile court.

The data in table 8.2 summarize the probability of conviction given arrest, the probability of incarceration given conviction, and the combined probability of conviction and incarceration by offender age for arrests for an index offense. The table shows that 46 percent of all index offense arrests resulted in conviction and 52 percent of the convictions resulted in incarceration. Overall, 24 percent of the index offense arrests resulted in the conviction *and* incarceration of an offender.

Table 8.2 suggests that age influences the probability of conviction between the juvenile years and the immediately succeeding young adult years. Juvenile index offense arrests resulted in conviction (adjudication) 40 percent of the time. The probability of such a conviction for offenders aged 18 to 21 is 61 percent, and the difference between these two age periods is statistically significant ($p <$ .02). Differences between other age groups, in terms of the probability of conviction, do not reach the .05 level of significance. Nevertheless, the probability of conviction is uniformly higher for arrests during the adult years.

Given conviction, the probability of incarceration is also higher in the adult years in comparison to the juvenile years, although none of the age-group differences are statistically significant. Given conviction for an index offense, 43 percent of the juveniles were incarcerated, while the probability of incarceration for the adults varies between .57 and .58.

The cumulative probability of conviction and incarceration, given arrest for an index offense, is displayed in the last column. Probabilities range from .17 to .35 and are highest for men aged 18 to 21. The differences between juveniles and young adults are statistically significant, but none of the other juvenile/adult age-group comparisons are significant. Nevertheless, the probabilities are higher for all the adult categories.

The findings of table 8.2 suggest that age may have been a significant factor in the likelihood of conviction and incarceration following arrests for index offenses. Combined conviction and incarceration probabilities are higher during the adult years than in the juvenile years, but this is due entirely to differences between juveniles and young adults aged 18 to 21. Differences between juveniles and older adults aged 22 to 30 and among the adult groups are not significant. In general, the highest conviction rates are associated with the young adults.

Lower probabilities of conviction and incarceration during the juvenile years were no doubt partly a function of the less serious prior records of the juvenile arrestees. It takes time to accumulate arrests, and on the average the juvenile offenders simply did not have the opportunity that the older offenders had to develop serious arrest records. Given the known direct relationship between prior record and criminal justice system sanctions, juveniles were expected to receive less harsh sanctions than adults.

The findings displayed in table 8.2 for the Philadelphia cohort sample are consistent with findings for Los Angeles. Greenwood, Petersilia, and Zimring (1980) found that 18-year-olds were more likely than older offenders to be convicted and incarcerated, with only some slight indication of leniency for the offense of burglary. However, the authors' review of the evidence also indicated that in two other jurisdictions—Franklin County, Ohio, and New York City—some leniency was shown to young adult offenders. Thus the jurisdiction itself apparently has an effect on the relationship between age and the application of criminal sanctions.

Although the data in table 8.2 indicate that the young adult offenders aged 18 to 21 received comparatively harsh treatment, a second factor or set of factors suggests that the observed differences may not be a function of offender age. The findings displayed here took place over a relatively long period. The first recorded arrest for a cohort sample member occurred in 1952; the last occurred in 1975, a span of twenty-three years. Most of the index arrests analyzed here occurred during the sixteen-year period between 1959 and 1974, and the behavior of the juvenile and adult justice systems may have changed in relevant ways during that period. Thus a time-period explanation, although less plausible than an age explanation, cannot be ruled out.

The data available do not permit confident interpretation of the relative effect that offender age and time period had on the likelihood of conviction and incarceration following an arrest for an index offense. Although it appears that adults were more likely to be convicted and incarcerated, it is also likely that prior record explained part of the observed age differences, and it is also possible that period effects influenced the observed patterns of dispositions.

Justice System Performance for One-Time, Recidivist, and Chronic Offenders

Table 8.3 provides conviction and incarceration probabilities for the index offense arrests of one-time offenders, recidivists (those arrested two to four times), and chronic offenders. The conviction and incarceration probabilities did not differ for the one-time and recidivist offenders. For the one-time offenders and the recidivists, 24 percent and 31 percent of the index offense arrests, respectively, resulted in convictions. On the other hand, half of the index arrests for the chronic offenders resulted in convictions, a proportion significantly different from that associated with either the one-time offenders or the recidivists.

The probability that incarceration would follow conviction was .29 for the one-time offenders and .28 for the recidivists. The chronic offenders, however, were much more likely to be convicted and incarcerated. The difference is statistically significant beyond the .05 level.

The difference between the probabilities of incarceration for the offender groups is not surprising. It is expected that convicted offenders with serious records will be more likely to receive prison sentences. The reason for the difference in conviction probabilities between the offender groups is not so apparent. If we view the adjudication process as operating in a legalistic manner—functioning to determine the legally defined guilt or innocence of an offender—we would expect conviction to be just as likely for an offender with a nonserious criminal history as for a chronic offender. If, however, the adjudication process functions from a crime-control perspective (Packer 1964) rather than from a legalistic perspective, then the findings shown in table 8.3 are not surprising. Apparently the criminal justice system attends to the offender's record not only at the sentencing stage but also earlier, in its deliberations concerning guilt or innocence.

TABLE 8.3   Probabilities of Conviction and Incarceration for Index Offense Arrests of One-Time, Recidivist, and Chronic Offenders

Offender Status	Number of Index Offense Arrests	Probability of Conviction (N)	Probability of Incarceration (N)	Probability of Conviction and Incarceration
One-time offenders	29	.24 (7)	.29 (2)	.07
Recidivists	94	.31 (29)	.28 (8)	.09
Chronic offenders	630	.50 (316)	.57 (179)	.29
Total	753	.47 (352)	.54 (189)	.25

Summary

The data describing how the criminal justice system handled the arrests of the 1945 Philadelphia cohort sample indicate that both legal and extralegal factors influenced outcomes. According to these data, serious offenses and offenders with more previous arrests were treated more harshly by the system. Slightly fewer than half the sample offenders arrested for index offenses were convicted; slightly more than half of those convicted were incarcerated. Overall, about one-quarter of the index offense arrests of the sample resulted in the imprisonment of an offender. However, the likelihood of the conviction and incarceration of arrested offenders with serious criminal records was much greater than the conviction and incarceration of offenders with less serious records.

The data also indicate that race had an effect on certain dispositions. Controlling for offense type and for criminal record, the data indicate that early in the adjudication process, and also at the sentencing stage, the nonwhites fared worse. They were more likely to be held for court action and to be incarcerated after arrest. The data do not show significant differences between the nonwhites and whites at the court stage of adjudication, however. Racial discrimination was more likely to operate at points in the system where visibility and formal rules were less influential.

The data provide some evidence that age or juvenile/adult criminal justice system differences influenced conviction and incarceration probabilities. Adult offenders were treated more harshly than juveniles. These differences, however, were not consistently significant, and the effects of criminal record and other factors could not be controlled in the age/outcome analysis.

The data discussed in this chapter show that the criminal justice system functioned rationally if the goal of the system was to sanction serious offenses and offenders more harshly. The data also indicate that the criminal justice system was apparently not free of racial bias in its handling of the 1945 cohort members who were arrested. Both of these outcomes manifest the crime control philosophy and racial attitudes that characterized the period when the cohort sample's arrests took place.

9 Some Policy Implications of Sample Arrest Patterns
James J. Collins

The preceding analysis described the official criminal careers of the sample members during their juvenile and adult years. Before continuing the analyses by examining the interview data, we shall discuss some policy implications that can be drawn from the analysis of the official data. In doing so, we shall repeat some data presented in previous chapters, but the discussion will be couched in terms of policy issues rather than data analysis.

Recent crime control deliberations have emphasized incapacitation as a viable approach to crime control (Petersilia, Greenwood, and Lavin 1978), on the assumption that the overall crime rate can be reduced if serious, repetitive offenders are withdrawn from the general population. Although intuitively appealing, such an approach is viable only if individual criminal careers conform to certain patterns. It is imperative, therefore, to describe accurately the criminal careers of offenders, a task well suited to the sample data and one to which we now turn.

Arrest Patterns

Forty-seven percent (459) of the cohort sample had officially recorded police contacts for nontraffic offenses by age 30. A total of 2,249 arrests were recorded against the sampled cohort members; 33 percent (753) of these arrests were for index offenses,[1] and 10 percent (226) were for the personal injury offenses of homicide, forcible rape, aggravated assault, and robbery. Table 9.1 shows the age distribution. The peak age for both the number of persons arrested and the number of arrests (columns 1 and 2) is 16. More cohort sample members were arrested at this age, and they were charged with more offenses and more index offenses than at any other age. Age 15 accounts for the next highest totals of both persons arrested and arrests. The number both of persons arrested and of arrests for all offenses diminished rapidly after age 16.

Other research data confirmed that juveniles are disproportionately responsible for arrests. Shannon (1977, 1979) examined birth cohorts of 1942 and 1949 for Racine, Wisconsin, and his results closely paralleled the findings for the Philadelphia cohort sample. Shannon's data showed that more of the 1942 cohort members were arrested at age 16 than at any other age. In the 1949 cohort, more members were arrested at age 17; the next highest age for the number of arrested offenders was 16.

1. Index offenses are criminal homicide, forcible rape, aggravated assault, robbery, burglary, larceny, and auto theft.

Official crime data indicate that juveniles and young adults are disproportionately likely to be arrested. According to the *Uniform Crime Reports* (*UCR*) for 1982, 18 percent of all persons arrested were under age 18; 34 percent were under age 21; and 53 percent were under age 25. Although the simple relationship between age and arrest rates is relatively clear, the interpretation of this relationship in terms of incapacitation is confounded by a number of important questions—for example, the size of the offender population and the magnitude of the individual crime rate. These questions have important policy implications (Blumstein, Cohen, and Nagin 1978), and official crime data do not allow the straightforward estimation of either offender population size or individual offense rates because the data cannot be summed for unique individuals under the

TABLE 9.1 Number of Arrests, Mean Arrests, and Offense Seriousness Scores by Age

Age	Number of Persons Arrested (1)	Number of Arrests, All Offense Categories (2)	Mean Number of Arrests (3)	Number of Index Offense Arrests (4)	Mean Number of Index Offense Arrests (5)	Mean Offense Seriousness Score[a] (6)
≤13	167	216	1.5	70	.32	121
14	98	147	1.5	33	.34	112
15	139	224	1.6	65	.45	125
16	170	292	1.7	72	.42	112
17	117	183	1.6	50	.43	124
18	96	126	1.3	44	.45	258
19	96	139	1.4	46	.48	273
20	88	127	1.4	36	.41	277
21	69	116	1.7	39	.57	398
22	56	81	1.4	29	.52	382
23	63	97	1.5	50	.79	396
24	62	113	1.8	45	.73	367
25	54	95	1.8	41	.76	486
26	47	85	1.8	33	.70	444
27	43	74	1.7	36	.84	582
28	31	51	1.6	25	.81	530
29	33	53	1.6	24	.73	567
30	17	30	1.8	15	.88	447
Total	459[b]	2,249	4.9[c]	753	1.60[d]	246

[a] Seven percent of the offenses could not be scored for seriousness because information was missing or incomplete in the police files. In addition, juvenile status offenses were not included in the mean scores for age 18 and below. Including these nonserious offense scores would have overstated differences between offenses committed before and after age 18.

[b] This figure is not a column total but is the total number of unique individual arrestees in the cohort sample.

[c] Column 2 divided by column 1; see note b.

[d] Column 4 divided by column 1; see note b.

UCR system. The Philadelphia cohort data do permit such an estimation, however, since individuals constitute the units of analysis.

The mean arrest estimates in columns 3 and 5 of table 9.1 are instructive in this regard; they indicate that there is very little variation by age when all arrest types are considered. The mean number of arrests between ages 14 and 30 varies between the narrow range of 1.3 and 1.8. According to the data, the *number* of active offenders—not their offense rate—explains the disproportionate involvement of juveniles and young adults among the offender population.

On the other hand, when only index offenses are considered, the age-specific mean number of arrests varies by age. Column 5 of table 9.1 shows that the mean number of index offenses committed at each age increases gradually from ages 13 to 21 and then, after a small decline, increases sharply to a value of .79 at age 23. Following that, the estimates remain relatively high until age 30. Overall, index offenses were far more likely to be committed during the adult years.

These findings are consistent with those of Blumstein and Cohen (1979) who used official data for Washington, D.C., to estimate the effects of age on the individual offense rates of officially active offenders. Analyzing *UCR* data for the years 1966–73, they created four artificial "age cohorts" and then examined the relationship of age and offense rates. They found that, with regard to age, arrest rates *increased* for some crime types and were stable for others. Thus the Blumstein and Cohen findings also suggested that the size of the active offender population—not the individual offense rate—is the more important determinant of the official crime rate.

In addition to age-specific arrest rates it is also informative to examine the issue of offense seriousness. Age-specific seriousness scores for offenses are included in the last column of table 9.1. These scores indicate clearly that the offenses committed by older offenders were much more serious than those of younger offenders. The mean score more than doubles between ages 17 and 18[2] and more than doubles again by age 27.[3]

Summarizing the findings from table 9.1, we see that 47 percent of the sample members had at least one recorded arrest by age 30. As reported elsewhere, more individuals were arrested and more arrests were recorded at age 16, after which both decreased with age. The mean number of arrests for all offenses does not vary over a wide range, indicating that the number of active offenders—not their *rate* of offending—is the paramount factor in explaining the age distribution of arrests. There is, however, a direct relationship between age and mean *index* of-

2. Juvenile status offenses were excluded from this analysis; thus the increase in seriousness scores from ages 17 to 18 was not due to the influence of status offenses.

3. The consistency of the age-graded findings for both arrest and seriousness score data provided some assurance that the findings were not simply a result of police-charging practices. Some research evidence suggests that police-charging practices for juveniles are often ambiguous (Klein, Rosensweig, and Bates 1975), and such ambiguity could affect the results of comparing arrest data over age. The alternative measures of offense seriousness used here (offense type and seriousness score) indicate that arrests during the adult years tended to be for more serious criminal behavior than were juvenile arrests. This finding permits greater confidence that the arrest data are a true indication of age-specific offense seriousness.

fense arrests. If an offender remained criminally active, there was a high probability that his arrests would be for index offenses. The seriousness scores also confirm the relative seriousness of arrests after the juvenile years. These scores increase substantially after age 17 and throughout the young adult years.

Offender Status and Arrest Patterns

Table 9.2 classifies the sample offenders, on the basis of their total career arrests, as one-time offenders, recidivists, or chronic offenders. Although the chronic offenders represent only 15 percent of the total sample and 32 percent of the official offenders, they are notable for their disproportionately large share of arrests, especially serious ones. Seventy-four percent of all arrests and 82 percent of all index offense arrests were charged to the chronic offenders. By age 30 these offenders averaged more than eleven total arrests and more than four index arrests each.

Comparing the seriousness scores for the offender groups also confirms that arrests of the chronic offenders tended to be much more serious than arrests of the one-time offenders and recidivists. Offenses of the one-time offenders have an average seriousness score of 153, while those of the recidivists and chronic offenders have average scores of 160 and 278, respectively.

The chronic offenders also committed more serious offenses *within* offense categories. Their index offenses involved more serious elements, such as the use of weapons, property loss, and personal injury. Overall, index offenses charged to the chronic offenders average 461 seriousness score points, while those charged to the one-time offenders and recidivists average 336.

The self-reported offense data collected from the cohort sample also confirm

TABLE 9.2   Arrest Patterns by Offender Status

Offender Status	Total Number of Arrests	Mean Number of Arrests	Number of Index Offense Arrests	Mean Number of Index Offense Arrests	Mean Offense Seriousness Score	Mean Number of Self-Reported Index Offenses[a]
One-time offenders (N = 155)	155	1.0	29	0.2	153	8.6
Recidivists (N = 159)	423	2.7	94	0.6	160	8.3
Chronic offenders (N = 145)	1,671	11.5	630	4.3	278	21.2
Total	2,249	4.9	753	1.6	246	14.2

[a] These mean estimates are based on the self-reports of 232 cohort sample offenders who were interviewed at age 26. The self-reported offensive behavior of the cohort sample is discussed in detail in later chapters of this volume.

that the chronic offenders were more seriously involved in criminal behavior. Based on their own reports, the chronic offenders reported committing an average of 21.2 index offenses by age 26. The one-time offenders and recidivists reported committing only 8.6 and 8.3 index offenses, respectively, by age 26. The self-reports from the cohort sample indicate that the chronic offenders committed two and one-half times as many serious offenses as the other two offender groups.

Probabilities of Recidivism

The probability of arrest and the time that elapses between arrests are important aspects of the arrest patterns of the sample offenders. Table 9.3 shows the probabilities associated with arrests, for all offense types and for index offenses, for the first to the twentieth offense rankings. As indicated, 47 percent of the sample were arrested at least once before age 30. Given a first arrest, there is a 66 percent chance that a second arrest will occur; 304 of the 459 first offenders were subsequently arrested. Of those arrested a second time, 72 percent were arrested a third time. The probability of a subsequent arrest increases to 80 percent after the third arrest and remains high—more than 80 percent for most of-

TABLE 9.3   Probability of Recidivism and Time between Arrests by Arrest Rank: All Arrests and Index Offense Arrests

Arrest Rank	Total Number of Persons Arrested (1)	Probability of Arrest (2)	Probability of Index Offense Arrest (3)	Time between Arrests (Years) (4)
1st	459	.47	.22	—
2d	304	.66	.27	2.2
3d	218	.72	.32	1.5
4th	174	.80	.36	1.1
5th	145	.83	.33	1.2
6th	122	.85	.33	1.1
7th	102	.84	.35	1.2
8th	91	.89	.39	1.1
9th	80	.88	.33	0.8
10th	72	.90	.42	0.8
11th	64	.89	.41	1.0
12th	50	.78	.46	0.7
13th	45	.90	.56	0.8
14th	43	.96	.44	0.9
15th	35	.81	.37	0.8
16th	27	.77	.37	0.9
17th	24	.89	.42	1.0
18th	20	.83	.30	0.7
19th	18	.91	.72	0.4
20th	16	.89	.63	0.9

fense ranks. Once an individual was arrested a third time, these data indicate that there was a very good chance he would be arrested again.

Column 3 indicates the probabilities associated with subjects being arrested for an *index* offense at each rank. Twenty-two percent of the cohort sample were arrested for an index offense by age 30. Twenty-seven percent of those who were arrested for a first offense of *any* kind were subsequently arrested for an index offense, and of those who experienced a second arrest, 32 percent were subsequently arrested for an index offense. The probabilities associated with ranks 4 through 9 vary between .33 and .39 and after the tenth arrest they escalate somewhat, but the number of cases upon which they are based becomes too small to generate a stable pattern. Overall, the likelihood that an individual will be arrested for an index offense increases with offense rank and, from the third offense on, remains relatively high.

Column 4 of table 9.3 provides a measure of arrest intensity for cohort offenders. Although the second arrest occurred an average of 2.2 years after the first, the time between the second and third arrests averaged 1.5 years. The time interval further declined to 1.1 years between the third and fourth arrests. In general this measure of offense intensity indicates that the time between arrests diminished as the number of arrests increased. After the eighth arrest, the subsequent arrests occurred after one year or less had elapsed.

The findings presented in table 9.3 provide consistent evidence about the pattern of recidivism. After the first few arrests there is a very high probability that subsequent arrests will follow, and there is a one-third or better chance that arrests will be for the relatively serious category of index offenses. Furthermore, not only do arrest and serious arrest probabilities increase for recidivists, but these arrests tend to occur closer together. More than two years typically pass between the first and second arrests, but only nine months pass between the ninth and tenth. (See chap. 7 for a fuller description of the time dimensions.)

Age, Race, and Arrests

Table 9.4 compares the arrest patterns of the white and nonwhite subjects. The nonwhites were disproportionately more likely to be arrested and were responsible for a disproportionate number of arrests. Although constituting only 28.6 percent of the cohort sample, they represented the 43 percent of the sample offenders who were charged with 61 percent of all of the officially recorded offenses. The mean number of arrests for the cohort sample members who were arrested at least once is 3.3 for the whites and 7.1 for the nonwhites. Although not shown in table 9.4, the nonwhites were also responsible for a high proportion of the index offenses: they accounted for 70 percent of all the index offense arrests.

The age-specific seriousness scores for the whites and nonwhites shown in the last two columns of table 9.4 clearly illustrate the more serious offensive behavior of the nonwhite subjects. The age-specific seriousness score data are generally consistent with the findings discussed for table 9.1—that is, seriousness

TABLE 9.4 Arrest Patterns and Seriousness Scores by Age and Race

Age	Persons Arrested Whites (1)	Nonwhites (2)	Number of Arrests Whites (3)	Nonwhites (4)	Mean Number of Arrests Whites (5)	Nonwhites (6)	Seriousness Score Whites (7)	Nonwhites (8)
≤13	76	91	87	129	1.1	1.4	120	112
14	49	49	60	87	1.2	1.8	67	132
15	75	64	96	128	1.3	2.0	122	106
16	90	79	129	163	1.4	2.1	62	134
17	59	52	81	102	1.4	2.0	91	147
18	46	48	57	69	1.3	1.4	193	309
19	46	48	59	80	1.3	1.7	148	368
20	31	55	39	88	1.3	1.6	78	368
21	23	49	41	75	1.8	1.5	393	401
22	24	35	36	45	1.5	1.3	281	456
23	21	41	34	63	1.6	1.5	251	479
24	22	41	39	74	1.8	1.8	240	426
25	22	35	33	62	1.5	1.8	522	470
26	6	40	13	72	2.7	1.8	304	463
27	12	31	20	54	1.7	1.7	514	616
28	6	23	16	35	2.7	1.5	480	548
29	10	22	11	42	1.1	1.9	399	608
30	6	11	16	14	2.7	1.3	416	598
Total	263[a]	196[a]	867	1,382	3.3[b]	7.1[c]	174	291

[a] Not a column total; these figures are the total number of unique individual arrestees in the cohort sample.
[b] Column 3 divided by column 1; see note a.
[c] Column 4 divided by column 2; see note a.

scores increased with age. However, the seriousness score data in table 9.4 also show that arrests of the nonwhites tended to be for far more serious offenses. At most ages the nonwhite arrests have higher seriousness scores, and the racial difference is especially noticeable during the adult years. For all but one year (age 25) of the 18–30 age span, the nonwhite seriousness scores exceed the white seriousness scores.

Comparing the arrest patterns by age and race reveals other differences. The arrests of the whites were more likely to occur during the juvenile years; 52 percent (453 of 867) of the arrests of whites, compared with 44 percent (609 of 1,382) of the arrests of nonwhites, occurred before age 18.[4] Although the numbers of arrests (columns 3 and 4 in table 9.4) were higher for the nonwhites at each age, the total number of offenders for the juvenile years was higher for the whites. At ages 18 and 19 the number of offenders for the racial comparison was approximately equal, but after age 19 many more nonwhites were arrested at each age up to 30. Furthermore, as indicated by columns 5 and 6, during the teenage years the nonwhites accumulated more arrests per capita, but fewer nonwhites were arrested. During the adult years the mean numbers of arrests per offender for the two groups approximated each other.[5] Thus, for those offenders who remained active into the adult years there was no apparent racial effect on the number of arrests.

In summary, the data in table 9.4 show that, based on their representation in the population, the nonwhites were disproportionately arrested and also experienced more arrests per capita. During the teenage years more whites were arrested, but the nonwhites were charged with more offenses per capita. Arrests of the whites were more likely to occur in the adult years. The mean number of adult arrests to age 30 tended to be similar for both groups. As measured both by the proportion of all arrests for index offenses and by their seriousness scores, however, the arrests of the nonwhites were for more serious offenses.

Implications for Crime Control

The arrest patterns described here suggest some implications for crime control policy, although the use of official crime data as the basis for drawing policy inferences must always be tentative.[6] Official data are a product of complex orga-

---

4. This white/nonwhite difference is significant beyond the .001 probability level under the chi-square test of statistical significance.

5. At ages 26, 28, and 30 the mean number of arrests for the whites is relatively high, but those estimates were also less stable because only six white subjects were arrested at each of those ages.

6. In this chapter we have not attempted to adjust arrest frequencies or means for "down time," or time not at risk. Some sample members were incarcerated for periods of time and thus were not at risk of being arrested for criminal behavior in the community for parts of the years covered here. These corrections have not been made because estimates of the incapacitation effect are not computed here and because the effect of not making the time-at-risk correction is conservative for the inferences drawn. The time-at-risk data show that adults and chronic offenders were more likely than the juvenile and nonchronic offenders to have been incarcerated and thus not at risk for periods of time. The disparity between the juvenile and adult and between the nonchronic and chronic arrest seriousness measures would have been magnified further by correcting for time at risk.

nizational behavior, and record-keeping practices vary between jurisdictions and change over time. We believe, but cannot be sure, that the 1945 Philadelphia cohort sample is also representative of birth cohorts in other urban places. Despite limitations that derive from the representativeness of the official crime data and the Philadelphia cohort sample, we believe it is useful and appropriate to draw tentative criminal justice policy inferences from the findings presented in this chapter. The policy implications suggested below are based on two assumptions: (1) control of more forms of personal crime should be a priority, and (2) justice system resources are scarce and ought to be expended on the basis of some set of priorities.

Juvenile Crime

The supposed tendency of the criminal justice system to treat juvenile arrests with more tolerance than adult arrests seems to be supported by the data. Such a policy implication is logical in two respects. First, juvenile arrests tend to be for less serious offenses. They are less likely to be for index offenses and, on the average, have lower seriousness scores. But where juvenile offenses are as serious as adult offenses, offenders should probably be treated equally.

A second reason why it is not appropriate for crime control to focus on juvenile crime is related to the efficient use of criminal justice resources. Because the disproportionate responsibility of juveniles for arrests is explained mostly by the number of officially active offenders rather than by their rate of offending, a crime control policy focusing on active juvenile offenders would not be as cost effective as one focusing on adult offenders. Any crime control approach focused on juvenile offenders will be comparatively expensive because it will have to deal with more individuals.

A Career Criminal Approach

The data analyzed above indicate that a relatively small percentage of offenders are responsible for a disproportionately large share of arrests. Results of the research for the juvenile years found that 6 percent of the entire cohort were responsible for 53 percent of all illegal acts charged to the cohort. These early findings were influential in the creation of career criminal programs (CCP) sponsored by the Law Enforcement Assistance Administration (Work 1974). CCPs are designed to focus resources for prosecution on the serious or recidivist offender under the assumption, supported by the cohort data and other data, that crime control efficiency will be enhanced by such a focus. If chronic offenders can be convicted and incarcerated, the incapacitative effect per unit of incarceration time served will be maximized. The relationship between individual offense rate, criminal justice system performance, and incapacitative effect has been demonstrated empirically by Shinnar and Shinnar (1975).

Blumstein and Moitra (1980), in criticizing the use of probability in recidivating as a basis for the CCP approach, analyzed the 1945 Philadelphia cohort data for the juvenile period and computed probabilities of recidivism using a geometric distribution. They found that the probability of recidivism is constant after the third arrest and inferred that recidivism rates are of little predictive value in distinguishing "career criminals" from those who desist from criminal activity. It is our position, however, that simple recidivism probability estimates are not, by themselves, an adequate basis for assessing the value of a CCP strategy. Specifically, based on several dimensions of the 1945 Philadelphia cohort sample data to age 30, the CCP strategy receives support. There are four factors that, taken together, suggest a CCP approach is appropriate:

1. As table 9.3 indicates, after the third arrest there is approximately an 80 percent chance that subsequent arrests will follow. An important implication of this high, relatively constant recidivism probability is that the "false positive" rate, if recidivism probability is a basis for special prosecution efforts, will be relatively low.

2. The probability that a subsequent arrest after the third arrest will be for an index offense is high and continues to escalate. Table 9.3 shows that the probability of an index offense rearrest ranges between .36 and .72 after the third arrest.

3. The time that elapses between arrests decreases with accumulating arrests. Table 9.3 shows that 2.2 years elapsed between the first and second arrest, while 1.1 years elapsed between the third and fourth arrest.

4. Arrests of chronic offenders develop much higher seriousness scores than arrests of nonchronic offenders. Table 9.2 provides these estimates and indicates that the arrests of chronic offenders are more likely than the arrests of one-time or nonchronic offenders to involve serious offense elements such as victim injury and property loss.

Despite our argument that the empirical evidence supports a CCP approach to crime control, we also acknowledge that certain factors make it difficult to implement such a strategy. For example, it has been shown that offense rates, especially serious offense rates, eventually decrease with age. Other research data that go beyond age 30 have confirmed that the direct or stable relationship between serious offensive behavior and age is eventually reversed (Boland and Wilson 1978; Petersilia, Greenwood, and Lavin 1978; Peterson, Braiker, and Polich 1980; Pittman and Gordon 1958). Older offenders are comparatively unlikely to commit serious offenses. Thus relatively few years of the adult life span provide an opportunity to maximize the incapacitative effect of incarceration.

A second factor that complicates the implementation of an incapacitative focus on chronic offenders is related to the criminal justice system itself. The criminal justice system usually operates in a complex bureaucratic setting where change is difficult. A recent evaluation of four career criminal programs found that the programs produced little change in the incarceration levels of career criminals compared with levels before the implementation of CCPs (Chelimsky and Dahmann 1980). Apparently the adjudication process was already dealing with the serious offender in a comparatively efficient manner. Using the Philadelphia birth cohort sample data, Collins (1981) also examined criminal justice system performance with chronic and nonchronic offenders and found that the system performed most efficiently against chronic offenders.

In general, although our data indicate that an incapacitation policy for adult recidivist offenders is empirically valid on the basis of crime control considerations, such a policy needs to be implemented carefully. The CCP approach should focus generally on the young-adult age span, and careful attention should be paid to the operational criminal justice system aspects of these programs.

Racial Implications

The findings presented in this chapter, which compared the arrest patterns of the whites and nonwhites in the cohort sample, are not an appropriate basis for policy interpretation. Although the nonwhites were involved more seriously in criminal activity as measured by the arrest data, it is clearly not acceptable to use these empirical findings as the basis for recommending differential treatment of nonwhites by the criminal justice system.

When we consider the policy implications of the racial comparisons discussed here, the need for a systematic theoretical understanding of the findings is clear. This need applies to all the empirical findings presented here, but it is especially clear when race—not age or previous record—is to be the basis for policy interpretation. Societal values do not and should not permit policies that provide for harsher treatment on the basis of race. Some argue convincingly that minorities are already treated more harshly by the criminal justice system, but that is an issue related primarily to the practice—not the policies—of criminal justice.

Summary

Several major summary points emerge from the descriptive analysis of the arrest patterns of the 1945 Philadelphia cohort sample described in this chapter. First, the data suggest that the number of officially active offenders was more important than the individual offense rates of these offenders in accounting for the official crime rate and, further, that the percentage of sample members who remained officially active in crime dropped dramatically after the juvenile years. Second, those who remained officially active in crime tended to be arrested for progressively more serious offenses, with a high probability of recidivism and a shorter time period between arrests. Third, the arrests of the whites were likely to occur during the juvenile years. Based on age-specific mean arrest rates and age-specific offense seriousness scores, however, the offenses of the nonwhites tended to be more serious. Furthermore, as indicated by our data up to age 30, the disproportionate involvement of the nonwhites in official crime increased with age.

Two major policy interpretations seem consistent with the empirical findings. First, the seriousness and distribution of arrests during the juvenile years suggest a more lenient adjudication policy toward juvenile arrests. Second, despite some data ambiguity and difficulties in implementing programs, the results suggest that special prosecution policies for chronic recidivists are appropriate and that the records of serious, violent juvenile offenses should be considered in sentencing offenders age 18 and older in the adult criminal court.

10 Race and Class Differences in Official and Self-Reported Delinquency
Paul E. Tracy, Jr.

The accumulation of knowledge in any scientific discipline is achieved mostly through empirical research conducted in well-defined substantive areas. For criminology these areas principally involve documentation of the character and extent of criminal activity and description of the offending population. Although these broad contexts give rise to other research issues, settings, and methods, the underlying goal is the same: the collection and analysis of data essential to understanding the relationship between criminality and the social structure of society. In confronting this task, the criminologist has most often relied on official statistics on crime and offenders that could be found in police, court, and prison records. The most common source has been the *Uniform Crime Reports* (*UCR*) of the FBI. Compiled annually since 1930, the *UCR* employs a crime classification system that is purported to represent meaningful measures of both the amount and the quality of crime, particularly the more serious offenses.

Despite the frequency with which they have been used, there is ample literature to indicate that official crime data are beset with problems related to both the reporting and the classification of crime (see, for example, Cressey 1957; Robison 1966; Wolfgang 1963). Official data may not adequately reflect the true amount or quality of crime, and offenders who are officially processed by the criminal justice system may constitute a biased sample of the total population of offenders (see, for example, LaFave 1962; Piliavin and Briar 1964; Terry 1967a,b).

These issues have serious implications. For example, it has been suggested that criminologists, unlike scholars in most other spheres of research, have relied upon terms, concepts, and definitions of units of investigation they did not establish, a practice that, if continued, could delay the growth of more sophisticated knowledge of crime (Wolfgang 1963, 725). Also, official data constitute a sample of persons and events with an unknown degree of bias concerning the types of delinquents and delinquencies, which may be over- or underrepresented. Consequently, reliance on official data constrains the disentangling of factors that explain criminal behavior from those that explain why some offenders are officially processed and labeled as delinquents (Hood and Sparks 1970, 12).

Therefore, relying exclusively on police data and other official offender statistics may bias research endeavors and theoretical developments essential to such research. As long as the focus is on such a restricted range of the phenomenon, it is problematic whether criminology will be able to properly describe and subsequently explain criminal behavior.

In light of these concerns, other measures have been used to map the trends and patterns of criminal activity. The self-report approach to the study of crime and delinquency has been suggested as a way to avoid the problems associated with police data. Soliciting information directly from respondents concerning crimes for which they have never been arrested may obviate the biases of official data. According to Hood and Sparks, self-report studies serve three important functions:

> First, they make possible an assessment of the *number of people* in the population as a whole who commit (or have committed) various deviant acts and the frequency with which they have done so. Secondly, by abolishing the artificial dichotomy between delinquents and nondelinquents under which all of the latter are presumed "innocent," they lead to the conception of delinquency—ranging from the completely innocent to the completely committed. Thirdly, and most important of all, they enable a comparison of those who have been officially labelled as delinquent—who have a record—with those who have not. (1970, 46)

Short and Nye have expressed similar sentiments about the inherent potential of self-report studies:

> Certain theoretical and immediately practical advantages to this type of study are apparent. In the study of juvenile delinquency, for example, the extent and nature of various types of delinquent conduct and its variability can be investigated. This, in contrast to the usual procedure of assuming that a group of institutionalized children are "delinquent," and comparing them with a group of non-institutionalized children who are defined as "non-delinquent." Further, such investigations *can* be made in all *segments* of the population, rather than in the socio-economically biased institutionalized or officially apprehended group. (1958b, 208)

Thus the self-report approach represents a strategy in which the prevalence of offenders and the overall incidence of crime can be measured and analyzed while at the same time avoiding the artificial dichotomy between delinquents and non-delinquents that confounds offensive behavior with official responses. Any attempt to delineate the determinants and correlates of criminal behavior is thereby enhanced.

Pioneering Studies of Hidden Delinquency

Initial self-report studies attempted to substantiate the existence of violations that did not come to the attention of the police or other official agents (see Murphy, Shirley, and Witmer 1946; Porterfield 1943; Schwartz 1945; Wallerstein and Wyle 1947). The results indicated that the number of delinquent acts actually far exceeded the number of acts officially recorded. Further, delinquents who were processed in an official capacity underrepresented the total population of offenders in crucial aspects.

Pioneering studies of hidden delinquency were less than sophisticated in both the scope of the investigation and the methods used. Nevertheless, they did provide valuable evidence in support of the growing suspicion that official statistics do not adequately reflect the extent of criminality. Moreover, by using self-report measures, these studies obtained data that questioned the artificial dichotomy of official delinquency versus nondelinquency.

The most important early use of the self-report technique was the work of Nye and Short (1957). Their attempt to scale the phenomenon of reported delinquency was a major impetus to the use of various other scales in the postpioneer period of hidden delinquency studies. From a list of twenty-one items that constituted both criminal and antisocial behavior, they developed scales of seven, nine, and eleven items,[1] which they claimed possessed both face and concurrent validity. The latter was demonstrated in the scales' ability to distinguish between groups known to be different along the dimension of delinquent behavior. The authors also found a moderate degree of unidimensionality for the seven-item scale (1957, 329–30).

This innovative investigation was important in two respects. First, Nye and Short demonstrated that self-reported offenses could be scaled using the familiar Guttman scaling approach and, consequently, that individuals could be ranked in terms of criminality as a variable rather than as just a dichotomous attribute, which obscures important differences. Second, etiological analysis was enhanced because the incidence of delinquent behavior could be examined in light of the configuration of offenses. That is, they could study the pattern of offensive behavior rather than isolated offenses, which might not reflect the full range of a person's criminality.

Social Class and Self-Reported Delinquency

Delinquency has customarily been portrayed as a lower social class phenomenon.[2] Indeed, official police statistics consistently suggest an inverse relation between social class and delinquency. Many researchers, however, have used the self-report technique to examine this association further, believing that reported offenses would serve as a better measure of offensive behavior by eliminating the potential social class selection bias in the police handling of offenders. In effect, of all the topics in the area of hidden delinquency, the issue of SES has been the most frequently studied and the most controversial.

Nye, Short, and Olson (1958) were the first researchers after the pioneer era to

1. The three scales were as follows: The seven-item scale included (1) drove a car without a license; (2) took things of less than $2 that did not belong to you; (3) bought or drank beer, wine, or liquor; (4) purposely damaged or destroyed property that did not belong to you; (5) skipped school without a legitimate excuse; (6) had sex relations with a person of the opposite sex; and (7) defied your parents' authority. The nine-item scale added (8) ran away from home, and (9) took things of medium value ($2 to $50). The eleven-item scale added (10) took things of great value (more than $50), and (11) used or sold narcotics.

2. A recent review by Braithwaite (1981) summarized much of the relevant literature. An opposing view can be found in Tittle, Villemez, and Smith (1978).

report the controversial finding that they could not reject the null hypothesis of no significant differences in the reported delinquency of boys and girls in different socioeconomic strata. There were no significant differences between classes regardless of whether they used a four-point scale (never to very often) or a dichotomy (did or did not) to order the frequencies of offenses and whether or not they tested proportions in each scale category.

The approach of Nye, Short, and Olson has been replicated by many other researchers, who reported similar findings. Dentler and Monroe (1961) found no significant SES differences for 912 Kansas junior-high-school students on a five-item theft measure. Clark and Wenninger (1962) reported no significant interclass differences for thirty-eight offenses among 1,154 school students in four Illinois communities. However, they did find significant differences in the quantity and quality of illegal acts between communities of different SES levels. Akers (1964) attempted an almost exact replication of the Nye, Short, and Olson study among 836 junior-high-school students in an Ohio community and also failed to uncover significant differences. He obtained a correlation coefficient of $-.0012$ between SES and delinquency scores, suggesting the absence of any relationship. Slocum and Stone (1963) reported that SES was not an intervening variable between the significant relationships of several sociodemographic factors and delinquent behavior. The results of the preceding investigations have been confirmed by other researchers using a variety of different techniques (see, for example, Arnold 1966; Hirschi 1969; Vaz 1966; and Winslow 1967).

Unlike the previous studies, which did not detect an inverse relationship between SES and delinquency, another group of investigations resulted in significant SES differentials. Erickson and Empey (1965) obtained a significant correlation between lower-class position and delinquency, measured by three scales. In light of the low values for the coefficients, however, Erickson and Empey employed analyses of variance, revealing that delinquency was not really much greater for low-status respondents but was only less prevalent at the higher level of SES compared with both low and medium SES. However, Voss (1966) reported opposite results. Among junior-high-school students in Honolulu, the higher SES stratum had significantly higher scores for a composite delinquency measure and for vandalism.

In terms of offense seriousness, Fannin and Clinard (1965) showed that the incidence of violent offenses (e.g., robbery and assault) was greater for lower-class than middle-class respondents. According to Gold (1966), lower-class subjects reported a greater frequency and seriousness of hidden delinquency. Elliott and Voss (1974) reported that they obtained significant SES differences for the junior-high-school years but not for the high-school years.

Race and Self-Reported Delinquency

One of the most frequently cited correlates of official delinquency is race. Most research using official offense data (especially police data) indicates much higher offense rates for nonwhites (see, for example, chaps. 3–5 of this book).

Similarly, victimization studies show nonwhites to be overrepresented, particularly in common-law personal crimes (Hindelang 1978). Despite the evidence, it is not clear whether the higher rates of official delinquency exhibited by nonwhites may be explained by a greater involvement in crime or by differential handling by the police. One explanation is that nonwhites commit proportionately more offenses, or offenses of greater gravity, and thus are more prone to arrest. On the other hand, the differential selection thesis suggests that nonwhites are arrested more frequently owing to racial bias on the part of the police rather than the level or seriousness of nonwhite delinquency. Thus, as with the correlation of SES and delinquency, the self-report technique appears to be a valuable tool for addressing the relative delinquency exhibited by whites and nonwhites. Compared with SES, however, the question of racial differences in hidden delinquency has been investigated by only a few self-report studies.

Gould (1969) studied 374 junior-high-school boys in Seattle with both official and self-reported offense data. He found that race (white vs. nonwhite) was strongly related to official delinquency, but race and self-reported offenses were virtually independent. In a similar small-sample study ($N = 201$), Chambliss and Nagasawa (1969) found that nonwhite high-school boys were arrested three times as often as their white counterparts. Yet when self-reported delinquency was examined, whites had the greater involvement. Hirschi (1969) studied 800 nonwhite and 1,300 white boys in California high schools and found a distinct difference between the races with respect to official delinquency: 42 percent of the nonwhites, compared with 18 percent of the whites, had police records in the two years before the research. However, the nonwhite boys were only slightly more likely than the white boys (49 percent vs. 44 percent) to report hidden delinquent acts.

Gold and his associates conducted two national surveys of youth that compared the self-reported delinquency of white and nonwhite youths (by sex and social status). In the first survey, Williams and Gold (1972) found that nearly equal proportions of white (64 percent) and nonwhite (62 percent) boys reported frequent delinquent acts, but nonwhites reported more serious acts (42 percent vs. 53 percent). The second survey, by Gold and Reimer (1975), repeated the previous findings that the mean frequency of self-reported delinquency was the same for both races (6.6), but nonwhites had higher mean seriousness scores than whites (4.1 vs. 3.0).

The findings of self-report research generally have presented a picture of delinquency very different from that reflected in the official data. The predominance of lower-status and nonwhite persons shown in the arrest data is not confirmed when self-reported acts are used as the criterion for measuring delinquent behavior. This discrepancy suggests two major implications: first, since self-report and official data appear to measure different dimensions of delinquency, the discrepancy may be due to the domains covered by the two data sources; second, the discrepancy can be viewed as indicating differential handling of offenders by the police and other official agents.

Some observers, however, have concluded that the discrepancy between the two classes of offense measures is illusory and have further suggested that past self-report research has not been substantial enough to document sufficiently the form and extent of the discrepancy, if it exists at all (Hindelang, Hirschi, and Weis 1979). The findings of a recent self-report survey supported this view. Elliott and Ageton (1980) found both race and class differentials using a new self-reported delinquency measure.[3]

Limitations of Previous Research

That self-report surveys of hidden delinquency have been used for over twenty years suggests that this mode of research constitutes a proven method of investigation. Such is not the case. The failure is due to limitations in the composition of the studies. Weaknesses have been perpetuated because researchers have not devoted sufficient effort to eliminating deficiencies readily detectable in previous investigations. The self-report technique represents such an attractive alternative to official police data that many studies were initiated and replicated before enough attention was paid to their limitations.

The principal limitations of previous hidden delinquency studies involve the following issues: the conceptualization of research objectives, the operationalization and measurement of major concepts, and the extent of legitimate generalization. Although the deficiencies are not necessarily limited to these topics, the most significant weaknesses can be examined within these contexts.

Conceptualization

Despite the importance of proper conceptualization of the objectives of research, many self-report researchers failed to pay enough attention to clarifying their objectives. One of the areas lacking clear objectives concerned the distinction between the concepts of "prevalence" and "incidence" (see Biderman 1972). Although prevalence refers to the number of persons in a status and incidence refers to the number of events, many studies have not distinguished whether the focus is on criminal events or on the persons involved in those events (McClintock 1970, 17).

The distinction between measures of prevalence and of incidence is important. Either orientation can document the existence of hidden offenses. However, when the major objective involves a comparison of subgroups in terms of their offensive behavior, recognition of the crucial difference between prevalence and incidence becomes mandatory. Comparing the proportion of offenders within designated subgroups (e.g., SES or race categories) who report hidden offenses or who fall into certain scale positions ignores the crucial factor of the quantity of offensive behavior. Likewise, relying solely on the volume of offenses a subgroup commits obscures the issue of how many group members are responsible for the violations. We argue here that a desirable procedure entails comparing the

3. Because their study represents a methodological advance over previous research, its results will be discussed later in this chapter. The next section reviews the limitations of previous studies as a backdrop to that discussion.

prevalence of offenders in the various categories of incidence as well as examining the overall incidence of offenses.

A second major problem in the area of conceptualization concerns "durable states." Many studies confound a durable, persistent state of delinquency with the admission of what could be a potentially isolated offense or pattern of offensive behavior that has been abandoned. Thus it is necessary to examine a respondent's offenses over a long period to ensure that he currently occupies a violator status or at least did so for a sufficient time. Failure to recognize or allow for exiting from the offender state may lead to the misclassification of respondents and yield erroneous conclusions.

Measurement

A particularly troublesome aspect of previous self-report research has been the measurement of the crucial variable—offensive behavior. This measurement has been limited in important respects, and consequently the extent of fruitful analysis, both statistical and substantive, has been restricted. Three principal components of the measurement process warrant attention: the offenses that make up the self-report inventories, the available response set, and the various scaling efforts.

Several observers believe that most self-report inventories are too limited in the range of items used (McClintock 1970; Reiss 1973). Many studies overweight the inventories with trivial offenses. This practice has two major consequences. First, because serious offenses are ignored, the self-report technique cannot be used to investigate how many serious offenses and offenders remain undetected. Second, it will not be possible to differentiate degree of offensive behavior across classes of various target groups.

Beyond these items, the design of the response categories is a limiting feature of previous self-report studies. Usually the respondent is constrained to place himself in a frequency category that represents a range of values (e.g., never, sometimes, frequently, or very frequently). Respondents may misinterpret such categories, leading to serious misclassifications. Further, the use of discrete categories prevents an analysis of incidence data and prescribes instead the analysis of prevalence measures within arbitrary levels of incidence. Finally, using ordered categories of at most the ordinal level of measurement precludes the more powerful statistical techniques requisite for causal analysis and the explanation of observed relationships.

Perhaps the most problematic aspect of the measurement process of previous studies concerns the validity of scaling hidden delinquency. Although the early scaling efforts (Dentler and Monroe 1961; Nye and Short 1957) were a stimulus to a wider application, there may have been too great a reliance on this approach. Hardt and Bodine (1965) argued that hidden delinquency may be multidimensional (or even nondimensional) and may not conform to the single-dimension requirement of Guttman scaling. And Gould (1969) demonstrated that certain self-reported offenses cannot be scaled at all.

Although a scale may achieve an empirical ordering of events, the interpretation of such an ordering rests with the conceptualization of the scale items and their capacity to present a composite picture of some behavior. Scaling measures have monopolized the focus of previous self-report research, and consequently only particular configurations of delinquency were examined. However, the value of self-report research inheres in its ability to delve into the full range of offenses, not just those violations that lead to official police action. To restrict the investigation of offensive behavior to scalable offenses necessarily ignores offense patterns that cut across scales or are multidimensional. This situation retards the proper utilization of this valuable approach to the study of delinquency and perpetuates the kind of limited information on criminal behavior that is maintained in the official crime statistics.

Extent of Legitimate Generalization

A crucial problem with previous self-report studies concerns the population to which results may legitimately be generalized. For example, samples drawn in large urban areas, where crime rates are usually highest, or samples that comprise racially heterogeneous groups are rare. These types of samples are requisite for investigating whether the differential arrest rates of nonwhites are due to their higher level of offensive behavior or to a selection bias in the police decision to arrest. Further, the use of in-school samples necessarily eliminates dropouts and truants, who may exhibit higher levels or seriousness of hidden delinquency. Thus these exclusions limit the extent to which the results of past studies can be generalized to substantively meaningful social groupings of juveniles.

The abundance of hidden delinquency surveys among juveniles has no parallel in the research on undetected crime among adults. Restricting the scope of self-report research to juvenile samples has two major consequences. First, the extent of hidden crime among adult subjects who may be committed to persistent and serious violations generally remains unmeasured, and such factors as education, SES, and unemployment, which may be associated with adult offensive behavior, go untested. Second, the extent to which juvenile offensive behavior (official and self-reported) influences the likelihood of subsequent violations in adults cannot be measured. Therefore the "criminal career" concept has not been used in a longitudinal fashion.[4]

The Present Study

In the present investigation we reexamine the topics of previous self-report studies and analyze previously underresearched areas. Thus this research departs from the basis of previous studies in crucial aspects.

First, the conceptualization of the objectives of this study dictates that we

4. See Thornberry and Farnworth (1982) for a detailed examination of the relationship between social status and both delinquent and adult criminal behavior. They found that the discrepancy between self-reported and official measures was more apparent than real and concluded that both data sets indicated inverse relationships between social status and criminality.

need both prevalence and incidence data. Incidence data are used to document the overall extent of hidden offenses, and in addition, the prevalence measures are incidence specific. That is, we analyze the proportions of subjects who fall into various ranges of overall incidence and who exhibit various commission frequencies. Thus we claim that an integration of both orientations (the number of persons and the number of events) is necessary to achieve a comparative analysis that is both sound and fruitful.

Second, we measure hidden offensive behavior through a twenty-four-item inventory that constitutes one of the most representative sets of offenses used. We include a greater range of offenses to reflect both the "index" and "other" crime categories of the FBI classification system and thus prevent an overweighting of trivial offenses. In addition, we use two measures of offense seriousness to enhance the depiction of a subject's offensive behavior. This research assumes that if self-report studies are to be of value, they must determine the extent to which serious offenses go unrecorded by the police and more serious violators fail to be processed by the criminal justice system.

Third, the subjects of this investigation constitute a heterogeneous population, by race and SES, and are residents of a large urban area. Therefore the potential for generalization to a substantively meaningful population is greater than in previous studies. Further, the data for this study concern both hidden and official offensive behavior. Unlike previous research, the sample is studied and compared in terms of alternate offense domains.

The Major Variables

Delinquency status was determined from the subjects' official police records, rather than from the interviews, to avoid possible response error. We coded the status as delinquent versus nondelinquent on the basis of whether the subject had ever been arrested in Philadelphia between ages 10 and 17.

Official arrests were also taken from the official police record. Data were available on the number and types of official arrests through age 17.

SES was measured in terms of the occupational prestige of the respondents' fathers. We chose occupation as the SES indicator because it has proved to be the single most important measure of social class (Kahl and Davis 1955). We used this particular scale because it has been demonstrated to be a reliable and valid indicator of occupational prestige and thus of SES (Reiss and Rhodes 1961).

Self-reported offenses were represented in the inventory by twenty-four crimes that constituted ordinal level measures. These offenses covered a range from very minor (disturbing the peace) to very serious (homicide and rape).[5]

5. The self-report items consisted of criminal homicide, rape, robbery, aggravated assault, attempt to assault with a weapon, burglary, theft from a person, shoplifting, simple assault, joyriding, illegal possession of a gun, illegal possession of a knife, receiving stolen property, passing a bad check, vandalism, heroin use, smoking marijuana, possession of heroin, possession of marijuana, public drunkenness, soliciting for prostitution, assisting in the arrangement of an abortion, disturbing the peace, and setting off a false fire alarm.

Seriousness of offenses was measured through two external criteria. First, we used the offense hierarchy depicted in the *UCR* classification system to group the self-reported offenses into categories of seriousness (crimes against persons or property).[6] Second, we computed the seriousness of the self-reported offenses by the Sellin-Wolfgang seriousness scale. Derived from a study of psychophysical scaling, the seriousness scores denote the relative mathematical weights of the gravity of different crimes (Sellin and Wolfgang 1978).

Findings
Official Juvenile Delinquency

Most self-report studies collect data only on the unofficial offenses committed by the subjects; they ignore the official dimension of delinquency. The consequence of this practice is important. In the absence of data concerning both official and hidden dimensions of delinquency, the valid interpretation of self-report findings is compromised. Because it is not known whether the respondents differ with respect to the official measure of delinquency, analysis of the correlates of hidden delinquency becomes problematic. For example, many self-report studies compare self-reported delinquency across race and social class categories, and when the *expected* differences are not found the results are interpreted as signifying problems with official data. But the proper context in which to view self-report findings includes official data. It is one thing not to find race and class differences for groups that have significant associations with the official measures. By treating these situations as synonymous, researchers may misinterpret their data and thus find a discrepancy between official and self-report data that is more apparent than real. To avoid these problems, the prevalence and incidence of *official delinquency* for the subjects of this study are displayed in table 10.1 by race and SES.

The prevalence data indicate that the nonwhite cohort members were much more likely to be classified as delinquents. The ratio of nonwhite-to-white delinquency was about 1.5:1. On the other hand, the prevalence data for the three SES levels indicate that lower-status subjects were only slightly more likely than their middle- or higher-status counterparts to be recorded as delinquent. Moreover, the incidence data show significant race and SES differences in the frequency of official offenses. The nonwhites were arrested more than three times as often as the whites. The magnitude of the differences was less by SES, but the data nonetheless indicate that low-SES subjects had about 1.8 times more offenses.

These relationships can be specified further by examining the pattern of differences obtained when race and SES are controlled. The race-by-SES data indicate that, for the medium and high SES levels, the nonwhites were classified as delinquent about twice as often as the whites. In terms of the frequency of arrest, the ratios of nonwhite-to-white offenses were 4.1:1 and 4.6:1 at the medium and high SES levels. Although the prevalence of delinquency among low-status

6. The first five items were considered serious offenses against the person, while the sixth through eighth represented offenses against property.

TABLE 10.1   Percentage Delinquent and Mean Number of Delinquent Events by Race and SES

	N	%	$\bar{X}$	F	Probability
Race					
Whites	453	28.0	0.54	39.02	≤.0001
Nonwhites	114	42.1	1.78		
SES					
Low	184	35.3	1.14		
Medium	195	29.7	0.63	4.27	≤.01
High	188	27.7	0.62		
Race by SES					
Low					
Whites	118	35.6	0.83	5.35	≤.01
Nonwhites	66	34.8	1.69		
Medium					
Whites	169	26.6	0.44	17.62	≤.0001
Nonwhites	26	50.0	1.84		
High					
Whites	166	24.1	0.43	18.92	≤.0001
Nonwhites	22	54.5	2.00		
SES by race					
Whites					
Low	118	35.6	0.83		
Medium	169	26.6	0.44	4.47	≤.01
High	166	24.1	0.43		
Nonwhites					
Low	66	34.8	1.68		
Medium	26	50.0	1.84	0.06	n.s.
High	22	54.5	2.00		

subjects was about equal for both races, there were significant incidence differences indicating that the nonwhites had about twice as many official offenses.

The race by SES data were instructive in two respects. First, among the whites, low SES respondents were more likely to be designated delinquent and to have more frequent contact with the police than their medium and high SES counterparts. Second, the prevalence of delinquency among the nonwhites varied directly with SES, but the incidence of juvenile crime was about equal across SES levels.

In sum, there were significant race and SES differences in both the likelihood of being delinquent and the number of police contacts. The differences were stronger by race but were distinct for both groups. With these findings established, we can address the question of self-reported delinquency.

Correlates of Hidden Delinquency

Table 10.2 presents the results of one-way analyses of variance on the mean frequency of self-reported delinquent events (summed across the twenty-four

TABLE 10.2   Mean Frequency of Self-Reported Delinquency by Race and SES

	N	$\bar{X}$	SD	F	Probability
Race					
Whites	453	70.06	149.01	0.77	n.s.
Nonwhites	114	56.06	165.01		
SES					
Low	184	68.35	142.43		
Medium	195	68.53	148.67	0.03	n.s.
High	188	64.82	165.79		
Race by SES					
Low					
Whites	118	78.63	165.64	1.72	n.s.
Nonwhites	66	49.98	83.87		
Medium					
Whites	169	75.47	158.43	2.78	n.s.
Nonwhites	26	23.42	20.28		
High					
Whites	166	58.46	345.60	2.10	n.s.
Nonwhites	22	112.86	124.91		
SES by race					
Whites					
Low	118	78.63	165.64		
Medium	169	75.47	158.43	0.80	n.s.
High	166	58.46	124.91		
Nonwhites					
Low	66	49.98	83.87		
Medium	26	23.42	20.88	1.88	n.s.
High	22	112.86	345.60		

items) by race and SES.[7] Like most self-report studies and in contrast to the recent work by Elliott and Ageton (1980), the present research found no significant race or SES differentials for a global self-report scale. In fact the group means across SES categories were so similar that they could be viewed as virtually identical. Further, the scores by race not only were not significant but also were not in the expected direction, since the mean for the whites was higher than that for the nonwhites.

When the data are viewed by race across SES and vice versa, the basic findings are confirmed. The whites had higher scores at the low and medium SES levels, while the nonwhites had a higher average number of offenses at the high SES level; but none of the differences were significant. In terms of SES, the

7. One-way and two-way ANOVAs were used so that the analyses would be comparable to those reported by Elliott and Ageton (1980); because the two-way analyses did not reveal effects different from those obtained with the one-way ANOVAs, we reported only the latter. However, we used separate one-way ANOVAs for the various race and SES combinations to show any contingent effects.

whites exhibited the usually expected inverse trend, but the nonwhites did not; again, the differences were not statistically significant.

Measuring Offense Seriousness

One of the significant contributions achieved by Elliott and Ageton (1980) concerned the self-report inventory. Unlike most self-report inventories, theirs was constructed with great attention to item selection. As a result, the forty-seven items were more comprehensive and much more representative of the universe of delinquent acts than previous scales. They concluded that the results they obtained, compared with other studies, may be a function of differences in the measures employed (1980, 107). Nowhere were these differences more apparent than with respect to serious offenses.

In addition to a total self-reported offense measure, Elliott and Ageton constructed six subscales, two of which (predatory crimes against the person and property) encompassed the serious set represented by the *UCR* part I offenses. The inventory in the present research also included such offense types, and we constructed scales similar to those later adopted by Elliott and Ageton. The results of these analyzes are given in table 10.3.

Table 10.3 indicates that the nonwhites reported a significantly higher number of crimes against the person; the ratio was over 2:1. When SES was controlled, however, it appeared that the discrepancy was almost totally accounted for at the high SES level. That is, there were no significant race differences at the low or medium SES levels, but there was a distinct discrepancy among the high SES respondents, where the nonwhites reported almost six times as many serious crimes against the person. Turning to SES, table 10.3 shows no significant differences across levels generally or for either racial group.

Data for the crimes against property subscale (not shown here) indicate no significant differences for either race or SES. As was true for total self-reported delinquency, we see the *unexpected* finding, that the white subjects had the higher frequency overall and at each SES level.

These results are in sharp contrast to those reported by Elliott and Ageton, who found significant class differences in crimes against the person and a significant race effect for crimes against property. The analyses reported above indicated no SES differences for either of the subscales overall or for race-specific comparisons. On the other hand, we found a significant race effect for the crimes against the person subscale but not for the crimes against property subscale (the opposite of that reported by Elliott and Ageton).

It should be clear that the use of subscales does not automatically handle the problem of the relative frequency with which items are reported and the effect this has on scale values. Thus even a potentially valuable subscale can be vitiated if some less serious offenses are reported so often that the more serious offenses are overshadowed. One way to handle this problem is to employ standard scores so that the contribution of any one item (regardless of the frequency with which it is reported) to the total scale is the same as that of any other item.

TABLE 10.3   Mean Frequency of Self-Reported Offenses against the Person by Race and SES

	N	$\bar{X}$	SD	F	Probability
Race					
Whites	453	1.68	6.71	6.920	≤.01
Nonwhites	114	3.74	9.88		
SES					
Low	184	2.81	7.87		
Medium	195	2.06	7.80	1.560	n.s.
High	188	1.44	6.73		
Race by SES					
Low					
Whites	118	2.43	7.74	0.770	n.s.
Nonwhites	66	3.50	8.10		
Medium					
Whites	169	1.90	8.12	0.540	n.s.
Nonwhites	26	3.11	5.29		
High					
Whites	166	0.93	3.57	8.170	≤.001
Nonwhites	22	5.22	16.92		
SES by race					
Whites					
Low	118	2.43	7.74		
Medium	169	1.90	8.12	1.850	n.s.
High	166	0.93	3.57		
Nonwhites					
Low	66	3.50	8.10		
Medium	26	3.11	5.29	0.316	n.s.
High	22	5.22	16.92		

Elliott and Ageton followed this procedure and produced some different findings. After weighting the data, they found that the results for social class were the same as when the unadjusted frequencies were used—class was related to total self-reported delinquency and the crimes against the person subscale. However, the weighted data showed that the nonwhites had significantly higher scores for the crimes against the person subscale, which was not the case with the unstandardized data. Elliott and Ageton further found that the original race effect for total self-reported delinquency was distinctly weaker after the frequencies were standardized (1980, 105).

Another way to address the problem of relative seriousness given the comparatively low frequency of serious offenses is to weight the offenses by some measure of gravity. In this way offenses contribute to the scale according to how serious they are relative to other offenses. In this research the items in the self-report inventory were weighted according to a system developed by Sellin and Wolfgang (1978). The results of their weighting procedure are given in table

TABLE 10.4   Mean Seriousness of Self-Reported Delinquent Events
by Race and SES

	N	$\bar{X}$	SD	F	Probability
Race					
Whites	453	1.28	1.00	6.17	≤.01
Nonwhites	114	1.55	1.07		
SES					
Low	184	1.30	1.03		
Medium	195	1.32	0.92	0.43	n.s.
High	188	1.40	1.11		
Race by SES					
Low					
Whites	118	1.16	0.99	6.13	≤.01
Nonwhites	66	1.55	1.07		
Medium					
Whites	169	1.24	0.85	9.22	≤.001
Nonwhites	26	1.83	1.19		
High					
Whites	166	1.42	1.13	0.54	n.s.
Nonwhites	22	1.23	0.87		
SES by race					
Whites					
Low	118	1.16	0.99		
Medium	169	1.24	0.85	2.48	n.s.
High	166	1.42	1.13		
Nonwhites					
Low	66	1.55	1.07		
Medium	26	1.83	1.19	1.84	n.s.
High	22	1.23	0.87		

10.4, which indicates that the nonwhites had a much higher average offense seriousness for the full self-report inventory,[8] signifying that, regardless of the overall frequency of offenses, the nonwhite events appeared to constitute a more serious offense set than those reported by the white respondents. With respect to SES, however, the mean scores indicated that the seriousness of the reported offenses was approximately the same across SES levels.

Table 10.4 also shows that controlling for race uncovered no suppressed SES effects. For both whites and nonwhites the average seriousness scores across SES categories were not significantly different. There were, however, race differences by SES. That is, at both the low and medium SES levels the nonwhites had significantly higher mean seriousness scores. Among the high SES subjects the scores showed no significant race effect.

8. The data given in table 10.4 represent the average seriousness of the self-reported offenses achieved by weighting the items, multiplying each weight by the frequency of commission, summing the products across the twenty-four items, and then dividing by the total number of offenses reported.

Levels of Incidence

We noted earlier that one of the principal weaknesses of many self-report studies concerns the response set. Because most research has constrained respondents to place themselves in discrete categories of offense incidence, the distribution of reported offenses has been severely truncated. The effect of this procedure is to hide the high-frequency offender and thus to prevent one of the most important comparisons in self-report research.

In this regard one of the significant differences between the research conducted by Elliott and Ageton and previous studies is that the former used an open-ended response set that let them compare subjects at various points along the frequency distribution. With these comparisons, Elliott and Ageton showed that the original differences by race and class for the continuous data were due mostly to race and class effects at the high end of the frequency continuum (1980, 104). The ratio of nonwhites to whites at the high frequency level was 2.3:1 for the crimes against property subscale. Similarly, the differences between low- and middle-class subjects showed a ratio of 2.1:1 for total reported delinquency and 3:1 for crimes against the person.

The present study also utilized an open-ended frequency format to allow for the discrimination of subjects at various levels of self-reported offense incidence.[9] These data are displayed in tables 10.5 through 10.7 for the total, person, and property offenses. Generally the results confirm those obtained with the mean frequency data, but the discrete comparisons reveal several effects not previously observed.

Table 10.5 shows that the percentages of subjects across the various levels of self-reported delinquent events were unrelated to race and SES. This was also the case when the SES data were examined separately by race. These findings replicated those obtained with the continuous data (table 10.2). However, when SES was controlled a significant difference emerged that was not evident earlier. That is, at the medium SES level a distinct discrepancy existed: 23 percent of the white subjects were classified at the two highest frequency levels, compared with none of the nonwhites. The other two SES levels exhibited no such race effect.

The results displayed in table 10.6 confirm, yet extend, the findings reported in table 10.3 for the crimes against the person subscale. That is, table 10.6 shows that, as was the case with the continuous data, the nonwhites differed significantly from the whites. Beyond the lowest frequency level, the proportion of the nonwhites was at least twice as high as that of the whites. However, the data by SES show that the (not significant) inverse trend reported in table 10.3 attained significance when levels of frequency were examined. With the exception of the slightly higher ten to twenty offenses category for the medium SES subjects, the percentages at the other frequency levels indicated that the low SES subjects

9. To make the results of the discrete measure analyses as comparable as possible to those of Elliott and Ageton (1980), we used the marginal distributions of their data for the total, person, and property offenses to construct the class intervals for the discrete measures of this research.

TABLE 10.5 Percentage of Respondents at Specific Levels of Total
Self-Reported Delinquency by Race and SES

| | N | Frequency of Offenses | | | |
		0–50	51–84	85–299	300+
Race					
Whites	453	70.6	9.9	13.9	5.5
Nonwhites	114	76.3	7.9	12.3	3.5
SES					
Low	184	71.2	9.2	14.7	4.9
Medium	195	70.8	9.2	14.9	5.1
High	188	73.4	10.1	11.2	5.3
Race by SES					
Low					
Whites	118	70.3	11.0	12.7	5.9
Nonwhites	66	72.7	6.1	18.2	3.0
Medium					
Whites	169	68.6	8.3	17.2	5.9
Nonwhites	26	84.6	15.4	0.0	0.0
High					
Whites	166	72.9	10.8	11.4	4.8
Nonwhites	22	77.3	4.5	9.1	9.1
SES by race					
Whites					
Low	118	70.3	11.0	12.7	5.9
Medium	169	68.6	8.3	17.2	5.9
High	166	72.9	10.8	11.4	4.8
Nonwhites					
Low	66	72.7	6.1	18.2	3.0
Medium	26	84.6	15.4	0.0	0.0
High	22	77.3	4.5	9.1	9.1

were much more likely to be frequent offenders in terms of offenses against the person.

Like table 10.3, table 10.6 shows that when race was controlled there was no significant trend by SES. When SES was controlled, table 10.6 replicates the earlier finding that much higher proportions of nonwhites were frequent offenders. But the table also shows that this was the case at the medium SES level as well, which supports the mean differences (not significant) found in table 10.3. The nonwhites at both the medium and high SES levels were about twice as likely to have committed at least two offenses.

This analysis, for self-reported offenses against property, also replicates the original finding that there were no significant race differences. As before, the white subjects exhibited more frequent involvement, but the percentages were not sufficiently different to maintain a race effect.

In sum, analysis of various levels of the frequency of self-reported total, per-

TABLE 10.6 Percentage of Respondents at Specific Levels of Self-Reported
Crimes against the Person by Race and SES

	N	Frequency of Offenses			
		0–1	2–9	10–20	21+
Race					
Whites	453	81.9	14.1	2.2	1.8
Nonwhites	114	63.2	27.2	6.1	3.5
SES					
Low	184	72.3	20.1	3.8	3.8
Medium	195	77.4	16.9	4.6	1.0
High	188	84.6	13.3	0.5	1.6
Race by SES					
Low					
Whites	118	77.1	16.1	3.4	3.4
Nonwhites	66	63.6	27.3	4.5	4.5
Medium					
Whites	169	79.9	16.0	3.0	1.2
Nonwhites	26	61.5	23.1	15.4	0.0
High					
Whites	166	87.3	10.8	0.6	1.2
Nonwhites	22	63.6	31.8	0.0	4.5
SES by race					
Whites					
Low	118	77.1	16.1	3.4	3.4
Medium	169	79.9	16.0	3.0	1.2
High	166	87.3	10.8	0.6	1.2
Nonwhites					
Low	66	63.6	27.3	4.5	4.5
Medium	26	61.5	23.1	15.4	0.0
High	22	63.6	31.8	0.0	4.5

son, and property offenses by race and SES categories largely supported the
findings obtained when mean frequency data were examined. There were no significant differences by race or SES for offenses concerning the frequency groups
for total self-reported delinquency. The exception pertained to the medium SES
level, where whites exhibited greater involvement in frequent delinquent acts.
For serious offenses against the person the findings showed distinct differences
by race. Overall, nonwhites were much more likely to be classified at the higher
levels of incidence. The nonwhite predominance also persisted at both the medium and high SES levels. Also, a significant inverse trend by SES was obtained
for the discrete incidence measure but not for the continuous data.

Comparing the Correlates of Official and Hidden Delinquency

The initial findings section of this chapter showed that there were distin-
guishable correlates concerning the prevalence and incidence of official juvenile
delinquency. We reported that a higher percentage of nonwhite subjects had been

recorded as delinquent and that they had a significantly higher frequency of arrests. We also reported that the nonwhites held these positions at each SES level for both frequency of arrest and percentage delinquent (except for low SES subjects, where the prevalence was virtually the same by race). The official data by SES showed that low SES subjects were slightly more likely to be delinquent and to be arrested more frequently.

If this research had available only a global scale of self-reported delinquency, then we would conclude that a discrepancy existed between the official and the self-report measures, a conclusion offered by most of the previous self-report studies. This conclusion would derive from the findings that there were neither race nor SES differences in the total self-reported delinquent events. Further, this conclusion would be supported whether we analyzed mean frequency data or compared discrete incidence levels. Thus, for all comparisons by race and SES, the correlates of official delinquency would not be replicated when reported offenses were used as the criterion of delinquency. However, when we examined the seriousness and frequency of self-reported events, we found a close correspondence between the correlates of delinquency obtained from the official and the self-report data.

As noted above, nonwhites had a significantly higher prevalence and incidence of official juvenile delinquency. Support for these differences came from two measures of the severity of the self-reported offenses. First, nonwhites reported a significantly higher frequency of violent offenses against the person (table 10.3). Because offenses against the person are more likely to be reported to the police by victims and have much higher arrest clearance rates, offenders who committed such crimes were thus more likely to risk an official arrest. Second, the weighting of the offense inventory by seriousness scores (table 10.4) indicated that, on the average, the seriousness of offenses reported by the nonwhite respondents was significantly greater than for the whites. If the police were more likely to arrest persons whose offenses were serious, then the higher severity scores exhibited by the nonwhites confirmed their greater potential for arrest. In addition to these two measures of offense seriousness, the discrete frequency data for the crimes against the person subscale (table 10.6) further showed that the nonwhites were much more likely to be classified at the very high incidence levels.

In comparisons, the data showing the relationship between official and unofficial measures of delinquency by SES were less convincing. Low SES subjects were only slightly more likely to be delinquent but had almost twice as many police contacts as subjects from the medium and high SES levels. The seriousness measures for the self-reported offenses also showed only slight SES differences. Low SES subjects reported only a few more offenses against the person and property than the high SES subjects. Further, the average seriousness of reported offenses for the low SES group was slightly lower.

Perhaps the most illuminating finding of the official offense data is that the nonwhites were more delinquent at all SES levels. The global scale of self-reported delinquency, on the other hand, showed that the whites actually reported higher frequencies. Yet, once again, the crimes against the person subscale and the weighted seriousness data showed the nonwhites to have significantly more serious offenses. However, support for this conclusion required the use of both seriousness measures. That is, the predominance of nonwhites in the official data was confirmed by the average seriousness scores for the low and medium SES levels. The race difference among the high SES subjects was supported by the crimes against the person subscale. It should be noted, however, that the cases where the race difference in official delinquency was greatest (medium and high SES) showed the greatest disparity in mean reported offense seriousness. The race effect for these two SES levels was further supported by the discrete frequency data for the crimes against the person subscale (table 10.6). Here the data showed that much greater proportions of medium and high SES nonwhites reported the two highest incidence levels.

Results
Official Delinquency and Self-Reported Delinquency

Incidence Measures   Tables 10.7 to 10.9 report the results of three-way analyses of variance for delinquency status, race, and SES and four measures of self-reported delinquency. These analyses are intended to show whether persons who have been treated as delinquents have significantly higher mean scores for a global measure of delinquency and three measures of offense seriousness than subjects who have never been arrested. We expected that, on the average, official delinquents would have a higher incidence of hidden delinquency and would report a higher frequency of serious offenses.

Table 10.7 shows that the expectation was correct in terms of the mean number of total self-reported offenses. As a group, the delinquents committed about twice as many offenses as the nondelinquents ($\bar{X}$ = 104.2 vs. 50.7). In addition to this overall effect, the table clearly indicates that the delinquency status difference held for both races and all SES groups. The white delinquents had consistently higher frequencies across SES levels than the white nondelinquents. The same result obtained for the nonwhites. The ANOVA results in the bottom panel of table 10.7 show that only delinquency status had a significant main effect and that none of the interaction effects were significant.

In addition to a higher frequency of offenses generally, we might also expect that official delinquents would exhibit a higher incidence of serious offenses than their counterparts who were not arrested. Thus groupings of offenses that reflect the type of offense likely to come to the attention of the police and result in an arrest should reveal higher mean frequencies among delinquents than among nondelinquents. These data are given in table 10.8 for self-reported offenses against the person and in table 10.9 for self-reported offenses against property.

As in the previous table, the results reported in table 10.8 indicate that the official delinquents committed about twice as many serious offenses against the person as the official nondelinquents ($\bar{X}$ = 3.1 vs. 1.6). However, this table shows that the delinquency status effect was stronger among the whites. In addi-

TABLE 10.7   Mean Number of Total Self-Reported Offenses by
Official Delinquency Status, Race, and SES

Race and SES	Nondelinquents		Delinquents	
	N	$\overline{X}$	N	$\overline{X}$
Whites	326	53.71	127	112.03
Low	76	57.03	42	117.71
Medium	124	60.74	45	116.08
High	126	44.79	40	101.52
Nonwhites	66	35.89	48	83.79
Low	43	33.58	23	80.65
Medium	13	20.07	13	26.76
High	10	66.40	12	151.58
Total	392	50.71	175	104.29

	d.f.	F	Probability
Main effects	4	4.31	$\leq.002$
Delinquency status	1	16.27	$\leq.0001$
Race	1	1.93	n.s.
SES	2	0.04	n.s.
Two-way interactions	5	1.05	n.s.
Delinquency status by race	1	0.15	n.s.
Delinquency status by SES	2	0.08	n.s.
Race by SES	2	0.10	n.s.
Three-way interactions	2	0.32	n.s.
Delinquency status by race and SES	2	0.32	n.s.

tion, regardless of delinquency status, the nonwhites reported a higher incidence of offenses against the person.

Inspection of the subgroup means reveals these differences. The nonwhite delinquents reported about 2.3 times as many offenses as their nondelinquent counterparts, while for the whites the ratio of 1.5:1 was much lower. Considering SES for the nonwhites, the delinquents had the higher mean number of offenses across all three SES levels. The largest discrepancy occurred at the highest SES level, where the nonwhite delinquents reported about 6.5 times as many offenses as the nonwhite nondelinquents. For the whites, however, the delinquents predominated only at the low SES level, where they showed a mean number of offenses that was 2.7 times higher than that of the nondelinquents. At the highest SES level, the white delinquents and nondelinquents reported similar levels of offenses against the person, and at the medium SES level it was the white nondelinquents who had the higher scores (1.66 vs. 1.99).

The ANOVA results given in the bottom panel of table 10.8 confirm these mean scores. Although the delinquency status differences were significant, the race effect was equally important. Further, it also appeared that the race and delinquency status effects were additive. Thus, being nonwhite and officially

TABLE 10.8   Mean Number of Self-Reported Offenses against the Person by Official Delinquency Status, Race, and SES

Race and SES	Nondelinquents		Delinquents	
	N	$\bar{X}$	N	$\bar{X}$
Whites	326	1.45	127	2.29
Low	76	1.48	42	4.14
Medium	124	1.99	45	1.66
High	126	0.89	40	1.07
Nonwhites	66	2.42	48	5.56
Low	43	2.62	23	5.13
Medium	13	2.61	13	3.61
High	10	1.30	12	8.50
Total	392	1.61	175	3.19

	d.f.	F	Probability
Main effects	4	3.08	$\leq .01$
Delinquency status	1	3.95	$\leq .04$
Race	1	4.22	$\leq .04$
SES	2	0.62	n.s.
Two-way interactions	5	1.25	n.s.
Delinquency status by race	1	1.34	n.s.
Delinquency status by SES	2	0.98	n.s.
Race by SES	2	0.84	n.s.
Three-way interactions	2	1.48	n.s.
Delinquency status by race and SES	2	1.48	n.s.

delinquent resulted in an appreciably higher level of serious offenses against the person.

The results given in table 10.9 for offenses against property also show a delinquency status effect. The delinquents reported almost three times as many property offenses as the nondelinquents ($\bar{X} = 21.84$ vs. 7.69). However, the race effect shown in table 10.9 was the opposite of that found for offenses against the person; the whites reported significantly more offenses against property, and the delinquency status difference was more pronounced.

The white delinquents reported slightly over three times as many property offenses as their nondelinquent peers. By SES the ratio was 2.4:1 at the low level, 3.6:1 at the medium level, and 3:1 at the high level. Among the nonwhites, the delinquents reported 2.8 times more offenses than the nondelinquents, which was only slightly less than the overall ratio obtained for the whites. However, the nonwhite results by SES showed less consistent differences. That is, at the low SES level the nonwhite delinquents reported 4.5 times the offenses of their nondelinquent counterparts, but at the medium and high SES levels the ratios were only 1.2:1 and 1.3:1, respectively.

Thus self-reported offenses against property showed the same delinquency status difference obtained for a global scale and for person offenses. Compared

TABLE 10.9   Mean Number of Self-Reported Offenses against Property by Official Delinquency Status, Race, and SES

Race and SES	Nondelinquents		Delinquents	
	N	$\bar{X}$	N	$\bar{X}$
Whites	326	8.43	127	25.70
Low	76	10.38	42	25.00
Medium	124	6.91	45	25.33
High	126	8.75	40	26.85
Nonwhites	66	4.03	48	11.64
Low	43	4.09	23	18.69
Medium	13	3.76	13	4.76
High	10	4.10	12	5.58
Total	392	7.69	175	21.84

	d.f.	F	Probability
Main effects	4	6.09	$\leq.001$
Delinquency status	1	20.61	$\leq.0001$
Race	1	5.30	$\leq.02$
SES	2	0.47	n.s.
Two-way interactions	5	0.34	n.s.
Delinquency status by race	1	1.16	n.s.
Delinquency status by SES	2	0.01	n.s.
Race by SES	2	0.17	n.s.
Three-way interactions	2	0.55	n.s.
Delinquency status by race and SES	2	0.55	n.s.

with offenses against the person, which were higher among the nonwhites, property offenses were predominantly committed by whites.

As an alternative to grouping offenses by type as a measure of seriousness, the severity of the self-reported offenses was computed by a weighting scheme.[10] Compared with the other two measures of offense severity, the results of the quantitative measure did not yield the expected delinquency-status effect; the average severity of offenses reported by the delinquents ($\bar{X} = 14.4$) was only slightly higher than that reported by the nondelinquents ($\bar{X} = 12.9$). This finding was virtually the same when the delinquents and nondelinquents were compared by race and by race across SES levels. In all instances, the offense severity was only slightly higher for the delinquents than for the nondelinquents.

High-Frequency Offenders   Although the preceding analyses generally showed that the official delinquents exhibited a higher mean incidence of self-reported offenses, it is important to investigate the relation between delinquency status and various discrete levels of self-reported delinquency. In this way the high-frequency offender could be isolated and studied separately from offenders

10. The self-reported offenses were weighted for seriousness by the Sellin-Wolfgang index.

who reported far fewer offenses.[11] Differences between delinquents and non-delinquents should be most pronounced at the upper end of the frequency continuum. The discrete data are reported in tables 10.10 to 10.12 for the global delinquency measure and the two groupings of serious offenses (person and property).

Table 10.10 shows, for all groups but the nonwhites, that a relationship existed between delinquency status and levels of total hidden delinquency. For the whites, the percentage of delinquents was much lower at the lowest level of hidden delinquency and much higher at the two levels of more frequent hidden offenses. The results by SES showed that the delinquency status effect was strongest at the medium SES level, with smaller differences at the other two levels. Among the nonwhites, the delinquents predominated at the high-frequency level, but overall the delinquents did not exhibit the differences in proportions achieved by the whites.

Table 10.11 indicates that when the frequency of self-reported offenses against the person was classified into three levels, delinquency status was significant only among the whites. For this group, the delinquents were more likely to report a few offenses or to report frequent involvement. For the nonwhites and the three SES levels, the delinquents predominated at the high-frequency level but differed little from the nondelinquents at the level of occasional involvement (i.e., from one to four offenses). Overall, the white delinquents were most dissimilar to the white nondelinquents, while the delinquents seemed to differ from the nondelinquents at the high frequency level for all groups.

Table 10.12 repeats the finding for property offenses observed in table 10.10 that delinquency status and frequency level were significant for all groups but the nonwhites. The data were particularly pronounced at the highest of the four frequency levels. Among the whites, the delinquents were almost three times more likely to be classified as high frequency. By SES, the results showed the percentage of the delinquents at the highest frequency level was three times higher for low and medium SES and two times higher for high SES than the percentage of the nondelinquents.

The results shown in table 10.12 do not exhibit the expected effect among the nonwhites, who were only slightly less likely than the nondelinquents to be non-offenders or infrequent offenders. The nonwhite delinquents were also only slightly more likely than the nonwhite nondelinquents to have reported moder-

11. When collapsing a continuous variable into discrete categories, the specific cutoff points are arbitrary. In the present analysis we decided to employ class limits that would place high-frequency offending at the extreme of the distribution. For total self-reported offenses the percentages we used to construct the three groups were 60 percent, 30 percent, and 10 percent. For the offenses against the person subset about 70 percent of the subjects had never committed such an offense; thus the remaining two categories comprised 20 percent and 10 percent of the subjects. The offenses against property subset posed a problem. About a third of the subjects had not committed property offenses, thus defining the first group. About 40 percent of the subjects had committed these offenses a few times, thus constituting the second level. The two remaining levels contained 20 percent and 10 percent of the respondents. Although arbitrary, these marginal percentages allowed the high-frequency level to comprise no more than 10 percent of the subjects, thus reflecting very frequent offending.

TABLE 10.10 Percentage of Respondents at Specific Levels of Total Self-Reported Delinquency by Official Delinquency Status, Race, and SES

| | Race | | | | SES | | | | | |
| | Whites | | Nonwhites | | Low | | Medium | | High | |
Offense Level	Nondelin-quents	Delin-quents	Nondelin-quents	Delin-quents	Nondelin-quents	Delin-quents	Nondelin-quents	Delin-quents	Nondelin-quents	Delin-quents
0–27	65.3	41.7	69.7	54.2	62.2	44.6	67.2	39.7	68.4	51.9
28–144	25.8	39.4	27.3	37.5	28.6	41.5	26.3	43.1	23.5	30.8
145+	8.9	18.9	3.0	8.3	9.2	13.8	6.6	17.2	8.1	17.3
χ^2	22.20		3.46		5.26		13.67		5.37	
	$(p \leq .001)$		(n.s.)		$(p \leq .07)$		$(p \leq .001)$		$(p \leq .06)$	
Gamma	0.41		0.32		0.29		0.47		0.32	

TABLE 10.11 Percentage of Respondents at Specific Levels of Self-Reported Offenses against the Person by Official Delinquency Status, Race, and SES

| | Race | | | | SES | | | | | |
| | Whites | | Nonwhites | | Low | | Medium | | High | |
Offense Level	Nondelin-quents	Delin-quents	Nondelin-quents	Delin-quents	Nondelin-quents	Delin-quents	Nondelin-quents	Delin-quents	Nondelin-quents	Delin-quents
None	72.7	59.8	56.1	50.0	65.5	55.4	67.2	51.7	76.5	65.4
1–4	21.2	30.7	25.8	22.9	22.7	26.2	24.1	36.2	19.1	23.1
5+	6.1	9.4	18.2	27.1	11.8	18.5	8.8	12.1	4.4	11.5
χ^2	7.09		1.28		2.24		4.10		3.91	
	$(p \leq .02)$		(n.s.)		(n.s.)		(n.s)		(n.s.)	
Gamma	0.26		0.14		0.20		0.27		0.27	

TABLE 10.12 Percentage of Respondents at Specific Levels of Self-Reported Offenses against Property by Official Delinquency Status, Race, and SES

| | Race | | | | SES | | | | | |
| | Whites | | Nonwhites | | Low | | Medium | | High | |
Offense Level	Nondelin-quents	Delin-quents	Nondelin-quents	Delin-quents	Nondelin-quents	Delin-quents	Nondelin-quents	Delin-quents	Nondelin-quents	Delin-quents
None	36.5	20.5	34.8	31.3	36.1	29.2	35.0	20.7	37.5	19.2
1–13	48.8	50.4	60.6	54.2	49.6	49.2	54.0	50.0	48.5	55.8
14–24	6.7	7.1	4.5	6.3	8.4	3.1	5.1	10.3	5.9	7.7
25+	8.0	22.0	0.0	8.3	5.9	18.5	5.8	19.0	8.1	17.3
χ^2	22.58		5.96		8.86		11.73		7.45	
	($p \le .001$)		(n.s.)		($p \le .03$)		($p \le .008$)		($p \le .05$)	
Gamma	0.36		0.18		0.18		0.39		0.36	

TABLE 10.13 Percentage of Respondents at Specific Levels of Selected Self-Reported Offenses by Official Delinquency Status, Race, and SES

| | Race | | | | SES | | | | | |
| | Whites | | Nonwhites | | Low | | Medium | | High | |
Offense Level	Nondelin-quents	Delin-quents	Nondelin-quents	Delin-quents	Nondelin-quents	Delin-quents	Nondelin-quents	Delin-quents	Nondelin-quents	Delin-quents
Rape										
0	98.5	96.9	92.4	89.6	94.1	93.8	98.5	98.3	99.3	92.3
1+	1.5	3.1	7.6	10.4	5.9	6.2	1.5	1.7	0.7	7.7

Robbery										
0	93.6	88.2	78.8	72.9	87.4	81.5	90.5	84.5	94.9	86.5
1–2	3.4	6.3	9.1	14.6	4.2	9.2	5.1	10.3	3.7	5.8
3+	3.1	5.5	12.1	12.5	8.4	9.2	4.4	5.2	1.5	2.1
Aggravated assault										
0	76.4	68.5	72.7	64.6	77.3	63.1	71.5	65.5	78.7	75.0
1–2	17.2	24.4	18.2	22.9	16.0	26.2	19.7	27.6	16.2	17.3
3+	6.4	7.1	9.1	12.5	6.7	10.8	8.8	6.9	5.1	7.7
Weapon threat										
0	94.5	90.6	83.3	85.4	86.6	92.3	94.2	82.8	96.3	92.3
1+	5.5	9.4	16.7	14.6	13.4	7.7	5.8	17.2	3.7	7.7
Burglary										
0	85.0	66.1	87.9	77.1	83.2	69.2	83.9	75.9	89.0	61.5
1–2	9.2	22.0	9.1	18.8	10.9	20.0	11.7	12.1	5.1	32.7
3+	5.8	11.8	3.0	4.2	5.9	10.8	4.4	12.1	5.9	5.8
Larceny										
0	74.2	62.2	69.7	75.0	70.6	69.2	77.4	65.5	72.1	61.5
1–7	19.3	29.1	30.3	20.8	23.5	23.1	18.2	31.0	22.1	26.9
8+	6.4	8.7	0.0	4.2	5.9	7.7	4.4	3.4	5.9	11.5
Shoplifting										
0	41.7	26.0	45.5	35.4	44.5	33.8	38.7	25.9	44.1	25.0
1–9	41.1	44.1	47.0	52.1	39.5	47.7	46.7	44.8	39.7	46.2
10–19	10.1	14.2	7.6	4.2	10.1	4.6	9.5	13.8	9.6	17.3
20+	7.1	15.7	0.0	8.3	5.9	13.8	5.1	15.5	6.6	11.5

ately frequent involvement (fourteen to twenty-four offenses). It appears that these three slight differentials overshadowed the pronounced difference at the highest frequency level, where 8 percent of the delinquents and none of the nondelinquents could be classified, and thus the delinquency status effect was not significant among the nonwhites.

Although the groupings of the person and property offenses were useful as a measure of offense seriousness, they were nonetheless limited because the two groups of serious offenses masked a range of seriousness. It is instructive, therefore, to compare the prevalence of the delinquents and nondelinquents at discrete levels of the seven offenses that constituted the person and property offense subsets.[12] These data are reported in table 10.13. It is apparent from the data shown in this table that, among the whites, the official delinquents consistently exceeded the nondelinquents at the highest frequency levels for all seven offenses. The discrepancy varied by type of offense, however. For aggravated assault and larceny, the delinquents outnumbered the nondelinquents at the highest frequency level by ratios of $1.1:1$ and $1.3:1$, respectively. The ratio of the delinquents to the nondelinquents was $1.7:1$ for robbery and weapon threats and at least $2:1$ for rape, burglary, and shoplifting at the highest incidence level.

It is also apparent from table 10.13 that the results for the nonwhites and the three SES levels were very inconsistent. Among the nonwhites, the delinquents showed a higher percentage of high-frequency offending for aggravated assault, burglary, larceny, and shoplifting. Yet the delinquents and nondelinquents showed about the same prevalence for rape and robbery, but with the nondelinquents having the higher share of high-frequency offending. The results across SES categories were similarly varied. For most of the offenses, the delinquents showed higher proportions than the nondelinquents at the high-frequency level. In other instances the proportions were very close. In four cases the nondelinquents showed the greater prevalence (i.e., weapon threat at low SES, aggravated assault and larceny at medium SES, and burglary at high SES).

Predicting Delinquency Status   An alternative way of examining the correspondence between official and unofficial measures of delinquency is to treat official delinquency status as the dependent variable. Compared with the previous analyses, which focused on the delinquents and nondelinquents in terms of a variety of self-reported offense measures, the succeeding data are used to determine whether the various hidden-delinquency data allow us to discriminate between delinquents and nondelinquents. In other words, the self-report data are assumed to represent the behavioral context of delinquency, and differences in this behavior should be associated with a greater likelihood of being classified as delinquent by the police at least once. Thus, if official delinquency status is a

12. The class limits for the seven relatively serious offenses were very straightforward. About 75 percent of the subjects had committed none of the offenses, thus setting the first level. In order to isolate high-frequency offending for serious offenses, we used a 5 percent class size; therefore the intermediate group represented the difference between the two percentages.

function of delinquent behavior, one might expect to be able to predict this status with a series of variables that measure delinquent behavior.

Table 10.14 displays the percentage of respondents who were never arrested for the three summary measures of hidden delinquency. In all instances the data show the expected trend that as frequency of offenses increased the percentage of undetected offenders decreased. This result obtained for both the whites and the nonwhites and across the three SES levels. Despite this trend, the data given in table 10.14 show that most of the offenders escaped detection regardless of the frequency of their delinquency.

TABLE 10.14 Percentage of Respondents Never Arrested at Specific Levels of Three Self-Reported Offense Scales by Race and SES

	Race		SES		
Offense Level	Whites	Nonwhites	Low	Medium	High
Total self-reported offenses					
0–27	80.1	63.9	71.7	80.0	77.5
28–144	62.7	50.0	55.7	59.0	66.7
145+	54.7	33.3	55.0	47.4	55.0
Self-reported offenses against the person					
0	75.7	60.7	68.4	75.4	75.4
1–4	63.9	60.7	61.4	61.1	68.4
5–80	62.5	48.0	53.8	63.2	50.0
Self-reported offenses against property					
0	82.1	60.5	69.4	80.0	83.6
1–13	71.3	60.6	64.8	71.8	69.5
14–24	71.0	50.0	83.3	53.8	66.7
25–450	48.1	0.0	36.8	42.1	55.0

Given this finding, the other noteworthy result shown in table 10.14 concerns the racial differences in the proportions of undetected offenders. At each incidence level for all three offense measures, the whites were more likely to be non-delinquent. In terms of a global measure of hidden delinquency, over half of the high-frequency white offenders were never arrested, compared with just one-third of the nonwhites. For serious offenses against the person, over 60 percent of the whites, compared with 48 percent of the nonwhites, were nondelinquent at the highest incidence level. The results were most dramatic for the property offense subset. Among the high-frequency offenders, almost half (48.1 percent) of the whites were never recorded as delinquent. On the other hand, none of the nonwhites who were high-frequency offenders escaped detection.

The results by SES show that the majority of offenders escaped detection. Further, unlike the data by race, the results show no consistent pattern favoring a particular SES level. For the global measure, the medium SES subjects were the most likely to be caught for frequent delinquency. For the two subsets of offenses, the high SES offenders were caught more often for offenses against the person, while the low SES subjects were more likely to be caught for frequent offenses against property.

In light of these results, the final aspect of the analysis is to determine the ability of the self-reported offense measures to differentiate between official delinquents and nondelinquents. To accomplish this task, we used the multiple discriminant function procedure. The set of discriminating variables included race, SES, total self-reported offenses, average severity of the self-reported offenses, and the seven serious offenses referred to earlier. We performed three analyses. The first included all the subjects, while the other two examined the whites and nonwhites separately. The results of the discriminant function analyses are reported in tables 10.15 and 10.16.

Table 10.15 lists the standardized coefficients of the variables in the canonical discriminant function. The coefficients are present to reflect the relative importance of each variable to the derived functions. The standardized coefficients are analogous to the partial betas in multiple regression and thus lend themselves to a similar interpretation. The signs associated with these coefficients are indicative of a "push away from" or a "pull toward" a particular group. For the present analysis a negative sign reflects a pull toward nondelinquency, while a positive sign indicates a push toward official delinquency.

For all the subjects, the most important predictor of delinquency status was shoplifting, followed by burglary. The third most powerful discriminator was the subject's race. Total self-reported offenses and robbery were somewhat useful to the derived function, while the other variables were weak predictors and, in fact,

TABLE 10.15   Standardized Discriminant Function Coefficients

Variables	All Subjects	Whites	Nonwhites
Race	0.50343	—	—
SES	−0.16688	−0.39035	0.45868
Total self-reported offenses	0.40127	0.50382	−0.27792
Severity of self-reported offenses	0.13290	0.15834	0.07459
Rape	−0.02136	−0.11410	−0.06094
Robbery	0.30481	0.15759	0.47489
Aggravated assault	−0.10552	−0.40074	0.39958
Weapon threat	−0.08789	0.20911	−0.56609
Burglary	0.56765	0.73594	0.30669
Larceny	−0.10147	−0.07491	−0.17601
Shoplifting	0.59641	0.66218	0.57807
Canonical correlation	0.2464	0.2431	0.3312
Wilk's lambda	0.9392	0.9408	0.8902
χ^2	35.07	27.18	12.437
Probability	.0002	.002	.256

TABLE 10.16   Distribution of Actual and Predicted Group Membership for Official Delinquency Status

		Predicted			
	Actual	Nondelinquents		Delinquents	
	N	N	%	N	%
All subjects					
Nondelinquents	392	303	77.3	89	22.7
Delinquents	175	104	59.4	71	40.6
Whites					
Nondelinquents	326	239	73.3	87	26.7
Delinquents	127	70	55.1	57	44.9
Nonwhites					
Nondelinquents	66	48	72.7	18	27.3
Delinquents	48	28	58.3	20	41.7

reflected a pull toward nondelinquency. The canonical correlation (.25) suggested only a weak association between the predictors and delinquency status. Last, the value of Wilk's lambda (.94) indicated that the discriminating power in the set of predictors was very small. Thus the rankings discussed above should be interpreted in light of a relatively weak set of predictors.

The data by race show about the same overall effects. The set of predictors was correlated only weakly with delinquency status, and the higher correlation was observed for the nonwhites. The set of discriminating variables had relatively little power, although the discriminating ability was slightly greater for the nonwhites. In terms of the relative importance of the predictors, the results varied by race. For the whites the two best predictors were burglary and shoplifting, while for the nonwhites the two strongest variables were shoplifting and weapon threat (with the latter representing a pull toward nondelinquency). Another difference was that SES and aggravated assault exerted a push toward nondelinquency for the whites but a pull toward official delinquency for the nonwhites. The reverse was true for total self-reported offenses, which pushed the whites toward official delinquency and pulled the nonwhites toward nondelinquency.

These data did not suggest a successful effort to discriminate between nondelinquents and delinquents on the basis of hidden offense measures. Table 10.16 reports the results of this effort. For all the subjects, the discriminant function predicted that 89 nondelinquents appeared more like the delinquents and that 104 delinquents had scores similar to those of the nondelinquents. These numbers translated into a false positive rate of 22.7 percent and a false negative rate of 59.4 percent. The results by race were similarly unimpressive. Among the nondelinquents of both races, 27 percent were classified as delinquent because their discriminant function scores looked more like those of the delinquents. In addition, the discriminant analysis classified about 55 percent of the white delinquents and 58 percent of the nonwhite delinquents into the nondelinquent group.

These results indicated that both the nondelinquents and the delinquents committed frequent and serious offenses. The distributions of the hidden offense measures were so similar for the two groups that the self-report data did not discriminate successfully between those who were and those who were not arrested for delinquent acts. Behaviorally, then, delinquency status did not appear to be associated with appreciably more frequent or more serious acts of delinquency.

Summary

The first part of this chapter examined the relationship between race and SES and a series of self-reported delinquency measures. As in prior research, this study has attempted to isolate correlates of hidden delinquency with respect to the prevalence and incidence of self-reported offenses for a global scale. Unlike most previous research, this study also examined possible race and SES differences in the seriousness of self-reported offenses and analyzed the official dimension of delinquency that served as an important context for viewing the self-reported offense data.

As in the vast majority of previous self-report studies, the findings reported here do not indicate significant offense differences by either race or SES for a global measure of hidden delinquency. The mean frequencies across SES groups were almost identical, and more important, whites rather than nonwhites exhibited higher group means, although the difference was not significant. The results were much the same when we examined discrete incidence data. The proportions of subjects that fell at the various levels of incidence were very similar by both race and SES, indicating that none of the groups had a disproportionate share of high-frequency offenders.

When we examined the seriousness of the self-reported offenses, however, race repeatedly emerged as a significant factor. Nonwhites had a much higher mean number of serious offenses against the person than whites; the ratio was over 2:1. In addition, nonwhites also exhibited a significantly higher mean seriousness score for the Sellin-Wolfgang index. These race differences were further supported by the finding that nonwhites had appreciably higher proportions of subjects than whites at the high-incidence levels of the crimes against the person subscale.

When we viewed the self-reported offense results together with those of the official delinquency data, we reached a conclusion different from that proposed by previous researchers. Generally, previous studies concluded that because self-report data do not reflect the race and class differences maintained in official offense data, the race and class disparities in the latter cannot be explained in terms of behavioral differences in delinquency. Failure to support the differential involvement thesis led to the suggestion that the criminal justice system, like other sectors of society, discriminates against minorities and the poor. It followed, therefore, that race and SES differences in official data might be explained better in terms of a differential selection thesis. Put simply, nonwhites and lower-class persons are not really more delinquent but are just more likely to be arrested.

On the other hand, the results reported in this chapter did not indicate a discrepancy between official and self-reported offense measures. In fact, for nonwhites there was a close correspondence between the alternative offense domains. That is, nonwhites were significantly more likely to be delinquent and to be arrested frequently both overall and at each SES level. These official designations were supported by significant behavioral differences between the nonwhites and whites. The former had appreciably higher numbers of violent offenses and average seriousness scores, measures that were presumably associated with a greater likelihood of arrest.

The conclusion that the alternative offense domains are not discrepant must be made with caution. The data suggested that this was the case, but only by implication. That is, as a group the nonwhites appeared more offensive in both the official and the self-reported offense contexts, thus implying a correspondence. However, the issue can be investigated best by focusing directly on the relationship between official delinquency status and the nature and extent of self-reported delinquency by race and SES. In this way the actual correspondence between official and unofficial measures can be specified for the various groups.

The second part of this chapter investigated the relationship between official delinquency status and a series of self-reported delinquency measures. The major purpose of the analysis has been to test the congruence of alternative offense measures. The analysis consisted of two parts. First, the delinquents and nondelinquents were compared in terms of the incidence of self-reported offenses and the prevalence of high-frequency offending. Second, official delinquency status was treated as the dependent measure, with the self-report data used as predictors. Although the results were less than conclusive, they illuminated several important issues surrounding the alternative measures of delinquency.

From one perspective the results sustained the findings of prior research. The present data indicated that the number of self-reported delinquent acts committed by the official delinquents was significantly greater than for respondents not labeled delinquent. We observed this result for a global measure of hidden delinquency and two subsets of offenses (person and property) reflecting more serious delinquency. Of equal importance was that the delinquency status effect held for both races across SES levels. The data also indicated that delinquency status was associated with high-frequency offending. When the self-reported offense data were ordered by specific levels of incidence, official delinquents were more likely to be classified at the highest frequency level, regardless of race or SES.

These longitudinal results verified the findings of previous research that delinquents report a higher incidence of hidden delinquency than do official nondelinquents. More important, the data showed that this characteristic is not affected by race or SES (factors that were largely ignored in past studies). At first glance these data supported the claim that official police statistics properly reflect the more frequent and serious juvenile offenders. However, further analysis of the data revealed the opposite; that is, when we examined the percentage of respondents who were never arrested at various levels of self-reported delinquency, we found that substantial percentages of respondents had escaped detection. The proportions were smaller at the higher incidence level, but they were sufficient to indicate that high-frequency offending was no guarantee of having an arrest status. Similarly, the seriousness of the offenses did not ensure detection, because substantial proportions of the high-frequency offenders for person and property offenses had escaped arrest. We also found that self-reported offense measures, when used in a multivariate framework, could not readily discriminate between subjects who had an official police record and those who had no such label. This finding indicated substantial overlap in the distributions of hidden delinquency measures for all the delinquents and nondelinquents.

The implications of these data concerned three fundamental aspects of official police statistics: How valid and useful are police data as indicators of the incidence of delinquency, the correlates of delinquency, and frequent or serious offending?

Official police statistics underestimate the actual extent of delinquency. The subjects of this research were responsible for many thousands of offenses that went undetected or at least were ignored by the authorities. Of course, the police might consider many of these events too trivial to warrant an official arrest. Nevertheless, approximately one thousand offenses that would have been recorded by the police as *UCR* index offenses, if detected, remained hidden. Police statistics do not constitute a complete measure of crime occurrence, at least in terms of self-reports of actual offenses.

The official police data depicted higher arrest rates for the nonwhites in this study. Yet this group was not found to have consistently higher levels of hidden delinquency. The nonwhites had significantly more offenses against the person, but the whites had more offenses and property offenses. It seems, therefore, that the differential selection of nonwhites for arrest is a better explanation of the race discrepancy in arrest status than the traditional differential involvement thesis.

The last issue concerning the frequency and severity of delinquency confirms the inadequacy of police data and explains the race difference in arrest rates. That is, many frequent offenders and offenders who committed serious offenses were not listed as official delinquents. Subjects with a police record should constitute the most frequent or more serious violators. Among the whites, the majority of frequent or serious offenders were not caught. For the nonwhites, however, the percentage of such offenders who escaped detection was much smaller, and it was zero for some offense/frequency combinations. The police data, therefore, underestimated the actual prevalence and incidence of delinquency among the whites. On the other hand, the police data seemed to capture those nonwhites who were frequent and/or serious offenders.

A major conclusion these results suggested concerned the lack of representativeness of the police data. If hidden delinquency data represent delinquent behavior, then the official dichotomy of delinquent versus nondelinquent may not appropriately label the majority of offenders who engage in frequent or serious acts of delinquency. We also concluded not only that official data constitute a sample of the offenses committed but also that offenders who received official attention are only a sample of the persons who commit delinquent acts frequently and within a relatively serious context. This is especially true for whites.

Still, self-report instruments may not be tapping behaviors that are equivalent to those listed among offenses known to the police. When viewed apart from the actual situation, self-reported offenses may be perceived by respondents as serious, but may somehow not be equivalent to the behaviors that require police intervention. Moreover, it remains unclear whether self-reported behaviors are free from the problems that inhere in the solicitation of sensitive data from survey respondents. Because no validation checks for hidden delinquency are available, it remains a question whether self-reports are susceptible to underreporting or overreporting and whether such response errors are independent of response characteristics.

For these reasons it is difficult to conclude confidently that self-reported and official measures are or are not congruent, particularly in terms of the correlates of delinquency. It is also a mistake to conclude that "police contacts are most likely to concern youth who are involved in very serious or very frequent delinquent acts" (Elliott and Ageton 1980, 107). Until our knowledge base is considerably more advanced, research should focus on multiple measures of delinquency. If alternative measures of delinquency are not possible in certain contexts, then the results of such research must be interpreted in light of the problems inherent in the particular data being used. The use of limited delinquency measures can only perpetuate inconsistent and apparently contradictory findings concerning delinquency and its correlates.

11 Situational or Planned Crime and the Criminal Career

Edna Erez

The Problem and Theoretical Background

Recent criminological research has devoted considerable attention to criminal careers. Yet little notice has been given to an important aspect of such careers: the planning involved in committing crimes. This chapter examines that issue and discusses both the theoretical and the practical implications of planning.

A wide variety of theories, covering biological, psychological, social, and cultural explanations of criminal behavior, have been presented over the years. One of the basic assumptions in these theories is that crime is caused by some enduring characteristic that renders the individual different from law-abiding citizens. For example, constitutional predisposition (Mednick and Volavka 1980; Shah and Roth 1974), personality structure (Alexander and Staub 1956; Eysenck 1964; Halleck 1971), location in the social hierarchy (Cloward and Ohlin 1960; Merton 1957), cultural or subcultural heritage (Cloward and Ohlin 1960; Cohen 1955; Miller 1958; Wolfgang and Ferracuti 1982), and group affiliation (Matza 1964; Shaw and McKay 1942; Sutherland and Cressey 1974) have all been suggested at one time or another as the primary causal factor.

This emphasis on enduring factors has had one rather limiting consequence: the impact of situational factors on criminal outcomes has not been viewed as an important category for causal explanation. But the study of causation may be enhanced by focusing on the "here and now" (Lewin 1951) rather than on some state of affairs in the past. The "contemporaneity of causation" (Cartwright 1959) or the role situational factors play in criminal events may be assessed by addressing the issues of planning and spontaneity in crime. Indeed, theoretical work (Homans 1961) and a number of experimental studies (for example, Asch 1955; Mischel 1968, 1971) have indicated that situationally induced stimuli of relatively short duration can have major effects on behavior, values, and attitudes.

In criminology, however, situational aspects of crime have been treated as of secondary importance, considered mostly in terms of a category of "situational offenders" (for example, Corsini 1949; Lindesmith and Dunham 1941). Also, only a few criminologists have emphasized the utility of "situational" or dynamic explanations of criminal behavior (for example, Cohen 1966; Gibbons 1971; Sutherland and Cressey 1974).

The systematic inclusion of situational factors in criminological research, however, is certainly consistent with many theoretical perspectives. For example, some theorists have suggested that delinquency is not restricted to people of a particular kind (Matza 1964) and that delinquent behavior is episodic, purposive, and confined to certain situations. Delinquent acts may be prompted by short-term, situationally induced desires youngsters experience and may be designed for specific purposes, such as to obtain goods, to display courage in the presence of peers, to demonstrate love, or simply to "get kicks" (Hindelang 1972b). Some writers argue that portraying delinquency as the product of long-term motives deriving from frustrations far removed from the arenas where offenses occur is not warranted in light of the erratic nature of delinquent acts (Briar and Piliavin 1965; Matza 1964; Wolfgang, Figlio, and Sellin 1972).

These assumptions about the influence of situational factors are also consistent with control theories (Hirschi 1969), which construe delinquency as the consequence of an inability to resist temptation. The type of control or restraint varies with the particular theory: inadequate socialization or deficient superego (Alexander and Staub 1956), failure of social institutions such as the family or the school (McCord and McCord 1959; Nye 1958), or reduced commitment to conformity (Briar and Piliavin 1965; Hirschi 1969). Common to all of these theories, however, is the assumption that people confronted with certain situations may deviate unless the relevant controls are effective.

Situational factors are also relevant to deterrence theory. It is plausible to assume that the criminal who plans will be more responsive to the principles of deterrence. He is more likely to include in his calculations the consequences of being caught and the magnitude of the resulting punishment (Zimring and Hawkins 1973, 106–8).

The issue of planning is also important in the development of crime prevention policies (Sykes 1972). If offenders are mostly impulsive, making targets more difficult to obtain may prevent some crime simply by reducing the opportunity. Such a policy would not be as effective, however, if the offender population consists mostly of persons who plan their offenses, since increasing the difficulty of achieving certain targets may lead either to more sophisticated criminality or to the displacement of crime to other targets (Reppetto 1976).

Finally, the issue of planning and spontaneity in crime is important for studies of criminal careers. If planning is related to a career in crime, if it affects the manner, seriousness, and tempo of criminal activity, or if it affects the likelihood of apprehension, it should be considered as one of the variables of analysis. Indeed, there is some evidence that persons who carefully plan lawbreaking are likely to be underrepresented among prosecuted or convicted offenders (McClintock 1970).

Planning and Impulsivity in Crime: A Review of the Literature
Definitional Problems

The term planning implies problems of external and internal ambiguity (Kaplan 1964, 66). Planning may be conceptualized as a quantitative variable, as a continuum upon which individuals are placed according to the forethought evidenced in their acts. Planning, however, may denote not only quantitative differences but qualitative differences. Thus it is one thing to refer to unplanned action in terms of the absence of premeditation and quite another to talk about the accidental act. One may not necessarily plan an act but may still commit it willingly. Further, unplanned acts may be the result of involuntary involvement, such as those acts that arise from coercion (physical or mental), necessity, or recklessness. Likewise, planning may take place simultaneously with the act or just before it, but here the behavior is termed impulsive or spontaneous.

Various disciplines use the term planning in different ways and for different purposes. In criminal law, planning is discussed in the context of intent or *mens rea*, particularly with respect to premeditation. Nevertheless, controversies exist concerning the kind and amount of planning required to satisfy the element of premeditation, its forms, or its proof (LaFave and Scott 1972, 562–67). In the psychological literature, planning denotes any hierarchical process that can control the sequence in a chain of events (Miller, Galanter, and Pribham 1960, 12); planning is viewed as a basic attribute of human life, and planlessness is equivalent to death (1960, 16). Psychological studies evaluate planning within the context of character development and personality structure, and a qualitative distinction is made between short-range and long-range plans (Shapiro 1965). Impulsivity is viewed as the hallmark of certain character disorders, being linked to criminal behavior either through one neurotic style, the "impulsive style" (1965, chap. 5), or through the extreme end of impulsivity, psychopathy (Hare 1970).

In criminology, planning has been discussed as an indicator of criminal sophistication, and references to the professionalism and hardening of criminals have been based on the amount or quality of planning involved in a crime (Petersilia, Greenwood, and Lavin 1978). This multiplicity of meaning may result in disagreement concerning the classification of many events. For instance, an offender may think continually about committing a crime (for example, acquiring money in an illegal way) without having any specific plan or scheme to implement it. But when the right circumstances occur or the opportunity presents itself, he commits the crime. What appears to be spur-of-the-moment may have been in the offender's mind all along.

In the present analysis we adopt a very general definition of planning that encompasses many of the specific meanings just discussed. In everyday language, planning means formulating a scheme or a procedure for doing something before doing it or having an intention of acting (*Webster's Third New International Dictionary,* 1976). This meaning has been adopted for this chapter.

Empirical Evidence on Planning and Impulsivity in Crime

Planning and impulsivity may be viewed as personality traits or character components (Kipnis 1971; Shapiro 1965). In addition to the character of the person involved, however, the complexity of the offenses should be examined, since some crimes logically require much preparation. Embezzlement, theft by manipulating records, fraud, or complex burglaries typically require much more planning than unarmed robbery or theft. It is necessary, therefore, to distinguish between types of lawbreaking in exploring the presence and effect of planning.

Direct evidence about planning may be found in studies that have used data elicited from offenders by means of questionnaires or interviews (including interviews by the police for investigative purposes) and from people who have had firsthand experience with offenders, either through their work (for example, caseworkers) or through other associations (for example, ethnographic research).

Studies of planning among juvenile delinquents have reported that spur-of-the-moment involvement was most common; unplanned situations presented actors with the opportunity to violate the law. Only when events were serious and profit oriented was planning evident (Hindelang 1972b).

Studies of specific offenses (such as robbery and shoplifting) have distinguished between professional and opportunistic offenders. The former tend to plan crimes carefully; the latter are more likely to be impulsive, committing offenses randomly as opportunities arise (Cameron 1964; Conklin 1972). But in a study of incarcerated habitual felons, Petersilia, Greenwood, and Lavin (1978) found that neither intensive nor intermittent robbers exhibited any precrime planning behavior, although the intensive group seemed to give deliberate attention to avoiding arrest. Also, no association between planning sophistication and other offender attributes was apparent. Offenders who planned did not necessarily commit more offenses (a finding that might be expected given the low level of crime planning); they engaged in crimes opportunistically and with surprisingly low monetary gains. In this same vein, Peterson, Braiker, and Polich (1981) found that the most frequent reason prison inmates gave for committing crime was a "good opportunity."

Some studies of the social organization of offenses have revealed degrees of planning in offenses against property. Preparation for burglaries ranges from visiting a potential site through elaborate planning of all details, including means and routes of escape. Skilled burglaries tend to be planned social enterprises (Shover 1973). Similarly, the "smoothness" with which armed robberies take place depends on the level of planning, which varies from the robbery team's simple drive around the neighborhood to a series of complex maneuvers (Einstadter 1969).

On the other hand, crimes against the person, particularly homicide, tend to be impulsive and not clearly planned (Wolfgang 1975). Rape cases vary in the degree of planning; "chosen" situations, where the offender has some predisposition owing to his general criminal tendency or the encouragement of peers, can be differentiated from "unchosen" situations, where the influence of alcohol or other situational factors lead to the crime (Amir 1971). In general, the primacy of situational factors has been stressed for crimes of violence (Luckenbill 1977; Wolfgang 1975).

Overall, therefore, the weight of the empirical evidence from previous studies suggests that criminal behavior is not characterized by extensive planning. For property crimes the results are mixed, and for violent crimes they suggest that spontaneity is most common. We now turn to the data available in this study to see if previous results are replicated.

The Role That Planning and Situations Play in Crime

The role of situational factors in crime is addressed by two kinds of questions posed to the 567 respondents interviewed. The most direct questions concern the amount of planning, if any, that preceded the first and last offenses for which the respondent was arrested. Less direct questions pertain to the motives or reasons respondents gave for committing the crimes or the presence of any special events that preceded the crimes and might have triggered them. If these offenses occurred without any apparent reason, motive, or precipitating event, we assume they were unplanned.

The majority of the offenders (66 percent) reported that they committed their offenses impulsively, with little or no planning or forethought. The second largest group (17 percent) were more clearly nonplanners in that they claimed they did not plan, even instantaneously, or they perceived their acts as accidental. For analysis and comparison we shall treat both types as "impulsive."

Those who devoted any time to planning their crimes constituted only 17 percent of the sample. Crimes planned at least one day before the event constituted only 6 percent of the first offenses. For the remaining 11 percent of the group, planning took place only on the day of the crime.

Because we are dealing with the first offenses for which the respondents were arrested, age may explain the high percentage of impulsivity and the low percentage of planning and preparation. Table 11.1 demonstrates, however, that impulsivity characterizes criminal behavior in *all* age groups.

The breakdown of offenses leading to the last arrest by the amount of planning is not very different from that of the offenses leading to the first arrest. The majority (61 percent) were committed on the spur of the moment, while only 21 percent were planned. Again, age does not explain the preponderance of impulsivity ($\chi^2 = 1.62$; $p < .55$).

The tendency to commit offenses impulsively appears to be very stable. There is a significant relationship between the manner of committing the first-arrest offense and the last-arrest offense, as table 11.2 indicates. Those who responded that they planned their first-arrest offenses were more likely than those whose

TABLE 11.1   Age at First-Arrest Offense by Planning

Age Group	Impulsive		Planned		Total	
	N	%	N	%	N	%
6–11	6	100	—	—	6	3
12–17	119	86	19	14	138	63
18–20	38	72	15	28	76	24
21–26	19	83	4	17	23	10
Total	182	83	38	17	220	100

$\chi^2 = 6.95$; $p \leq .08$.

TABLE 11.2   Planning in Last-Arrest Offense by Planning in First-Arrest Offense

First-Arrest Offense	Last-Arrest Offense					
	Planned		Not Planned		Total	
	N	%	N	%	N	%
Planned	8	40	12	60	20	18
Not planned	16	17	78	83	94	82
Total	24	21	90	79	114	100

$\chi^2 = 3.94; p \le .05$.

first-arrest offenses were impulsive to plan their last-arrest offenses (40 percent vs. 17 percent); conversely, those reporting that their first-arrest offenses were not planned were more likely not to plan their last-arrest offenses (83 percent vs. 60 percent).

Reasons Given for the Offense

One factor that could explain the occurrence of an offense and undermine the significance of the situational elements is whether there was a particular reason for committing the crime or whether any special event preceded or triggered the offense. It is plausible, therefore, to expect an association between planning and the presence of a reason for committing an offense. Without announced reason, the fortuitous role of the situation becomes more significant.

Respondents were asked to specify their reasons for "getting into trouble" in the first- and last-arrest offenses. The question was open-ended; answers were collapsed into the categories presented in tables 11.3 and 11.4. For the first-arrest offense the most frequent reason was the search for excitement, followed by chance factors ("it just happened"). For the last-arrest offense the overwhelming reason was chance (89 percent). In examining the relationship between the presence of some reason given for that offense and planning preceding the offense, it was found that there was little association between them during the juvenile years. The only exception to the overall pattern concerned offenses for which the respondent still claimed innocence and said the arrest was a "police mistake." During the adult years, however, the expected relationship between

TABLE 11.3   Reasons Given for Committing First-Arrest Offense by Planning

Reasons	Planned		Not Planned		Total	
	N	%	N	%	N	%
Chance factors	5	21	58	79	63	28
Mistake by police	1	5	20	95	21	10
Excitement	24	23	79	77	103	47
Other	7	21	26	79	33	15
Total	37	17	183	83	220	100

$\chi^2 = 9.28; p \le .05$

TABLE 11.4 Reasons Given for Committing Last-Arrest Offense by Planning

Reasons	Planned		Not Planned		Total	
	N	%	N	%	N	%
Chance factors	10	11	80	89	90	89
Nonchance or rational reasons	6	54	5	45	11	11
Total	16	16	85	84	101	100

$\chi^2 = 10.8; p \leq .001.$

chance factors and unplanned events is observed. The reader should be aware of the very small number of "nonchance" offenses in interpreting this result.

Another way to illuminate the relative significance of situations compared with planning in criminal outcomes is to examine variation by type of offense. Previous research indicates that offenses against property are more likely to be planned than are other types of crime, since property crimes are instrumental. Crimes against the person, on the other hand, are mostly expressive; that is, they express emotions (for example, frustration, anger, lust) and therefore tend to be impulsive (Chambliss 1967).

Results for the first-arrest offenses indicate, however, that although theft was planned more frequently than other index offenses (most of which were offenses against the person), the nonindex offenses were planned twice as often as theft (table 11.5). The preponderance of planning in nonindex offenses in the first-arrest crimes becomes clearer if one recalls the reasons respondents gave for these offenses. Most of these crimes (for example, drinking, gambling, drugs, disorderly conduct) were offenses planned for the purpose of "having a good time," excitement, or relief from boredom.

For the last-arrest offenses, however, we discern no significant relationship between offense type and planning. Although planning appears more often in theft, the difference is not statistically significant.

The picture of crime that emerges from the description of first- and last-arrest offenses portrays criminal activity mostly as situational and unplanned. Even after we eliminate that portion of crime and delinquency that was due to age alone (status offenses committed for the purpose of "having a good time"), crime is seen as an activity that is not governed by long- or short-range plans or instrumentality; rather, it is likely to occur on the spur of the moment as perceived

TABLE 11.5 Offense Type by Planning: First-Arrest Offense

Offense Category	Planned		Not Planned		Total	
	N	%	N	%	N	%
Nonindex	45	33	90	67	135	61
Theft	5	16	26	84	31	14
Other index	5	9	49	91	54	25
Total	55	25	165	75	220	100

$\chi^2 = 13.43; p < .001.$

opportunities present themselves or as situations are conducive to law violations. Whether property offenses or crimes against the person, the law violations involved little thinking and reflection; no particular reason or justification is suggested to account for them.

The image that emerges from this analysis is one of individuals who act on the spur of the moment, whose criminality is more a function of lack of thinking in their daily activities or experiences than the result of planning, reflection, or deliberation. Crime is something that "happens" to them wherever they are rather than a course of action that they desire or aim for. We are not suggesting that these acts are committed involuntarily or that offenders are merely victims of their life circumstances. There is an element of choice in all activities that people engage in or become involved in, provided they are not coerced. What stands out here is the lack of "will" or prior decision to commit offenses and the inability to "resist" temptations or forgo opportunities.

Planning and the Criminal Career: Offense Number and Seriousness

Although most crime is situational or unplanned, there is a fraction that is planned. Our interest now is in studying the effect planning may have on the criminal careers of those whose offenses are planned and not merely a result of situational factors.

The effect of planning is addressed by examining the relationship between the way the crime was committed and the resultant harm or offense seriousness, and the relationship between the tendency to plan and the number of offenses in a criminal career. The empirical relationship between planning and the results of criminal conduct—as measured by seriousness and length of criminal record—is important for both theoretical and penal purposes. For example, mental state (or moral culpability) and harm (the degree of damage inflicted by the act) have been listed both as major determinants of perceptions of crime seriousness and as the two analytical components to be used in measuring the commensurability of punishment (von Hirsch 1976). The underlying assumptions are that these two factors are independent and that both should be considered in determining punishment, although the weight assigned to each has not been specified. Yet the relationship between the two has not been examined empirically. Furthermore, harm has been given almost exclusive priority over culpability both in the judgment of seriousness (Sellin and Wolfgang 1978) and in the determination of punishment by judges (Schulhofer 1974).

It is understandable that planned offenses portray a different image of offenders than is presented by cases in which the crimes were impulsive, though equally serious in their consequences. Planning is more than mere awareness or intent; thought and preparation suggest a person highly committed to criminality. The common view of offenders as lacking moral restraint and compassion for their victims best fits those who approach their crimes in a cool, methodical, planned fashion. As Immanuel Kant stated, rationality and planning are desirable personal attributes, but when applied to crime they are the attributes of a villain. In other words, planning may itself lead us to view the offender as more blameworthy or culpable than if the offense is committed on the spur of the moment and, though voluntary, is unplanned.

Planning, however, not only may indicate more blameworthiness owing to the forethought involved, but may also result in a higher degree of seriousness. If planned offenses result in more damage, injury, or loss, then planning contributes to both harm and moral culpability. If planned offenses actually result in the utmost loss, injury, or damage, then an implicit attribution of a degree of intentionality to criminal conduct proportional to its harmful consequences may underlie the judgment process. This possible explanation is supported by Sebba's (1980) finding that raters tend to assume intention when assigning scores to offenses in which intent was not specified. Our aim here is to explore these possibilities.

To examine the relationship between seriousness and planning, we compared the mean seriousness scores of the sample's first- and last-arrest offenses for crimes classified as planned or impulsive. For these crimes the detailed description of each offense by the respondents led to seriousness scores that took into consideration all the relevant factors, such as degree of injury or amount of damage or stolen property.

Each crime (first and last) was examined separately. We suspected that for the first-arrest offense, which was committed at an early age, the differences would not be as pronounced as for the last-arrest offense, which was committed in adulthood. The majority of offenses (60 percent) consisted of nonindex crimes; 15 percent were thefts, and the rest were other index offenses for both the first- and last-arrest offenses.

Table 11.6 indicates that planning was related to seriousness only for the last-arrest offense, confirming the hypothesis. The mean seriousness score of the planned last-arrest offense is appreciably higher than that of the impulsive last-arrest offense (375 vs. 212). In examining only property crimes, for which the hypothesis is most applicable, we found no significant relationship between planning and seriousness. But the variance of the two groups appears to be significantly different ($p < .007$). The impulsive offense scores ranged from 161 to 1,600, while the planned offense scores ranged from 287 to 300.

These preliminary results suggest that there is some practical justification for emphasizing the seriousness of the consequences of crime rather than the de-

TABLE 11.6   Seriousness by Planning for First-Arrest and Last-Arrest Offenses

| | Seriousness | | | | Significance |
	$\overline{X}$	SD	N	t	(One-Tailed Test)
First-arrest offense					
Impulsive	136	259	130	.567	$p < .25$
Planned	170	320	25		
Last-arrest offense					
Impulsive	212	314	74	1.600	$p < .05$
Planned	375	615	19		

gree of intent. For purposes of punishment, stepping over the threshold from law-abiding to law-violating behavior is the overriding factor. Once the intent is formed and legal culpability is determined, consequences of the act should be considered in determining the commensurability of punishment. Impulsive offenses may have results of minimal or utmost seriousness; planned crimes are not necessarily more serious.

Career Length and Planning: Official and Hidden Crime

In examining the relationship between planning and the number of offenses committed in a career, we hypothesize that planning results in fewer offenses. It is conceivable that the offender who prepares for the offense will commit fewer crimes in his criminal career, and the tempo of criminality will be inhibited somewhat by the carefulness and cautiousness of his activity. It is also conceivable that at least in property offenses, assuming that offenders are "satisfiers" (McPheters and Stronge 1976), planned offenses will yield more returns, thus requiring fewer crimes. At the same time, these characteristics of planned offenses would lead to more difficulties in detecting and apprehending lawbreakers and would result in fewer arrests compared with the number of offenses committed.

Impulsive offenders, on the other hand, are more likely to commit crimes indiscriminately, whenever opportunities arise or situations present themselves, and should exhibit more offenses in their careers. But the impulsivity of their crimes should lead to a higher ratio of arrests to offenses, for crimes committed on the spur of the moment are executed less carefully and thus are less likely to escape detection.

To study the effect of planning on the criminal career, we classified as planners those who planned their first- and last-arrest offenses, and the rest of the sample we classified as impulsives. As we showed earlier (table 11.2), subjects who planned their first-arrest offenses were more likely to plan their second offenses. We further assume here that those who planned both offenses exhibited a general tendency to plan their criminal affairs, although in any particular offense this assumption may not be realized. Our interest in this case is with planning as an attribute of the offender, not of the offense.

The total number of offenses each subject admitted committing was examined by the offense type: violent, property (for which the hypothesis is most applicable), and nonindex. Statistical tests showed no significant differences between the two groups in their number of property offenses. Comparing the groups with respect to violent crimes and nonindex crimes, however, yielded significant differences, as presented in table 11.7. Violent offenses embraced all types of assaultive, aggressive behavior, including threat or intimidation. The mean of the impulsive group is nearly twice that of the planned group. The bulk of the difference came from offenses such as carrying a switchblade or other weapon and sexual or other assault.

Similarly, comparing the groups with respect to nonindex offenses yielded significant differences. The mean number of nonindex crimes for the impulsive group is twice as large as that of the planned group. The bulk of the difference

TABLE 11.7   Differences in Means of Self-Reported Offenses between
Impulsive and Planned Offenders, Violent and Nonindex Offenses Only

	Offenders		
Offenses	Impulsive		Planned
Violent			
$\bar{X}$	757		350
SD	1143		696
N	169		23
t		1.66	
p		.05	
Nonindex			
$\bar{X}$	1398		687
SD	1465		1185
N	107		14
t		1.73	
p		.04	

came from offenses such as disturbing the neighborhood, being drunk in public, possessing and using drugs, making obscene phone calls, and visiting prostitutes. Comparing the ratios of arrests to self-reported offenses for these two groups did not yield statistically significant differences.

These results may illuminate the behavior of the impulsive offender more than the effect the tendency to plan has on the criminal career. We cannot claim that the individual who tends to plan differs from his impulsive counterpart in the *number* of property offenses he commits or in the likelihood of being arrested. The results, however, suggest that impulsive offenders violate the law more readily, behave more violently, and come into conflict with the law on many occasions in which specific situations are conducive to crime.

Summary and Conclusions

Our survey of the literature has led us to expect that criminal violations are mostly situational and that impulsive crime is more common than planned crime. Consistent with that literature, we find that in analyzing the description of first- and last-arrest offenses in the cohort sample, the overwhelming majority of offenses occurred without any planning. Only a small fraction of offenses were conceived beforehand.

One exception to this trend was nonindex status offenses committed during adolescence. These offenses tended to be planned with the object of "having a good time," "getting excitement," or "relieving boredom." The source of excitement, however, happened to be contrary to the law, which might add to its attractiveness.

The objective of relief from boredom in juvenile delinquency was noted and described by playwright Arthur Miller (1962, 51):

The boredom of the delinquent is remarkable mainly because it is so little compensated for, as it may be among the middle classes and the rich who can fly down to the Caribbean or to Europe, or refurnish the house, or have an affair, or at least go shopping. The delinquent is stuck with his boredom, stuck inside it, stuck to it, until for two or three minutes he "lives"; he goes on a raid around the corner and feels the thrill of risking his skin or his life as he smashes a bottle filled with gasoline on some other kid's head. In a sense, it is his trip to Miami. It makes his day. It is his shopping tour. It gives him something to talk about for a week. It is his life. Standing around with nothing coming up is as close to dying as you can get. Unless one grasps the power of boredom, the threat of it to one's existence, it is impossible to "place" the delinquent as a member of the human race.

As we focused on offenders who committed their crimes impulsively, without planning, certain attributes of their criminal behavior and careers emerged. These offenders exhibited a greater involvement in crime, coming into conflict with the law much more often than their counterparts who planned. To an extent, their criminal behavior appeared to be part of a life-style that involved readiness to resort to violence and disregard for community conventions about social order or acceptable behavior.

Despite the lack of planning in their crimes, the impulsive offenders committed offenses with very harmful consequences. The range of their crime seriousness scores was large and was significantly different from that of offenders who planned. Because the next opportunity that presents itself and the next crime they happen to commit are quite unpredictable, so too are the harmful consequences of their offensive behavior. Therefore an "accidental" view of the magnitude of crime seriousness is supported by the data.

Criminal law, by emphasizing harmful consequences in the determination of punishment, may be overcoming a difficulty presented by these impulsive offenders. Planning or any form of preparation to commit a crime is absent and cannot be used as a reason for sentence enhancement or considered an aggravating circumstance. To arrive at any measure of punishment commensurate with the crime, the consequences of behavior should be considered rather than the degree of intent or planning.

A corollary measure in addressing the problem of impulsive crimes is to reduce opportunities or to avoid precipitative situations. The remarkably high proportion of crimes of all types committed on the spur of the moment illuminates the importance of the microanalysis of offense situations.

12 Transitional Life Events and Desistance from Delinquency and Crime
Alicia Rand

Transitional Life Events and Criminality

The design of this cohort study allows for the collection and analysis of time-ordered data on official criminality. That is, in addition to information on each of the subjects' arrests, data are also available on the time intervals between arrests. Additionally, the interview schedule was designed to collect time-ordered data on presumed correlates of criminality so that the strength of the association between independent variables and criminality could be examined as well as the temporal order of those relationships.

The concern with the temporal order was furthered by the levels of desistance observed in the analysis of the juvenile data. Although 35 percent of the cohort members were found to be delinquent, nearly half of the delinquents were arrested only once, and only 6 percent were arrested five times or more. Moreover, although the rates of recidivism and chronicity increased when the exposure period was extended to age 30,[1] a substantial amount of desistance remained in these life careers. This chapter therefore examines variation in desistance rates as a function of a set of experiential and environmental life transitions, including marital and parental status, educational level, military service, and gang affiliation.

Unlike the origins of crime, the circumstances of desistance have rarely been described and analyzed. Criminology entertains diverse etiological theories of delinquency and crime, some of which see the origins of crime in social disorganization and social stress (Cloward and Ohlin 1960; Merton 1957), while others point to labeling (Lemert 1967), conformity to the norms of deviant subcultures (Cohen 1955; Matza 1964; Shaw and McKay 1942; Sutherland and Cressey 1974), cultural heritage (Miller 1958; Wolfgang and Ferracuti 1982), or biological factors (Figlio 1976; Shah and Roth 1974). However, little research has attempted to explain why people stop offending.

Although the phenomenon of desistance has received no specific theoretical or empirical attention, it appears to be strongly related to the maturation process. The Gluecks, in their follow-up of juvenile delinquent careers, observed that "with the passing of the years there was . . . both a decline in criminality and a decrease in the seriousness of the offenses of those who continued to commit

1. See chapters 3 and 4.

crimes" (Glueck and Glueck 1940, 89).[2] Age seems to be a factor in such changes in behavior; juvenile delinquency is often described as a transitory phase that passes as offenders grow older (Glaser 1972; Glueck and Glueck 1937, 1940; Radzinowicz and King 1977; van den Haag 1975). Nevertheless, chronological age per se does not satisfactorily account for changes in behavior; it is thought to contribute to the process of maturation, which in turn is credited with reducing criminality.[3] But because different individuals appear to achieve the same levels of maturation at different ages (Glueck and Glueck 1940), factors besides chronological age also must affect maturation.

In American society the late teens and early twenties are associated with the transition from adolescence to adulthood. The maturation process may be accelerated by such events as completion of education, marriage, and parenthood. On the other hand, events such as joining a gang, experiencing unemployment, and the like may delay maturation.

Such interrelationships should not be interpreted as evidence that a maturation effect based on chronological age does not exist. Rather, the question is whether certain life transitions produce changes in delinquent behavior that would not have occurred spontaneously because of growth by age alone. Therefore the main hypothesis of this chapter is that experiential and environmental factors resulting from an individual's life transitions may affect patterns of criminality. A set of specific hypotheses will be formulated and tested in relation to particular life events, using the interview data collected from the follow-up sample in combination with the official arrest records of the subjects.

Methodological Issues

This chapter investigates changing patterns of criminal behavior over the period from adolescence to adulthood; therefore juvenile status offenses in the data could bias the results by creating a false appearance of sudden "desistance" as the subjects reached age 18. Moreover, there are many relatively mild offenses, such as failure to pay a transportation fare or defiant trespassing, that are considerably more common among juveniles than among adults and that would further contribute to the unwanted effect produced by the status offenses. To facilitate more proper comparisons between offenses committed by juveniles and adults, therefore, we have retained only index crimes and those other offenses that have injury, theft, or damage components. As a result, the data are limited to 106 offenders and 315 serious offenses.

In addition to investigating patterns in the quantity and distribution of of-

---

2. Glueck and Glueck (1940) traced the delinquent and criminal careers of the original group of one thousand delinquents from the average age of just above 9 up to age 29. By the end of the third follow-up period, when the men reached an average age of 29, more than one-third had reformed.

3. Glueck and Glueck (1940) differentiated two forces acting within the process of maturation. One lies in the acquisition of the new personality traits that help the individual adapt successfully to the demands of society; the other originates in the loss of some of the individual's energy and aggressiveness as a result of the physiological "slowing down" of the organism with the passage of time.

fenses, we also examine the intensity of criminal behavior. One method of measurement is to compare the number of offenses committed before and after a particular life transition. Such a number, however, may reflect the age at which the transition occurred rather than the actual change in criminal behavior. For example, a subject who married at age 16 had less time to commit offenses before marriage than a subject who married at age 25, assuming that marriage is a factor in desistance. Another reason for not using the number of offenses as an outcome variable is that it does not reflect possible changes in the seriousness of delinquent behavior.

An indicator that is effective in detecting such changes is the Sellin-Wolfgang scale of offense seriousness (1978). Because the data are presented in a specified temporal ordering (before and after the event), however, particular caution must be exercised to control for the possible effect of "deterministic drift"—regular and persistent change occurring in the baseline data in the absence of any known intervention (Sechrest, White, and Brown 1979, 68). In these data it seems possible that age might precipitate such a phenomenon in relation to seriousness scores. To investigate this possibility, we examined the plot of the frequency distribution of mean seriousness scores from ages 9 to 26.

Figure 12.1 shows two age-differentiated levels of seriousness scores for the follow-up sample. For juvenile offenses up to and including age 17 we obtained a mean score of 243.3, while for adults age 18 and older the mean score was considerably higher, 444.4. This finding confirms the existence of drift in the data that could skew comparisons of seriousness scores before and after a particular event. Every time the offenders' ages crossed the boundary from juvenile

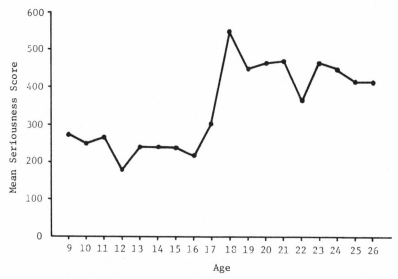

FIG. 12.1   Seriousness score by age of offender.

to adult status, an average increase of 200 points occurred, whether or not a given transitional event had taken place. To counteract such a distortion, we adjusted for the age factor in the scale of seriousness scores by subtracting 243.3 from all scores for juvenile offenses and 444.4 from all scores for adult offenses. As a result, the grand mean of the adjusted seriousness scores equals zero for all offenders; variations from the mean can be either larger or smaller than zero and are specified by a plus or minus sign. By introducing this precautionary measure we hope to minimize the "deterministic drift" produced by the age factor.

Each independent variable expressing a life event (family status, educational level, service in the armed forces, and gang affiliation) and obtained from the follow-up interviews was examined separately. With each of these sections, we take two general approaches. The first divides the subjects into two groups: those who experienced the event and those who never did. This division helps us compare the two groups' behaviors. Such an approach implies that the two groups are inherently disparate at the outset and that the differences in their behaviors are not necessarily affected by experiencing the transitional event, though such a possibility is not excluded. The second approach focuses only on the subjects who experience the event, and our concern is whether there were subsequent changes in their behavioral patterns. With this treatment the order of observations is important, for we were interested not only in the particular value of the observations, but also in the time or order of appearance. Thus the data base was divided into two observation periods: before the event and after the event. Such a collapsed data base is considerably more convenient to use and easier to interpret.

Both approaches are combined when we study differences in behavioral patterns of the four different comparison groups (those who never experienced the event, those who had experienced it, those who had not yet experienced it, and those who had already experienced it). To isolate the moderating effect of age in such comparisons, we used times-series techniques. We measured the dichotomous dependent variable, offender status, by the presence of arrest at each age within the period investigated. Moreover, given the strong association observed between race and official criminality, we conducted analyses for white and nonwhite subjects separately as well as analyzing the combined group.

Family Life and Criminality
Marriage

Establishing one's own family is the most obvious indicator of adult status. Marriage is viewed as an important transition into a conventional adult role in the community and, as a factor contributing to maturation, gives rise to two hypotheses.

Hypothesis 1: Young men who marry are less criminal than those who never marry. They commit fewer offenses; their offenses are less serious; and they desist from criminal behavior at an earlier age than the unmarried group.

This hypothesis is based on Elliott and Voss's finding that "for males marital status is the variable most highly associated with police contact. The police contact rate for unmarried males is more than three times the rate for married males" (1974, 126). According to Elliott and Voss, this finding was confirmed by self-report studies. The tendency of marriage to reduce criminal behavior was also reported by Bachman, O'Malley, and Johnston (1978).

Hypothesis 2: Young men become less criminal after marriage.

Although the first hypothesis does not exclude this assumption, it implies that there are differences between the two groups: those who ultimately marry and those who never do. The first group might carry values and attitudes that conform more closely to the prevailing social standards, and these attitudes may prompt them to be less criminal. In this case, hypothesized different rates of criminality might be affected not by marriage but by a set of personal characteristics preceding marriage. The second hypothesis, on the other hand, assumes a direct causal relationship between marriage and criminal behavior and predicts a reduction in such behavior after marriage.

The first hypothesis, that married men are less criminal than single men, is not supported by the data. Of the 106 subjects, the 59 percent who were married at least once were responsible for 57 percent of all of this group's offenses. The proportions are evenly distributed, and introducing race as a control variable fails to extract different patterns from the data. Sixty-four percent of the whites who were married accounted for 65 percent of the offenses committed by whites. Similarly, 54 percent of the nonwhites who were married accounted for 53 percent of the offenses attributed to nonwhites.

Even though there was no difference in the number of offenses committed by married and single men, there may be a difference in the seriousness of offenses between the two groups. Table 12.1 lends support to the hypothesis, indicating a statistically significant difference in seriousness scores between married and

TABLE 12.1   Mean Adjusted Seriousness Scores by Marriage and Race

	Number of Offenses	$\bar{X}$	SD	F	Probability
All					
Married	180	−50.16	244.33		
Never married	135	66.87	487.47	3.98	≤ .01
Total	315				
Whites					
Married	74	−50.81	148.31		
Never married	40	−35.30	263.99	3.17	n.s.
Total	114				
Nonwhites					
Married	106	−49.70	294.07		
Never married	95	109.90	550.93	3.51	≤ .01
Total	201				

single men. When race is introduced as a control variable, the results for the whites are not statistically significant. For the nonwhites, however, the mean score for those who never married is more than three times as high. It appears that the relationship between marriage and criminality is not a simple one: although there is no noticeable impact of marriage on the number of offenses, there is a strong effect on the seriousness score among the nonwhite offenders.

The last part of the first hypothesis postulates that men who marry desist from crime earlier than those who remain single. To examine this prediction, we compared the mean ages at the last offense for the two groups. The married men desisted from criminality more than a year and a half earlier than their single counterparts (age 19.2 vs. 20.9). This difference is statistically significant at the .05 level; however, when race is controlled the differences cease to be statistically significant. This finding indicates that the impact of race on age of desistance is stronger than the impact of marriage alone and that the marriage variable acts in this case as a proxy for race.

To test the second hypothesis concerning marriage—that young men are less criminal after marriage—we made before-and-after comparisons of the sample offenders' status. Offender status classifies the subjects into three categories according to their behavior after marriage: those who ceased to be offenders, those who continued to be offenders, and those who newly became offenders. Two-thirds of those who married were involved in criminal behavior before they married but did not continue such behavior after marriage. By contrast, almost one-sixth acquired criminal records only after marriage. A similar, only slightly higher proportion were involved in criminal behavior both before and after they married.

When race is introduced as a control variable, two distinctly different patterns emerge. Among the whites, 84 percent did not persist in criminal behavior after they married; only 8 percent began criminal careers at that time; and an equal proportion were offenders both before and after. For the nonwhites, marriage did not appear to be as strongly correlated with unlawful behavior. Although 42 percent abandoned criminal behavior after they married, 27 percent became offenders at that point, and 31 percent were involved in criminal behavior both before and after marriage. However, the standard of desistance used to measure changes in criminal behavior, which indicates only whether such behavior ceases or continues, cannot capture a possible change in the seriousness of offenses.

To examine whether the seriousness of criminal behavior was reduced after marriage as hypothesized, we compared mean seriousness scores for the periods before and after marriage. Contrary to the hypothesis, the differences in seriousness scores before and after marriage are not significant and are attributable to chance. However, offenses committed by the nonwhites showed an "improvement" of -45.57 points on the adjusted scale, and offenses committed by the whites became more serious after marriage (an increase of 30.63 points).

The appearance of separate, but not significant, trends for the two racial groups hinted by the data above may have been caused by age. If the whites and nonwhites married at different ages, their patterns of delinquent behavior might

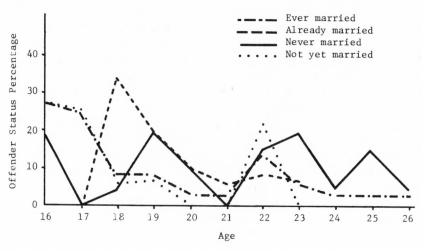

FIG. 12.2   Offender status by marriage, age, and race: whites.

have differed as a function not of marriage but of age. To eliminate the age effect, time-series displays using two configurations of the data base are shown in figures 12.2 and 12.3. Each contains a series of eleven observations per subject: one for each year from age 16 to age 26. The dependent variable is a dummy variable expressing the offender status and takes on the value of one if the subject committed one or more offenses in a given year and a value of zero if he did not. In the first configuration, the independent variable determines whether the subject ever experienced the event—that is, whether he ever married. The second and more elaborate data base forms two groups among the subset of men who ultimately marry: those not yet married and those already married.

The advantage of the time-series model is its capacity to deal with variables, such as age, that continue to change throughout the offenders' careers. Using this model, we can examine behavior patterns of each group within the same one-year intervals. The results presented in figures 12.2 and 12.3 show that the probability of becoming an offender is higher for the never-married men than for the ever-married group. This trend was particularly strong for the nonwhites (fig. 12.3).

We expected, in accordance with the hypothesized positive impact of marriage, a similar trend among those not yet married and those already married, but no definite trends can be found. Figure 12.2 shows that for the whites there is generally a lower probability of becoming an offender for those not yet married than for those already married. The pattern for the nonwhites, shown in figure 12.3, is less discernible, but for the initial and end categories of age the frequencies became quite small and hampered proper analysis.

Examining the relation between marriage and delinquent and criminal behavior shows no noticeable effect of marriage on the number of offenses and the age of desistance, but the existence of the association between the two variables is

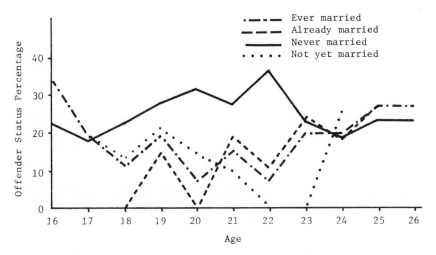

FIG. 12.3   Offender status by marriage, age, and race: nonwhites.

confirmed by a strong effect on the seriousness of offenses committed by the nonwhites. The mean seriousness score for the nonwhites who never married is more than three times as large as for those who did. Although we do not know why this pattern is not shared by the whites (their results were not statistically significant), trends for the two racial groups are considerably different.

This observation is confirmed by the finding that 84 percent of the whites (compared with only 42 percent of the nonwhites) committed no offenses after marriage. Marriage might have a genuine impact on criminality, but the opposite may also be true; that is, a person first abandons criminal behavior and consequently adjusts his life to a socially accepted mold that includes marriage. Another possibility is that the relationship between marriage and criminality might be a case of "C causes both A and B," where C may be employment, change of friends, and so forth. It would be interesting to examine the correlation of marriage and crime controlling for these variables. Unfortunately, attrition prevented the meaningful use of controls, since the cells became too small to yield statistically significant results.

Cohabitation

Marriage is considered an important transition from adolescence to adulthood. But with today's changing morality, cohabitation without formal matrimony has become increasingly popular and socially acceptable. It may be expected, therefore, that as a transitional event comparable to marriage, living with a woman could have a dampening effect on criminal behavior. For this reason the hypotheses below are similar to those for marriage.

Hypothesis 1: Subjects who have lived with a woman are less criminal than subjects who never lived with a woman.

141

Hypothesis 2: Subjects are less criminal after establishing a relationship with a woman than they were before.

Our data indicate that, contrary to the first hypothesis, living with a woman contributed to higher rates of criminality. Of all the sample offenders, 30 percent lived with a woman, and they were responsible for 46 percent of the offenses. The same pattern holds when we introduce race as a controlling variable. Both the white and the nonwhite offenders who lived with a woman were responsible for more offenses than their proportion in the population. Of the whites, the 22 percent who lived with a woman accounted for 31 percent of the offenses, while the 40 percent of the nonwhites who lived with a woman accounted for 54 percent of the offenses.

To examine the association between living with a woman and the seriousness of offenses, we examined differences in the mean seriousness scores between the two groups and found them not statistically significant. Moreover, all the differences were in the opposite direction from that hypothesized.

To test the latter part of the first hypothesis—that those who have lived with a woman desist at an earlier age than those who have not—we compared the mean ages at the last offense for the two groups. Contrary to expectations, those who lived with a woman desisted almost four years later than those who did not. This pattern held for both racial groups and was stronger for the whites.

To test the second hypothesis, that subjects are less criminal after cohabitation, the criminal behavior of the sample offenders was examined in the temporal sequence of these two periods. The hypothesis is not supported by the data. For the period following the establishment of a relationship with a woman, there were only slight differences in the proportions of those who desisted (28 percent), those who became offenders (34 percent), and those who persisted in criminality (38 percent). There was a higher proportion of white desisters (46 percent), but the trend was reversed for the nonwhites. Moreover, the small number of subjects who lived with a woman outside marriage suggested great caution in drawing strong conclusions from these findings.

Moreover, the seriousness data do not further support the hypothesis. Contrary to expectations, there is a considerable increase in mean seriousness scores after living with a woman. These findings coincided for the three groups examined, but they were statistically significant only for the whites, whose scores in this period increased more than twofold.

It appears that cohabitation is not similar to marriage in its effect on criminal behavior. Although marriage is negatively correlated with such behavior, cohabitation has the opposite effect. Not only did subjects who lived with a woman account for a higher number of offenses, they also desisted from criminal careers almost four years later than the other groups. For the whites, the seriousness of offenses also increased after they entered such a relationship.

Fatherhood

Like marriage, parenthood is an accepted indicator of adult status in our society. Because of the importance surrounding the institution of the family, the role of parent is endowed with approval and respect. Expectations associated with the role of father include a number of responsibilities, such as supporting the child financially and providing personal supervision and care. Such obligations should be conducive to relatively conventional activities. From this premise, we developed two hypotheses.

Hypothesis 1: Men who become fathers are less criminal than men who do not.

Hypothesis 2: The number and seriousness of offenses decline with fatherhood.

The first hypothesis found no support in the data. Of the sample offenders, 58 percent became fathers, and they were responsible for 64 percent of all the offenses. Controlling for race smoothed the ratio. Of the whites, the 45 percent who became fathers accounted for 43 percent of the offenses committed by whites; of the nonwhites, the 75 percent who became fathers accounted for 76 percent of the offenses committed by nonwhites.

We might expect that even though we found no differences in the number of offenses, there may have been differences either in the seriousness of the offenses committed or in the patterns of behavior exhibited before and after fatherhood. In general, the data did not support any strong and consistent relationship between fatherhood and criminality. We found no effect of fatherhood on the number and seriousness of offenses or on the length of the criminal careers. The only possible influence of fatherhood was seen in the fact that 81 percent of the whites desisted after becoming fathers. This proportion was almost identical to the 84 percent of the whites who desisted after marriage. Many men who married also became fathers; the correlation was thereby confused.

Overall, the relation between family life and criminality was complex. Marriage appeared to have a dampening effect on criminality, especially in terms of the seriousness of the offenses the nonwhites committed and the number of offenses the whites committed. Subjects classified as cohabitating had higher rates of criminality and desisted from criminal behavior at later ages. Parenthood, on the other hand, appeared to have a negligible impact on criminal behavior.

Education
High School

There is a widespread assumption that the school functions as a positive form of social control and is conducive to a better life adjustment. It is also thought that when the restraints imposed by school are removed from those who drop out, higher rates of delinquent behavior will emerge. Dropouts are presumed to be less likely than high-school graduates to obtain jobs, which also may contribute to their criminality. Such beliefs have resulted in the current policy of increasing educational opportunities for youths and encouraging dropouts to return to school as a means of preventing delinquency. Elliott and Voss challenged the conventional stereotype of delinquents and dropouts by claiming that "the school is the critical generating milieu for delinquency" and that "failure to achieve long-range educational and occupational goals is not a highly significant factor in delinquent behavior" (1974, 203; see also Mukherjee 1971). They asserted that, contrary to popular belief, failure to graduate does not lead to delinquency but delinquency leads to dropout, and that for both dropouts and graduates rates of delinquency decline upon leaving school. Similar results were reported by Bachman, O'Malley, and Johnston (1978, 178), who found no support for the contention that high delinquency rates are a consequence of quitting school. Given the high hopes and monetary investment focused on education, understanding the obviously complex relationship between delinquent behavior and education seems of primary importance.

The subjects in our sample pursued a large variety of educational options, ranging from vocational training to graduate school. The availability of this information made it possible to develop a set of hypotheses and to test them at each educational level. The analysis begins with the relationship between delinquency and education at the high-school stage.

> *Hypothesis 1:* High-school graduates engage in less delinquent behavior and have lower mean seriousness scores than high-school dropouts. High-school graduates also desist from delinquent careers at an earlier age than high-school dropouts.

This hypothesis is based on the findings of Bachman and his colleagues that delinquency correlates negatively with educational attainment.[4] Bachman's group stressed, however, that differences in delinquent behavior between those who drop out of high school and those who graduate are caused not by high-school experiences, but by factors operating before the students enter high school. Those who do well in school have different values and attitudes than those who do poorly and who are apt to drop out. The same values and attitudes that contribute to dropping out also contribute to delinquency. Bachman and his colleagues claimed that high-school experience seems neither to exacerbate nor to repair the effects of such characteristics. Although Bachman's group downplayed school as a factor contributing to a decrease in delinquency, Elliott and Voss (1974) went even further in their assumptions. Special attention is given to their assertion that dropping out does not lead to delinquency but delinquency leads to dropping out.

> *Hypothesis 2:* After leaving high school, through either graduation or dropping out, subjects engage in delinquent behavior less than during school enrollment. Also, the seriousness of their offenses is lower after leaving high school.

Table 12.2 confirms the first part of the first hypothesis, that high-school graduates are less delinquent than high-school dropouts. Almost half of the 106 offenders graduated from high school. They constituted 47 percent of the total

4. In 1966 Bachman and his colleagues (Bachman, Green, and Wirtanen 1977; Bachman, O'Malley, and Johnston 1978) developed a probability sample of high schools throughout the United States and created a panel of 2,213 boys from those entering tenth grade. The panel was surveyed at

Table 12.2 Criminality by High-School Graduation and Race

	Offenders		Offenses	
	N	%	N	%
All				
Graduated	50	47	91	29
Never graduated	56	53	224	71
Total	106	100	315	100
Whites				
Graduated	29	50	41	36
Never graduated	29	50	73	64
Total	58	100	114	100
Nonwhites				
Graduated	21	44	50	25
Never graduated	27	56	151	75
Total	48	100	201	100

and were responsible for only 29 percent of the offenses. There was only a small difference in the proportion of graduates to dropouts when race was introduced as a control. Exactly half of the whites and 44 percent of the nonwhites graduated. There was, however, a substantial difference in their delinquency patterns. While the white graduates were responsible for 36 percent of all the offenses committed by whites, the nonwhite graduates were responsible for only 25 percent of the offenses committed by nonwhites. It seems, therefore, that, although high-school graduation was negatively correlated with criminality, the impact on non-whites was considerably stronger.

We might also expect lower seriousness scores for high-school graduates than for dropouts. Contrary to the hypothesis, none of the differences between graduates and dropouts are statistically significant; moreover, all the differences are opposite to the direction hypothesized. The mean seriousness scores for the high-school graduates are about twenty-five points higher than for the high-school dropouts.

The final part of the hypothesis, that high-school graduates desist from criminality earlier than dropouts, also is not supported by the data. The mean differences in age of desistance are not statistically significant; the values are so close as to be almost identical.

Finding no support for the findings of Bachman's group,[5] we tested the second hypothesis—that after leaving high school subjects become less criminal—by examining behavior patterns and changes in them. In search of possible diverse trends, we considered two subsets, graduates and dropouts, separately within the

intervals of one year or more over an eight-year longitudinal span that included high school and five years beyond.

5. The disparity in findings may be explained, at least partially, by the fact that the Bachman group's operationalized definition of delinquency differed from ours (Bachman, Green, and Wirtanen 1977; Bachman, O'Malley, and Johnston 1978). For example, their studies included minor offenses, such as truancy, that we omit from the data.

temporal sequence of before and after leaving high school. Table 12.3 indicates only partial confirmation of the hypothesis. Graduation from high school did not mark a decrease in criminal behavior. However, introducing race as a control variable produced different trends for whites and nonwhites: 55 percent of the whites versus 24 percent of the nonwhites desisted after graduation; 38 percent of the whites versus 62 percent of the nonwhites embarked on delinquent careers at this point; and 7 percent of the whites versus 14 percent of the nonwhites were involved in crime both before and after graduation. It seems that although there was a certain decrease in criminal behavior for the whites after graduation, the reverse held for the nonwhites.

Table 12.4 presents similar trends for the dropouts. Although dropping out appeared to reduce criminality among whites, the effect for the nonwhites was strikingly opposite what we expected. Forty-one percent of the nonwhites remained criminal after dropping out, and the ratio of those who became criminal after dropping out to those who desisted was almost $3:1$. These data appear to contradict Elliott and Voss's (1974) thesis that departure from school reduces the dropouts' rate of criminal behavior. It is important, however, that we keep these findings in perspective, because the results, though provocative, were based on a small number of cases.

To test the final part of the second hypothesis, that the seriousness of offenses decreases after departure from high school, we compared the before-and-after seriousness scores for each subset in turn. Although the direction of the changes in seriousness scores before and after graduation appear to confirm the hypothesis, none of the results are statistically significant. In relation to the dropouts, the hypothesis found no support in the data. The differences for all the dropouts and

TABLE 12.3   Offender Status before and after High-School Graduation by Race

Offender Status	All		Whites		Nonwhites	
	N	%	N	%	N	%
Before only	21	42	16	55	5	24
After only	24	48	11	38	13	62
Both before and after	5	10	2	7	3	14
Total	50	100	29	100	21	100

TABLE 12.4   Offender Status before and after Dropping out of High School by Race

Offender Status	All		Whites		Nonwhites	
	N	%	N	%	N	%
Before only	20	36	16	55	4	15
After only	20	36	8	28	12	44
Both before and after	16	28	5	17	11	41
Total	56	100	29	100	27	100

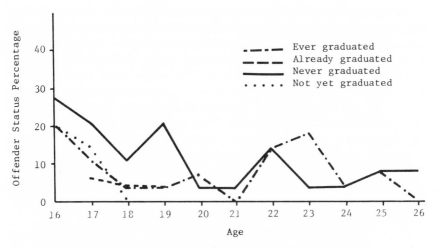

FIG. 12.4   Offender status by high-school graduation, age, and race: whites.

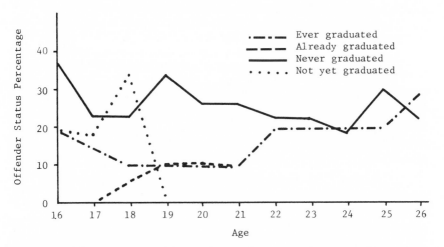

FIG. 12.5   Offender status by high-school graduation, age, and race: nonwhites.

for the nonwhites were opposite the predicted direction, and all were attributable to chance variations.

The time-series analysis presented in figures 12.4 and 12.5 shows that those who never graduated (the dropouts) had a considerably higher probability of becoming offenders than those who did graduate. This trend seemed particularly strong for the nonwhite subjects. Those who had already graduated were less delinquent than those who had not, but there were only a few years during which to observe this difference, because all the whites graduated between ages 17 and 19 and all the nonwhites graduated between ages 17 and 21. The whites began leaving school at age 15, and the last one dropped out at age 19. The first nonwhite dropped out before age 15 and the last one at age 18.

The finding that the high-school graduates accounted for fewer offenses than the dropouts supports Bachman, Green, and Wirtanen's statement (1977) that criminality correlates negatively with educational attainment. There was no evidence, however, that the graduates accounted for less serious offenses or that they desisted from criminal behavior earlier than the dropouts. There is also no evidence that graduating from high school suppressed criminality. Of the whites, whether or not they graduated, 55 percent did not engage in criminal behavior after they left school. For the nonwhites, leaving school appeared to produce the opposite results: 62 percent of the graduates and 44 percent of the dropouts began their criminal careers after leaving school. Only 15 percent of the nonwhite dropouts and 24 percent of the nonwhite graduates abandoned criminal behavior after leaving school.

College

We expected college experience to be negatively correlated with criminal behavior.

Hypothesis 1: Young men who attend college are less criminal and commit less serious offenses than those who never attend college. Those who attend college also desist from delinquent behavior at an earlier age than the group without college experience.

This hypothesis is based on the Bachman group's findings (Bachman, Green, and Wirtanen 1977; Bachman, O'Malley, and Johnston 1978) that the higher the level of education, the lower the level of crimes and that during the school years those destined for college are least disposed toward criminal behavior. Such an assumption suggests that there are differences in values, attitudes, self-esteem, aspirations, and behavior patterns between those who do and do not attend college.

Hypothesis 2: After attending college, subjects engage in criminal behavior less than they did before. The mean seriousness score of their offenses also decreases after attending college.

This hypothesis is based on the assumption that the requirements and expectations of college-level education instill and strengthen those attitudes that support conformity to the prevailing social norms, such as acceptance of authority, systematic work habits, organized planning for the future, and deferring instant gratification. Internalizing such values should contribute to a decrease in the amount and seriousness of criminal behavior.

Only 17 percent of the sample attended college, and these individuals were responsible for 9 percent of the total offenses. Of the whites, the 22 percent who attended college committed 18 percent of the offenses attributed to whites. Only 10 percent of the nonwhites attended college, and they were responsible for 3 percent of the offenses attributed to nonwhites. These results seem to confirm the first hypothesis, but the number of cases on which the results are based is small (eighteen). In addition, when we examine the seriousness scores of their offenses, contrary to the hypothesis, none of the differences are statistically significant.

Nor is the last part of the first hypothesis, that college students desist earlier than noncollege students, supported by the data. The age of desistance for the whites was almost the same for both students and nonstudents (18.3 and 18.1). Although the nonwhites who attended college seemed to desist earlier than those who did not attend, the difference could be attributed to chance (19.2 vs. 22.3).

To test the hypothesis that criminal behavior decreases after attending college, we examined the subset of eighteen college students. Observations from this subset were divided into two periods: before and including the year of departure from college and the years following departure from college.

Table 12.5 seems to confirm the hypothesis. Over two-thirds of the whites desisted from criminal behavior before the end of their college years; the remainder were divided almost evenly between those who became criminal after leaving college and those who engaged in criminality throughout both periods. For the nonwhites, the number of cases was too small to produce meaningful results.

TABLE 12.5   Offender Status before and after Attending College by Race

Offender Status	All		Whites		Nonwhites	
	N	%	N	%	N	%
Before only	11	61	9	69	2	40
After only	4	22	2	15	2	40
Both before and after	3	17	2	15	1	20
Total	18	100	13	99 [a]	5	100

[a] Does not sum to 100 percent owing to rounding.

The differences in the seriousness scores for these various comparisons also lend little support to the hypothesis. Although there appeared to be a decrease in seriousness scores for the whites after attending college, it was attributable to chance variations. Moreover, none of the other differences are statistically significant. Because of reservations resulting from the small number of cases, the time-series analysis employing college attendance as an independent variable seemed to be of limited use.

Vocational Training

The belief that educational and occupational success may offer an alternative to criminality has played a significant part in the proliferation of correctional rehabilitation programs. Many of these programs suggest that criminality is caused by some specific deficit of the individual, such as poor work habits and skills. By employing skill-development techniques, these programs seek to improve the offenders' chances of securing employment and thus, presumably, of joining the mainstream of law-abiding citizens.

Lipton, Martinson, and Wilks, in their critical evaluation of correctional programs, found that "there is evidence that vocationally oriented training programs for youthful offenders (over 16) both in institutions and in the community are associated with lower rates of recidivism than standard institutional care or standard parole. These programs appear to be most successful when they provide the offender with a readily marketable skill" (1975, 194).

In the present study, twenty-seven of the offender subjects (25 percent) attended trade schools, twenty-five (24 percent) took part in apprentice programs, and twenty (19 percent) participated in other skill-improvement programs, such as on-the-job training.[6] These training programs produced no statistically significant differences in the seriousness of criminality or in the age of desistance between those who took part in training and those who did not.

There was no support for the expectation that, after training, youths should become less criminal. Differences are not statistically significant; moreover, there is no clear trend to support the expectations. In general, therefore, vocational education appeared to be modestly but negatively correlated with criminality.

The Armed Forces
Service

Besides the family and school, service in the armed forces seems suited to encourage components of a mature personality. The routine and discipline of military service are designed to promote such qualities as postponement of immediate desires, the ability to learn from experience, and deference to authority. Such qualities are commonly assumed to have a negative correlation with criminal behavior. To examine this relationship, we tested two hypotheses.

Hypothesis 1: Young men who served in the armed forces are less delinquent and their offenses are less serious than those who never served. Those who served desist from criminal behavior earlier than those who did not.

This hypothesis is based on the Gluecks' findings that "the majority of youths who served enlistments either in the Army or Navy made a successful adjustment. . . . A considerably higher percentage of offenders did well in the Army or Navy than under probation or parole" (Glueck and Glueck 1940, 165).

Although a causal relationship may be inferred from the Gluecks' position, it seems reasonable to suppose that serious offenders are not accepted for enlistment. Such a policy should sort out the two subsets (those who enlisted and those who did not) by level of criminality. Thus differences in behavior between the two groups preceded the experiential effects of military service.

Hypothesis 2: Young men who served in the armed forces are less criminal after service than before in terms of number and seriousness of offenses.

---

6. Training in the armed forces will be described separately because of the different conditions under which it is conducted.

We inferred this hypothesis from Johnston and Bachman's findings that the direction of change among the young men's personality dimensions during military service seems positive (1970, 217). Although Johnston and Bachman found no dramatic changes in attitude and personality characteristics, they noticed increases in occupational aspirations and ambitions, a rise in self-esteem, and feelings of personal efficacy. Such changes are presumed to lead to the abandonment of criminal behavior, or at least to a decrease in seriousness (Glueck and Glueck 1937).

Of the 55 percent of the sampled offenders who served in the armed forces, 60 percent were white and 40 percent were nonwhite. The first hypothesis, that those who served in the armed forces are less criminal than those who did not serve, finds only partial confirmation. Table 12.6 shows the considerable impact of military service on the number of offenses for the nonwhite subjects. Although 48 percent of the nonwhites served in the armed forces, they were responsible for only 29 percent of the offenses committed by nonwhites. For the whites, however, no such impact was evident: the 60 percent who served in the armed forces accounted for 60 percent of the offenses committed by whites.

TABLE 12.6   Criminality by Military Service and Race

	Offenders		Offenses	
	N	%	N	%
All				
Served	58	55	126	40
Never served	48	45	189	60
Total	106	100	315	100
Whites				
Served	35	60	68	60
Never served	23	40	46	40
Total	58	100	114	100
Nonwhites				
Served	23	48	58	29
Never served	25	52	143	71
Total	48	100	201	100

The hypothesized difference in seriousness scores between the two groups finds no support in the data. None of the differences between the means of the various groupings are statistically significant; moreover, there is a considerable difference in seriousness scores for nonwhites, which runs counter to the hypothesis (those who served committed more serious crimes than those who were not in the military).

The last part of the first hypothesis predicted that men who served in the armed forces would desist from criminal behavior at an earlier age than those who did not serve. Table 12.7 shows that there was indeed a statistically significant difference of more than one and a half years in the predicted direction. When

TABLE 12.7 Mean Age at Last Offense by Military Service and Race

	Number of Offenders	$\bar{X}$	SD	F	Probability
All					
Served	58	19.12	4.34	1.17	≤ .05
Never served	48	20.81	4.01		
Total	106				
Whites					
Served	35	17.43	3.75	1.06	n.s.
Never served	23	19.26	3.64		
Total	58				
Nonwhites					
Served	23	21.69	3.96	1.05	n.s.
Never served	25	22.24	3.86		
Total	48				

TABLE 12.8 Offender Status by Military Service and Race

	All		Whites		Nonwhites	
Offender Status	N	%	N	%	N	%
Before only	32	55	25	71	7	30
After only	15	26	5	14	10	43
Both before and after	11	19	5	14	6	26
Total	58	100	35	99[a]	23	99[a]

[a]Does not sum to 100 percent owing to rounding.

race was introduced the difference for the nonwhites was reduced to half a year and was no longer significant. The whites who served in the armed forces, on the other hand, desisted nearly two years earlier than those who did not.

To test the second hypothesis, that the rate of criminality declines after serving in the armed forces, we focused only on the subjects who served in the military. Table 12.8 presents the criminal status for the period before and including the year of discharge from the service and for the remaining years. The trend for the whites confirmed the hypothesis, but the trend for the nonwhites did not. After discharge, 71 percent of the whites but only 30 percent of the nonwhites refrained from criminal behavior. Although the remaining whites were divided evenly between those involved in criminality throughout both periods and those who became criminal after discharge, the pattern for the nonwhites was distinctly different. Contrary to prediction, 43 percent of the nonwhites embarked on crime after leaving the service, and 26 percent continued their lawbreaking behavior after leaving the service.

The second part of the hypothesis, which predicted a decrease in seriousness after serving in the armed forces, found no support in the data. Not only were the differences in seriousness scores not statistically significant, but the means suggest an increase in seriousness scores following military service.

If age instead of military service accounted for the differences between those who did not serve and those who did, the criminality trends for the two groups should not have differed. Contrary to our expectation, the whites who served were criminal more often than those who did not serve, with one exception at age 18. This pattern was reversed for the nonwhites. The nonwhites who served were criminal less often than those who did not serve, up to and including age 22. These data enable us to test the first hypothesis, which postulates that those who never served and those who did are inherently different in their criminal behavior. Examining the pattern of criminality for the nonwhites, we found a clear and strong trend indicating that the group that served was involved in criminal behavior considerably less often than the group that never served.

Armed Forces Vocational Training

One of the activities made available in the military is job training, and two-thirds ($N = 38$) of the young men in the sample who served in the armed forces took advantage of this opportunity. The previous hypothesis, that vocational training is negatively correlated with criminal behavior, was not supported by the data. That military service is correlated negatively with criminal behavior found only partial and weak support, but we expected that the effect of vocational training would gain strength within the specific framework of the military. Whatever positive factors are carried by vocational training (skill development, improvement of work habits, etc.) should be reinforced and amplified by such components of military service as discipline and routine organization. From this premise we developed two hypotheses.

Hypothesis 1: Participants in armed forces vocational training are less criminal than other subjects. This assumption includes the amount and seriousness of offenses as well as the age of desistance, which indicates the length of criminal careers.

Hypothesis 2: Young men who participate in armed forces vocational training are less criminal after this experience than they were before. A decrease is expected not only in their criminal status but also in the seriousness of their criminal behavior.

While lending partial support to the first hypothesis, the data repeat the pattern evident in table 12.6, where the independent variable was military service. Again, there is no impact on the whites; but among nonwhites the armed forces vocational training participants appeared to be responsible for a smaller share of the offenses than the nonparticipants. One-third of all the nonwhites in the sample participated in the training, and they accounted for only one-fifth of the offenses committed by nonwhites.

The last part of the first hypothesis, that the vocational training participants

TABLE 12.9   Mean Age at Last Offense by Military Vocational Training
and Race

	Number of Offenders	$\bar{X}$	SD	F	Probability
All					
Participated	38	18.84	4.35	1.11	n.s.
Never participated	68	20.47	4.13		
Total	106				
Whites					
Participated	22	16.64	3.37	1.25	≤ .01
Never participated	36	19.08	3.77		
Total	58				
Nonwhites					
Participated	16	21.87	3.72	1.16	n.s.
Never participated	32	22.03	4.01		
Total	48				

desisted earlier than the nonparticipants, finds only partial confirmation in table 12.9. The whites who took part in training desisted almost two and a half years earlier than those who were not trained. The difference for the nonwhites, however, was not statistically significant; indeed, the two means were almost identical.

The second hypothesis, which predicts a positive change in the behavior of participants after armed forces vocational training, also found no clear support. The data confirm the predicted direction of the change for the whites: 73 percent desisted after training. The nonwhites, however, were divided almost evenly into the three temporal categories (before, after, and both before and after), and the training showed no effect on their lawbreaking behavior. These results should be treated with caution, because the number of cases in each category was small (two to twenty individuals, depending on the category).

Further results contrary to the second hypothesis, though congruent with the hypotheses concerning armed forces service as shown earlier, are found in both racial groups, where mean seriousness scores increased (although not significantly) after vocational training in the range of fifty to ninety points.

Although the linkage of service in the armed forces with criminal behavior seemed quite weak, the association of such behavior with armed forces job training appeared to be strong, but not as straightforward as we expected. In both instances, the nonwhites who participated accounted for a lower number of offenses than the nonwhites who did not participate; but neither service nor job training had an effect on the number of offenses the whites committed.

The Juvenile Gang

Although the role of the gang in juvenile crime has been discussed endlessly, there has been little systematic consideration of the patterns of delinquency for gang members before their identification with a gang, during the period of affiliation, and after disassociation from the gang. In an attempt to investigate the pattern, extent, and sequence of such behavior, we tested two hypotheses.

> *Hypothesis 1:* Boys who belonged to a gang are more delinquent
> and commit more serious offenses than boys who never belonged to
> a gang. Gang members also desist from delinquent behavior at a
> later age than those who never belonged to a gang.

This hypothesis is based on subcultural theories of delinquency such as those of Cohen (1955) and Cloward and Ohlin (1960), which create an image of the gang in which delinquency is mandatory for its members and heavily influenced by the lower-class culture (Miller 1958). Similarly, Wolfgang and Ferracuti (1982) suggested the existence of a subculture of violence in which high rates of violent crime are produced by shared cultural attitudes toward the use of violence.

> *Hypothesis 2:* After joining a gang, boys become more delinquent
> than before, and their offenses become more serious.

This hypothesis is based on Matza's (1964) concept of delinquency as drift. Matza argued that boys occasionally drift into delinquency to conform to the norms of their peer group, with whom they spend most of their time. Once they move out of adolescence, however, their delinquent behavior is reduced and only a few remain committed to delinquency.

Table 12.10 offers support for the first part of the first hypothesis: boys who join a gang are more delinquent than those who do not. The thirty-one boys who reported gang affiliation represented 29 percent of the total offender sample and were responsible for 50 percent of the offenses. The one-sixth of the whites who belonged to a gang accounted for one-third of the offenses committed by whites.

TABLE 12.10   Criminality by Gang Membership and Race

	Offenders		Offenses	
	N	*%*	*N*	*%*
All				
Gang members	31	29	158	50
Never gang members	75	71	157	50
Total	106	100	315	100
Whites				
Gang members	10	17	38	33
Never gang members	48	83	76	67
Total	58	100	114	100
Nonwhites				
Gang members	21	44	120	60
Never gang members	27	56	81	40
Total	48	100	201	100

Among the nonwhites, the 44 percent who were gang members accounted for 60 percent of the offenses committed by nonwhites. As expected, the gang members contributed more to delinquency than the nongang members. Although the nonwhites reported gang membership at a considerably higher rate, the effect described was particularly strong for the whites.

To test the second part of the first hypothesis, we examined the seriousness of offenses. We expected that those who belonged to a gang would have committed more serious offenses than those who never joined. Table 12.11 indicates that the hypothesis did not find support in the data. Not only were the differences in seriousness scores not significant, but they were also in a direction opposite that hypothesized for both races.

To test the last part of the first hypothesis, that boys who join gangs engage in delinquent behavior for longer periods of time than boys who were never gang members, we investigated the relationship between gang membership and duration of the delinquent career. Table 12.12 indicates partial confirmation of the hypothesis. Boys who belonged to a gang persisted in delinquent behavior almost three years longer than those who never joined. When race is controlled, however, it is clear that this effect is due to the impact of the nonwhite gang members, who continued their delinquent behavior almost three years longer than the nongang members. For the whites, however, the results are not statistically significant.

To test the first part of the second hypothesis, that gang members are more delinquent after joining a gang than before, we examined the data distinguishing between the "before" and "after" periods. Table 12.13 supports the hypothesis, indicating that 81 percent of the boys became delinquent after joining a gang. Although the effect was exceptionally strong for the nonwhites, the general trend remained the same for both racial groups: 90 percent of the nonwhites and 60 percent of the whites became delinquent after they became gang members. Not surprisingly, of all the gang members, those who were offenders before joining

TABLE 12.11   Mean Seriousness by Gang Membership and Race

	Number of Offenses	$\overline{X}$	SD	F	Probability
All					
Gang members	158	1.40	444.15	2.44	n.s.
Never gang members	157	−1.40	284.35		
Total	315				
Whites					
Gang members	38	−60.54	244.48	2.13	n.s.
Never gang members	76	−37.79	167.54		
Total	114				
Nonwhites					
Gang members	120	21.01	489.96	1.86	n.s.
Never gang members	81	32.73	359.05		
Total	201				

TABLE 12.12   Mean Age at Last Offense by Gang Membership and Race

	Number of Offenders	$\overline{X}$	SD	F	Probability
All					
Gang members	31	21.93	4.17	1.07	≤ .001
Never gang members	75	19.04	4.03		
Total	106				
Whites					
Gang members	10	18.60	4.25	1.30	n.s.
Never gang members	48	18.06	3.73		
Total	58				
Nonwhites					
Gang members	21	23.52	3.12	1.67	≤ .01
Never gang members	27	20.78	4.03		
Total	48				

TABLE 12.13   Offender Status before and after Joining a Gang by Race

	All		Whites		Nonwhites	
Offender Status	N	%	N	%	N	%
Before only	1	3	1	10	0	0
After only	25	81	6	60	19	90
Both before and after	5	16	3	30	2	10
Total	31	100	10	100	21	100

and desisted after joining a gang constituted only 3 percent of the subset. The remaining 16 percent embarked on delinquent behavior before joining a gang and subsequently continued.

We further hypothesized that boys commit more serious offenses after they join a gang. Our data, however, do not confirm this hypothesis, since differences between mean seriousness scores before and after joining a gang are attributable to chance.

These data do not reflect the fact that some who joined a gang might have subsequently left it. Disregarding this expresses the assumption that once a boy has joined a gang his behavior is permanently altered, without regard to his later withdrawal from the gang. This approach is not suitable for investigating Matza's (1964) concept of delinquency as drift. To examine his thesis, that leaving the gang could decrease delinquent behavior, we have to examine the behavior with respect to leaving rather than joining juvenile gangs. In table 12.14, therefore, the "before" period represents the period of time before joining the gang *and* the duration of gang affiliation up to and including the year of disassociation from the gang. The "after" period refers to the time period following disassociation.

In support of Matza's hypothesis, for the white subjects leaving the gang also

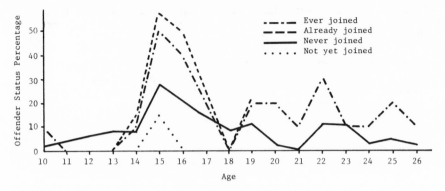

FIG. 12.6   Offender status by joining a gang, age, and race: whites.

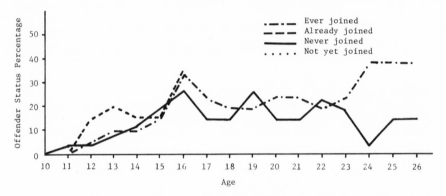

FIG. 12.7   Offender status by joining a gang, age, and race: nonwhites.

amounted to leaving delinquent behavior. Ninety percent of the whites committed no further offenses after leaving the gang, and none became delinquent at this point. For the nonwhites, however, no clear effect of leaving the gang was evident. One-third of the nonwhites commenced lawbreaking behavior after leaving the gang, while close to two-thirds persisted in delinquency and crime.

The data do not support the hypothesis that the seriousness of offenses decreases after subjects disassociate themselves from the gang. Table 12.15 shows that the difference in seriousness scores for whites was negligible, and there was

TABLE 12.14   Offender Status before and after Leaving a Gang by Race

	All		Whites		Nonwhites	
Offender Status	N	%	N	%	N	%
Before only	10	32	9	90	1	5
After only	7	23	0	0	7	33
Both before and after	14	45	1	10	13	62
Total	31	100	10	100	21	100

TABLE 12.15 Mean Adjusted Seriousness Scores before and after Leaving a Gang by Race

		Before			After			Difference		
Offenders	N	$\overline{X}$	SD	Probability	$\overline{X}$	SD	Probability	$\overline{X}$	SD	Probability
All	31	65.09	329.48	n.s.	93.98	416.76	n.s.	28.90	570.48	n.s.
Whites	10	−10.62	122.06	n.s.	−6.09	25.05	n.s.	4.52	127.02	n.s.
Nonwhites	21	102.94	392.21	n.s.	144.02	506.46	n.s.	41.09	698.41	n.s.

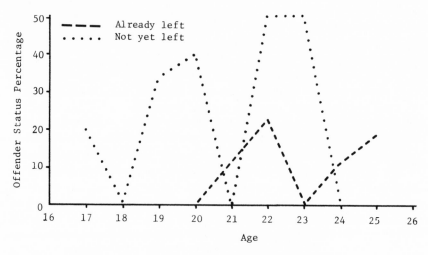

FIG. 12.8   Offender status by leaving a gang, age, and race: whites.

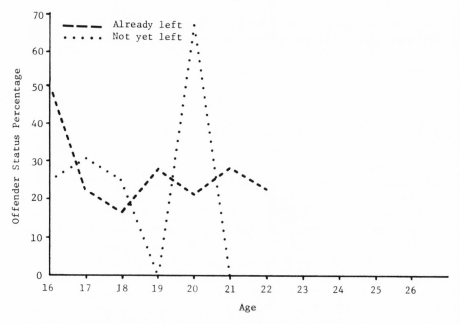

FIG. 12.9   Offender status by leaving a gang, age, and race: nonwhites.

a certain increase for the nonwhites. All the differences, however, were attributable to chance variations.

The time-series analyses presented in figures 12.8 and 12.9 show that the gang members have a considerably higher probability of becoming offenders. This trend, though more obvious for the whites, holds for both racial groups. Those who had already joined the gang were most delinquent, in sharp contrast with those who had not yet joined, for whom the probability of becoming offenders most often equaled zero. This trend indicated a strong positive relationship between delinquency and gang affiliation.

Examining the relationship between delinquent behavior and gang affiliation confirms the existence of a positive correlation between these two variables. As expected, the gang members commit more offenses than the nongang members, and the bulk are committed during their gang affiliation periods. As we hypothesized, leaving the gang seems to coincide with breaking away from delinquent behavior, though this effect is limited to the whites. For the nonwhites no such effect is observed, with the majority of the gang members (62 percent) committing offenses both before and after disassociation from the gang. By comparison, only 10 percent of the whites fall into this category.

Summary and Conclusion

Our major goal in this chapter has been to examine the role of life-transition events in the process of desistance from delinquent and criminal behavior. From this standpoint such events can be divided into three categories: those negatively correlated with illegal behavior, those positively correlated with illegal behavior, and those that do not appear to be correlated with illegal behavior.

The data revealed that the first category—negative correlation with criminality—included marriage, vocational training in the armed forces, and to some degree graduation from high school. Marriage had a strong effect on the seriousness of the offenses, but this effect was limited to the nonwhite offenders. The mean seriousness score for the nonwhites who never married was more than three times the mean for those who did. Although marriage did not appear to be correlated with the seriousness of the offenses of the whites, note that 84 percent of the whites did not commit offenses after marriage. For both racial groups, no significant effect of marriage was found on either the number of offenses or the age of desistance.

The high-school graduates accounted for fewer offenses than did the dropouts, which lends support to the Bachman group's finding (Bachman, Green, and Wirtanen 1977; Bachman, O'Malley, and Johnston 1978) that delinquency correlates negatively with educational attainment. There was no evidence, however, that high-school graduation affected the seriousness of offenses or the age of desistance.

Those whites who received vocational training in the armed forces desisted from criminality almost two and a half years earlier than their untrained counterparts. This strong association did not exist for the nonwhites, but the nonwhites who received training accounted for fewer offenses than those who did not.

The group of variables positively correlated with delinquent and criminal behavior included living with a woman and gang affiliation. Those offenders (of both races) who lived with a woman persisted in their criminal careers almost four years longer than those who had never done so. They were also responsible for more offenses than would be expected from their proportion in the sample. As expected, the data showed that gang members committed more offenses during their affiliation with the gang. For the whites, leaving the gang seemed to coincide with desistance, and gang membership was also related to the age of desistance. The white offenders who never belonged to a gang desisted almost three years earlier than those who belonged.

The association between criminal behavior and the other life-transition events examined—fatherhood, military service, vocational training, and college education—was found to be nonexistent.

Further tests encompassing larger offender populations are needed to test more fully the concept of a causal relationship between transitional life events and lawbreaking behavior. Samples including subjects who experienced different combinations of such events are needed to allow the use of proper controls. We also expect that certain life-transition events could have a different effect on the criminal behavior of an individual depending on the total number of offenses he committed. Larger samples would allow testing for such effects, and comparing offender and nonoffender populations with regard to life transitions would also be informative. The measures proposed here, if applied under the conditions described above, could indeed reveal that life-transition events have an important role in desistance from crime and delinquency. As it is, the follow-up data are suggestive of the influence life transitions have on criminality and indicate that this is a fruitful area for the continuation of longitudinal analyses.

13   Victims in a Birth Cohort

Simon I. Singer

The search for patterns of criminal conduct has historically been confined to examining the characteristics of offenders. With the advent of victimization surveys, however, attributes of both victims and offenders have been providing useful insights into the criminological processes. Although victimization data have expanded the criminological insights, relatively little attention has been paid to the interaction between individuals' experiences as victims and as offenders. This chapter examines that relationship along with others of interest to the study of victims of crime. Our purpose is not simply to tabulate the amount of crime committed against the cohort members, but to examine offenders as victims in relation to their social background, self-reported criminal involvement, and officially recorded arrests.

Some Methodological Issues

Unlike victimization surveys for which the reference period consists of a few years or less, respondents in the birth cohort follow-up were asked about their experiences during three general age periods: childhood (before age 12), adolescence (between ages 12 and 18), and adulthood (between ages 18 and 26, the time of the interviews). Although these large reference periods have the disadvantage of straining the respondents' ability to recall particular criminal incidents, they have the important advantage of increasing the chance of uncovering serious victimization incidents. In the National Crime Panel (NCP) victimization surveys, for example, samples consisting of thousands of respondents are necessary to better estimate the amount of serious crime. In the eight cities surveyed in 1972, based on a one-year reference period, 165,346 respondents reported only 789 serious assaults (Hindelang 1976, 107). Thus if surveys with much smaller sample sizes, like the birth cohort follow-up survey, are to uncover incidents of serious victimization, a larger reference period is justified.

But it is for good reason that shorter reference periods are used in the NCP surveys. Reverse record checks conducted by the United States Bureau of the Census (1970a,b), and United States Department of Justice, Law Enforcement Assistance Administration (1972), in which police-recorded victims were interviewed to measure their ability to recall reported victimizations, indicated that shorter time spans are better for measuring the occurrence of crime in a given period. Incidents that happened six months ago are remembered better than those that occurred more than a year before the interview. In addition, reverse record checks indicate that there is substantial variation in the types of incidents likely to be remembered; the more salient the event, the more likely it is to stand out in the recall process (Sudman and Bradburn 1974). Thus, simple assaults in the NCP retests are reported less reliably than are more serious offenses. There is also a tendency to report incidents in the nearest reference period that may actually have occurred in the preceding time period.

In general, therefore, as the recall period increases the precision of estimates tends to decline. In designing the follow-up interview, however, we decided that these factors did not outweigh our overriding objective—to uncover estimates of the *relative* frequency with which our subjects were victims of serious offenses. Thus we extended the reference period, and the data suggest that this technique can provide estimates that are accurate enough to assess the association between victimization and a variety of independent variables.

Surveyed Victimizations

The distribution of reported victimizations in the follow-up study has been presented in a paper by Thornberry and Figlio (1974). The purpose here is to reexamine the distribution of offenses in order to distinguish categories of incidents that we will examine later in terms of the victims' social backgrounds, official arrests, and self-reported delinquencies and crimes. Table 13.1 presents the proportion of the sample members experiencing each of the ten surveyed incidents in childhood, adolescence, and adulthood. To determine the frequency of victimization, we asked the respondents if the incident had occurred "never," "once or twice," or "three or more times." There was a substantial association between the type of incident and the age period. Minor assault and robbery generally decreased as the subjects became older, while property offenses increased. Major assaults, those involving a stabbing or a shooting, however, tended to peak in the teenage and early adult years.

The most trivial type of assault surveyed was being "pushed around." It was reported to occur most frequently in childhood; approximately two-thirds of the sample reported this type of victimization. The proportion declined slightly in the teenage years and then dropped sharply in adulthood.

Being "beaten up" was a less trivial but still relatively common event during childhood. By age, its pattern of occurrence was similar to that of being pushed around; nearly half of the sample members reported its occurring at least once before age 12, with the percentage declining to 39 percent in the teenage years and 14 percent in the adult years.

Serious injury with a weapon was relatively rare among the sample members compared with other types of assault. At some point in their lives, however, 134 sample members reported being the victims of either a shooting or a stabbing, with the majority falling into the less serious category of being stabbed. The probability of being stabbed was greatest in the teenage years, 10 percent, and fell to 7 percent during the adult years. Fewer subjects reported being shot, but the probabilities increased slightly with age. Only 2 percent of the sample mem-

TABLE 13.1 Frequency of Victimization by Type and Age Period ($N = 567$)

Type of Victimization and Age Period	Frequency					
	0		1–2		3+	
	N	$\%$	N	$\%$	N	$\%$
Pushed around						
<12	177	31.2	193	34.0	197	34.7
12–18	228	40.2	208	36.7	131	23.1
>18	464	81.8	72	12.7	31	5.5
Beaten up						
<12	298	52.6	154	27.2	115	20.3
12–18	347	61.2	164	28.9	56	9.9
>18	485	85.5	67	11.8	15	2.6
Cut or stabbed						
<12	549	96.8	17	3.0	1	0.2
12–18	512	90.3	51	9.0	4	0.7
>18	528	93.1	32	5.6	7	1.2
Shot						
<12	563	99.3	4	0.7	0	0.0
12–18	559	98.6	8	1.4	0	0.0
>18	557	98.2	8	1.4	2	0.4
Other violence						
<12	550	97.0	16	2.8	1	0.2
12–18	527	92.9	38	6.7	2	0.4
>18	536	94.5	26	4.6	5	0.9
Robbed						
<12	430	75.8	79	13.9	58	10.2
12–18	470	82.9	73	12.9	24	4.2
>18	535	94.4	26	4.6	6	1.1
Pocket picked						
<12	531	93.7	25	4.4	11	1.9
12–18	518	91.4	29	6.9	10	1.8
>18	506	89.2	49	8.6	12	2.1
Burglary						
<12	409	72.1	101	17.8	57	10.1
12–18	346	61.0	155	27.3	66	11.6
>18	266	46.9	221	39.9	80	14.1
Property damaged or destroyed						
<12	458	80.3	60	10.6	49	8.6
12–18	433	76.4	92	16.2	42	7.4
>18	315	55.6	185	32.6	67	11.8
Other offenses						
<12	560	98.8	4	0.7	3	0.5
12–18	551	97.2	14	2.5	2	0.4
>18	546	96.3	17	3.0	4	0.7

bers reported being shot as adults, 1.4 percent as teenagers, and 0.7 percent as children.

The age trend for robbery offenses was similar to that observed for simple assaults. Nearly one-quarter of the sample, 24 percent, reported being robbed during childhood, with the percentage declining steadily to 17 percent in the teenage years and 6 percent in the adult years. Robberies occurring three or more times also followed this pattern.

Pocket-picking, involving personal theft with contact but without the usual threat of violence, increased with age: 11 percent of the sample reported this type of offense during the adult years; but only 9 percent and 6 percent reported it for the teenage and childhood periods, respectively.

For other property offenses, the probability of victimization peaked in the adult years. Burglary victimizations were reported by the greatest number of sample members, 53 percent in their adult years. Acts of vandalism involving property damage or destruction were also reported most often in the adult years: 44 percent were experienced by adults, 24 percent by teenagers, and 19 percent by children.[1]

The distribution of these victimization data, in terms of their frequency of occurrence, their seriousness, and their age distribution, suggest that for analysis they can be collapsed into five more general categories. Two categories concern violent crimes. The first is the single item of being "beaten up," generally classified as "simple assault."[2] The second category involves serious injury from the use of a weapon—being shot or stabbed. This category falls under the *UCR* definition of "aggravated assault." In addition to these separate categories of violent offenses, we will use a more general one called "assaultive crimes." This category combines incidents of being beaten up, stabbed, or shot.[3]

The third and fourth categories concern primary face-to-face victimizations of robbery and having one's pocket picked. Both types of incident require some contact between victim and offender, though the latter is more subtle and less violent. Because of the different degrees of violence required for robbery and pocket picking, their separate classifications are warranted. For stylistic purposes, victimizations involving pocket picking will be referred to henceforth as "theft." The fifth and last category considered combines burglary with property damage or destruction and will be referred to as "burglary." Both aspects involve the loss of property, usually not in the presence of the victim, and thus neither involves face-to-face encounters between offenders and victims (Sellin and Wolfgang 1978).

1. The two miscellaneous categories, "other violence" and "other offenses," represented too few incidents to discern any clear pattern by age.

2. Because being "pushed around" is a relatively trivial type of incident, it serves no analytical purpose beyond its bivariate description by age.

3. The frequencies of responses to the categories "beaten up," "stabbed," and "shot" did not sum to the frequencies reported for the category of "assaultive crimes." Any subject who reported each of the separate types of victimization was counted only *once* in the "assaultive crimes" category.

In general, victims who experienced an incident three or more times did not differ in social background and crime-related variables from those who reported being victimized once or twice. Throughout the analysis, therefore, the data are presented in terms of the probability of *ever* being a victim.[4]

Race is a control variable for two reasons. First, throughout this study race has been shown to be the most important social background predictor of the frequency and seriousness of criminal offenses. Second, variation in the seriousness of surveyed victimizations is also related to race. Of critical concern, then, is the extent to which bivariate relationships between victimizations and other background variables remain when race is held constant.

To guard against unwarranted inferences that might arise in describing the characteristics of victims, we must perform a statistical test of significance. For nominal level data, the most common procedure is to employ a goodness-of-fit chi-square test. In multivariate analysis, however, it is difficult to determine the variables that contribute significantly to differences between observed and expected values. One way to determine the significance of a variable is to partition its effect by taking the natural log of the observed over the expected. By doing so, we can obtain the additive property of chi-square, referred to as a "likelihood ratio." The likelihood ratio and the goodness-of-fit chi-square follow the same theoretical distribution; thus we can measure the probability of independence at the standard .05, .01, and .001 levels of significance (Goodman 1978).

Tests of significance in the tables presented are based on likelihood ratios for the independent variables of interest, controlling for race. The tests are analogous to a test of partial association between two variables, controlling for the third. For example, a test of the relationship between area income and serious assaultive victimization is based on the effect of area income and victimization, contrasted with the complete model that includes race.

Results
Social Background

In the NCP surveys, rates of personal victimization are related to demographic characteristics such as race, age, sex, marital status, employment status, and family income. This section focuses on the relation between background characteristics and the probability of victimization. Three measures of social background are considered: SES (as measured in the original study), the subjects' marital status, and employment status. The general hypothesis guiding the analysis is that social background accounts for a significant proportion of victimizations involving direct contact between victims and offenders. For victims of burglary, we hypothesized no significant difference.

The suggestion that victims of violence differ significantly in social back-

---

4. In addition to these general rules for classification, we also used more specific rules for individual items. Because major violence is so rare during childhood, the data for the periods of under age 12 and from ages 12 to 18 have been combined throughout. This situation also obtained for theft (pocket picking), and these data have been combined for the childhood and teenage periods as well.

ground stems from a number of class-linked theories of crime and studies of victimization. Subcultural theory and conflict theory generally argue that victims of violence are disproportionately represented within lower-class populations (see Wolfgang and Ferracuti 1982). Empirical support for the proposed hypothesis exists in Hindelang, Gottfredson, and Garofalo (1978).

We begin by analyzing the effect of SES, determined by the median income of each subject's census tract of residence during high school. This measure divides the subjects into low and high SES categories and is the same measure used in earlier chapters to examine official criminality.

The distribution of victims by SES and race is presented in table 13.2. For victims of simple assault, the relationship between SES and the probability of being a victim was specific to the whites in the teenage years. Thirty-five percent from the high-income area were victims, compared with 51 percent from the low-income area. For the nonwhite subjects the relationship exhibited the opposite pattern.

For aggravated assult, the difference for the whites by SES was significant before age 18 and for all age periods combined. The chance of being a victim

TABLE 13.2   Victims by Race and SES

Type of Offense and Age Period	Whites				Nonwhites			
	High SES		Low SES		High SES		Low SES	
	N	%	N	%	N	%	N	%
Simple assault								
<12	151	45.6	66	54.1	7	50.0	45	45.0
12–18**	116	35.0	62	51.0	7	50.0	35	35.0
>18	44	13.3	20	16.4	3	21.4	15	15.0
Aggravated assault								
<18*	26	7.9	23	18.8	4	28.6	17	17.0
>18*	14	4.2	11	9.0	2	14.3	18	18.0
<26***	37	11.2	33	27.0	5	36.0	31	31.0
Assaultive crimes								
>18	49	14.8	25	20.5	4	28.6	28	28.0
Robbery								
<12	72	21.7	27	22.1	6	42.9	32	32.0
12–18	46	13.9	24	21.1	4	28.6	23	23.0
>18	18	5.4	5	4.1	1	7.1	8	8.0
Theft								
<18	30	9.1	15	12.3	2	14.3	15	15.0
>18	24	7.2	12	9.8	5	35.7	20	20.0
Burglary								
<12	107	32.3	35	28.7	5	35.7	40	40.0
12–18	142	42.9	57	46.7	4	28.6	48	48.0
>18	230	69.5	79	64.7	7	50.0	56	56.0

*$p < .05$.
**$p < .01$.
***$p < .001$.

was nearly twice as great for those in the low-income area. No other type of victimization was significant at the .05 level by SES and race. Overall, though, there appears to be a very modest relationship between social status and victimization once race is controlled.

In a recent empirical assessment of the relationship between intelligence and delinquency, Hirschi and Hindelang (1977, 283) commented on the importance of school-related variables for the study of criminality: "Their significance for delinquency is nowhere in dispute and is, in fact, one of the oldest and most consistent findings of delinquency research." Given their importance for explaining criminality, it is also worth considering the contribution of school-related variables in explaining the probability of being a victim of crime. The same factors that lead to criminality may also expose one to the risk of becoming a victim. For these purposes, education can be measured by the highest school grade completed, dichotomized at the point of whether or not the subject graduated from high school.

The difference between graduates and nongraduates by type of victimization is presented in table 13.3. In the adult years, the high-school dropouts were more

TABLE 13.3   Victims by Race and Completion of High School

Type of Offense and Age Period	Whites				Nonwhites			
	Nongraduates		Graduates		Nongraduates		Graduates	
	N	%	N	%	N	%	N	%
Simple assault								
<12	30	42.8	187	48.8	25	58.1	27	38.9
12–18	33	47.1	145	37.9	21	48.8	21	29.6
>18	12	17.1	32	13.6	10	23.3	8	11.3
Aggravated assault								
<18	10	14.3	39	10.2	10	23.3	11	15.5
>18**	8	11.4	17	4.4	11	25.6	9	11.1
<26***	17	24.3	53	13.8	19	44.2	71	23.4
Assaultive crimes								
>18**	16	22.9	58	15.1	17	39.5	15	21.1
Robbery								
<12	11	15.7	88	23.0	16	37.2	22	31.0
12–18	14	20.9	56	14.7	9	20.9	18	25.3
>18	5	7.1	18	4.7	6	17.3	3	4.2
Theft								
<18	6	8.6	39	10.2	6	13.9	11	15.5
>18	6	8.6	30	7.8	11	25.6	14	19.7
Burglary								
<12	20	28.6	122	31.8	19	44.2	26	36.6
12–18	34	48.6	165	43.1	20	46.5	32	45.1
>18	50	71.4	259	67.6	23	53.5	40	56.4

**$p < .01$.
***$p < .001$.

than twice as likely to be victims of aggravated assaults. This difference holds for both the white and nonwhite sample members and is significant at the .001 level.

If simple and aggravated assault are combined to form the category of assaultive crimes, the relationship is again significant during the adult years. Nearly 40 percent of the nonwhite high-school dropouts were victims, compared with 21 percent of the graduates. For the whites the difference is less substantial, with 23 percent of the nongraduates and 15 percent of the graduates becoming victims of violence. The relationship between robbery and educational level, while not significant at the .05 level, is in the direction expected, with nongraduates having a higher probability of victimization during the adult years.

The high-school graduates can be divided into those who continued their education and those who did not to analyze further the association between education and victimization. The differences in percentages followed the same trend for both the whites and nonwhites. Among the whites 11 percent of the nongraduates, 9 percent of the graduates, and 1 percent of those with some education beyond high school were victims; among the nonwhites 24 percent of the nongraduates, 18 percent of the graduates, and 4 percent of those with some education beyond high school were victims.

The last two measures of social background are employment and marital status. Because full-time employment and marriage usually follow the teenage years, we considered only victimization incidents after age 18.

The importance of employment and marital status is highlighted in the lifestyle exposure approach to explaining personal victimization. In Hindelang, Gottfredson, and Garofalo's analysis of the NCP surveys, the highest probability of personal victimization was for unemployed males between ages 16 and 19. The injury likelihood for this group was 47 percent, compared with 8 percent for those over age 19 and either married or widowed (1978, 116–17). Thus, if proximity and opportunity are important determinants for experiencing the direct consequences of a crime, then they should be reflected in the employment and marital status of victims.

Table 13.4, which cross-tabulates employment status by victimization, shows that nearly all the percentages were in the expected direction. Yet only major violence and theft are significant at the .05 level. For nonwhites, especially, the probability of being a victim of an aggravated assault was much greater for the unemployed. Among the unemployed nonwhites, 38 percent were victims, compared with 9 percent of the employed nonwhites. For the whites the difference was less dramatic, though still in the expected direction: 8 percent of the unemployed and 5 percent of the employed were shot or stabbed. For theft offenses, the differences were also greater for the nonwhite subjects (38 percent of the unemployed were victims compared with 15 percent of the employed) than for the white subjects (10 percent of the unemployed were victims compared with 8 percent of the employed).

Table 13.5 presents the relationship between marital status and victimization. In general, the data indicate that married persons had a lower probability of being victims. Although significant at the .05 level, the difference in marital

TABLE 13.4   Adult Victims by Race and Employment

	Whites				Nonwhites			
	Unemployed		Employed		Unemployed		Employed	
Type of Offense	N	%	N	%	N	%	N	%
Simple assault	10	20.4	54	13.4	6	17.6	12	15.2
Aggravated assault**	4	8.2	21	5.2	13	38.2	7	8.9
Robbery	4	8.2	19	4.7	4	11.8	5	6.3
Theft*	5	10.2	31	7.7	13	38.2	12	15.2
Burglary	35	71.4	274	68.0	16	47.1	46	58.2

*$p < .05$.
**$p < .01$.

TABLE 13.5   Adult Victims by Race and Marital Status

	Whites				Nonwhites			
	Single		Married		Single		Married	
Type of Offense	N	%	N	%	N	%	N	%
Simple assault**	33	18.5	31	11.3	11	18.0	7	13.2
Aggravated assault*	16	9.0	9	3.3	11	18.0	9	17.0
Robbery**	13	7.3	10	3.6	8	13.1	1	2.0
Theft**	18	10.1	18	6.5	18	29.5	7	13.2
Burglary	120	67.4	189	68.7	38	62.3	25	47.2

*$p < .05$.
**$p < .01$.

status for victims of aggravated assault was specific to the white sample members. Robbery was significant for both races, with more than twice as many single subjects as married subjects being victimized. Similar differences were seen for simple assault and theft.

Although marital status accounted for some of the variance in the probability of reported victimization, race was still the most important predictor. Moreover, this same general outcome held for the other social background variables examined. Race took precedence over any of the other variables, especially in distinguishing victims of serious violence. We note also that the social background variables, as expected, accounted for little of the difference between victims and nonvictims of property offenses.

Crime and Victimization

If the chance of personal victimization is a function of an individual's proximity to a potential offender, then participating in criminal activity should increase the risk of being a victim. Thus the critical question in this section is the extent to which victims are products of a life-style involving a subcultural adaptation to crime, in which being the predator and the prey are equally likely outcomes.

The follow-up indicators of crime were cross-classified with the type of victim experience: having a friend arrested, belonging to a gang, using a lethal weapon, committing a serious assault, and being arrested. We hypothesized that these variables, controlling for race, were all significantly related to being the victim of a personal crime. Victimization for property offenses, however, was hypothesized to be insignificant.

In the follow-up study, the sample members were asked the following question: "Think of the three closest friends you had during your high school days. How many of them were picked up by the police in that period?" Because there was no significant difference in the characteristics of victims between those with one or those with more than one friend arrested, the results from this question were dichotomized.

Table 13.6 cross-tabulates incidents by friends arrested and by race. The differences in the percentages of victims are in the direction expected, with victims more likely to report having had friends arrested. For victims of violence, the

TABLE 13.6   Victims by Race and Friend Arrested

| Type of Offense and Age Period | Whites | | | | Nonwhites | | | |
| | No Friend Arrested | | Friend Arrested | | No Friend Arrested | | Friend Arrested | |
	N	%	N	%	N	%	N	%
Simple assault								
<12***	117	43.0	100	55.2	19	34.5	33	55.9
12–18***	90	33.1	88	48.6	14	25.4	28	47.5
>18**	30	11.0	34	18.8	5	9.1	13	22.0
Aggravated assault								
<18**	24	8.8	25	13.8	5	9.1	16	32.6
>18***	10	3.7	15	8.0	3	5.4	17	28.8
<26***	55	13.8	15	27.8	16	21.3	20	51.3
Assaultive crimes								
>18***	33	12.1	41	22.6	8	14.5	24	40.7
Robbery								
<12	55	20.2	44	24.3	19	34.6	19	32.2
12–18*	34	12.5	36	12.8	12	21.8	15	25.4
>18	15	5.5	8	4.4	5	9.1	4	6.8
Theft								
<18	25	9.2	20	11.0	6	10.9	11	18.6
>18	20	7.3	16	8.8	8	14.5	17	28.8
Burglary								
<12	82	30.1	60	33.1	22	40.0	23	39.0
12–18**	105	38.6	94	51.9	23	41.8	29	49.1
>18	184	67.6	125	69.1	35	63.6	28	47.5

*$p < .05$.
**$p < .01$.
***$p < .001$.

relationship is significant in all three age periods. By race, the differences in percentages are especially strong for the nonwhites. During the teenage years, the nonwhite sample members who had had friends arrested were twice as likely to be the victims of simple assault; during the adult years the differences were also evident. For aggravated assault, the nonwhites with delinquent friends had substantially higher probabilities of victimization. Examining victimization for all assaultive offenses during the adult years, we again see that the differences are significant at the .001 level. Among the nonwhites with delinquent companions, 41 percent suffered some violence, compared with 15 percent of those without delinquent friends.

For the whites, the relationship between delinquent friends and victimization is less pronounced. Still, for aggravated assault during the teenage years one and a half times more victims had friends who were arrested. The combined category of assaultive crimes also shows that the whites with friends arrested were nearly twice as likely to be victims as those who reported having no friends arrested.

For the property offenses of robbery and burglary the relationship between having a friend arrested and victimization is specific only to the teenage years. For theft, the percentages show that the nonwhites with friends arrested were twice as likely to be victims as those whose friends were not arrested. Because of the small sample size, this difference is not significant at the .05 level.

An alternative method for examining the association between delinquent peers and victimization is to analyze the association between being a member of a juvenile gang and being a victim of criminal activity. Although theoretical explanations for the genesis of gangs vary considerably (see Cloward and Ohlin 1960; Cohen 1955; Miller 1958), it is clear that all these theories predict elevated levels of criminal activity for individuals who belong to gangs.[5] Given this association, it is reasonable to expect that gang members would also be more likely to be victims of crime.

Table 13.7 presents the relationship between belonging to a gang and victimization. By victim status, the nonwhite gang members reported more than three times as many simple assaults as the nonmembers in the adult years. For the nonwhite subjects aggravated assaults were more than twice as likely to occur for gang members during the juvenile and adult periods. For the white gang members the rate of aggravated assault was more than four times as great as for the white nonmembers in the adult years and twice as great for all age periods combined. When all forms of violence were combined after age 18, the difference was again highly significant: gang members were more than twice as likely as nonmembers to be victims, a relationship that held for both races.

The observed differences for other types of victimizations, such as burglary and theft, do not depart from what would be expected by chance. For robbery, however, a specific interaction effect seems to suppress the significance of gang membership. In general, a consistent relationship can be observed for the white subjects, but it is not statistically significant.

5. See chapter 12 for additional comments and empirical evidence on this issue.

TABLE 13.7   Victims by Race and Gang Membership

| Type of Offense and Age Period | Whites | | | | Nonwhites | | | |
| | Not a Gang Member | | Gang Member | | Not a Gang Member | | Gang Member | |
	N	%	N	%	N	%	N	%
Simple assault								
<12	182	45.7	35	63.6	35	46.7	17	43.6
12–18	150	37.7	28	50.9	28	37.3	14	35.9
>18**	52	13.1	12	21.8	6	8.0	12	30.8
Aggravated assault								
<18	42	10.5	7	12.7	10	13.3	11	28.2
>18***	16	4.0	9	16.4	8	10.7	12	30.8
<26***	55	13.8	15	27.3	16	21.3	20	51.3
Assaultive crimes								
>18***	58	14.6	16	29.1	13	17.3	19	48.7
Robbery								
<12	81	20.3	18	32.7	24	32.0	14	35.9
12–18	57	14.3	13	23.6	19	25.3	8	20.5
>18	19	4.8	4	7.3	6	8.0	3	7.7
Theft								
<18	42	10.5	3	5.4	13	10.4	4	10.2
>18	30	7.5	6	10.9	15	20.0	10	25.6
Burglary								
<12	125	31.4	17	30.9	28	37.3	17	43.6
12–18	172	43.2	27	49.1	34	45.3	18	46.2
>18	272	68.3	37	67.3	44	58.7	19	48.7

**$p < .01$.
***$p < .001$.

Overall, then, gang membership seems to be related to victimization for the violent offenses but not for the property offenses. This finding, in combination with the earlier results when the delinquent behavior of friends was examined, suggests that the subcultural link between criminality and victimization may be specific to violence. The finding also suggests that the availability of weapons may play a role in victimization, as it does in crime. Indeed, in suggesting the normative system they designated as a subculture of violence, Wolfgang and Ferracuti stated that "ready access to weapons in this milieu may become essential for protection against others who respond in similarly violent ways in certain situations, and . . . the carrying of knives or other protective devices becomes a common symbol of willingness to participate in violence, to expect violence, and to be ready for its retaliation" (1982, 159).

As part of the follow-up study, the respondents were asked if they had "used a weapon to threaten another person" during two age periods in their lives: before and after age 18. Combining these responses, we can examine the relationship between self-reported behavior on the use of weapons and experiences as a victim (see table 13.8).

The association between being victimized and using a weapon is significant at the .001 level for all forms of violence we surveyed. For whites who reported using weapons, the percentages of victimization for simple assault were 62 percent in childhood, 60 percent in adolescence, and 29 percent in adulthood; for those who did not use weapons, the percentages were 44 percent, 34 percent, and 11 percent, respectively. For nonwhites the differences were even more dramatic: The percentages of subjects who were victims were 64 percent in childhood, 49 percent in adolescence, and 24 percent in adulthood for those who used weapons; for those who did not use weapons the percentages were 33 percent, 28 percent, and 9 percent, respectively.

Although the absolute magnitude of the differences varied, the patterns just described for simple assault also obtained for aggravated assault and for the combined category of assaultive crimes. For both whites and nonwhites the probabilities of being victims of violent offenses were significantly higher for the subjects who reported using weapons.

TABLE 13.8   Victims by Race and Use of Weapons

Type of Offense and Age Period	Whites				Nonwhites			
	No Weapon		Weapon		No Weapon		Weapon	
	N	%	N	%	N	%	N	%
Simple assault								
<12***	158	44.1	59	62.1	22	32.8	30	63.8
12–18***	121	33.8	57	60.0	19	28.4	23	48.9
>18***	40	10.8	24	29.3	5	8.5	13	23.6
Aggravated assault								
<18***	13	3.6	12	12.6	8	11.9	12	25.5
>18***	30	8.4	19	20.0	8	11.9	13	27.2
<26**	35	9.4	35	42.7	8	13.6	28	50.9
Assaultive crimes								
>18***	46	12.4	28	34.0	10	16.9	22	40.0
Robbery								
<12	72	20.1	27	28.4	20	29.9	18	38.3
12–18***	43	12.0	27	28.4	14	20.9	13	27.7
>18***	14	3.8	9	11.0	1	1.7	8	14.5
Theft								
<18	35	9.8	10	10.5	7	10.4	10	21.3
>18**	26	7.0	10	12.2	7	11.9	18	32.7
Burglary								
<12**	106	29.6	36	37.9	23	34.3	22	46.8
12–18***	141	39.4	58	61.1	26	38.8	26	55.3
>18	250	67.4	59	72.0	31	52.5	32	58.2

**p < .01.
***p < .001.

Victimization differences by weapon use also held for property offenses. Robbery victimizations during the teenage and adult years were substantially higher for subjects who used weapons. Offenses of theft and burglary also yielded substantial and generally significant differences. Subjects who reported the use of weapons were far more likely than their counterparts to be victims of property offenses.

In general, weapon use was related to all types of victimization. Subjects using weapons were more likely to be victimized for both violent and property offenses than those who did not report the use of weapons.

We have examined the relationship between victimization and offensive behavior in a somewhat indirect fashion by looking at the link between victimization and delinquent peers, gang membership, and weapon use. We conclude this analysis by examining the possibility raised earlier that victims and offenders are drawn from the same population.

Our first measure of delinquency is based on the subjects' responses to the self-reported delinquency items. Because the majority of the respondents reported committing at least one of the more trivial offenses, we focus on those who reported committing serious acts of violence. Any subject who responded positively to any of the following self-report items is classified as a serious offender: "hurt someone badly enough to require medical treatment"; "forced a female to have sexual intercourse with you"; or "killed someone not accidentally."

Table 13.9 presents the relationship between being a victim and committing a serious assault by race and victimization status. The observed differences are in the expected direction, with victims of violence more often being offenders than nonoffenders. Aggravated assault was more than twice as likely to occur during the adult years to a sample member who was an offender. When incidents of violent victimization are combined in the assaultive crimes category, the observed differences in offender status are again highly significant. For the whites, 23 percent of the offenders were victims, compared with 14 percent of the nonoffenders; for the nonwhites, 46 percent of the offenders were victims, compared with 19 percent of the nonoffenders.

For victimizations involving property crimes, offender status was less important: for robbery the relationship was specific to the whites during their teenage years, with 13 percent of the nonoffenders being victims compared with 26 percent of the offenders. The only other significant difference was for theft during the adult years: the probability of being a victim was more than twice as great for the offenders, and this relationship held for both races.

Up to this point measures of delinquency and criminality have been confined to surveyed information contained in the follow-up study. It is possible that differences in the observed characteristics of victims are a function of response bias that survey methodologists might attribute to saying nay or yea (Sudman and Bradburn 1974). To control for this potential bias, we examined the relationship between arrest status, as measured by official arrest records, and self-reported incidents of victimization.

TABLE 13.9 Victims by Race and Self-Reported Serious Assault

Type of Offense and Age Period	Whites				Nonwhites			
	Not Assaulted		Assaulted		Not Assaulted		Assaulted	
	N	%	N	%	N	%	N	%
Simple assault								
<12**	176	46.2	41	56.9	33	41.8	19	54.3
12–18*	140	36.7	38	52.8	28	35.4	14	40.0
>18**	42	12.5	22	18.6	5	6.7	13	33.3
Aggravated assault								
<18	39	10.2	10	13.8	15	19.0	6	17.1
>18**	14	4.2	11	9.3	10	13.3	10	25.6
<26***	21	6.8	49	33.6	13	21.0	23	44.2
Assaultive crimes								
>18***	47	14.0	27	22.8	14	18.7	18	46.2
Robbery								
<12	82	21.5	17	23.6	22	27.8	16	45.7
12–18*	51	13.4	19	26.4	18	22.8	9	25.7
>18	15	4.5	8	6.8	5	6.7	4	10.3
Theft								
<18	35	9.2	10	13.9	10	12.7	7	20.0
>18**	19	5.7	17	14.4	13	17.3	12	30.8
Burglary								
<12	121	31.8	21	29.2	30	38.0	15	42.9
12–18	163	42.8	36	50.0	32	40.5	20	57.1
>18	219	65.4	90	76.3	40	53.3	23	59.0

$*p < .05.$
$**p < .01.$
$***p < .001.$

To our knowledge, only one other study has examined official arrest records of surveyed victims. In another Philadelphia cohort born in 1957, Savitz, Lalli, and Rosen (1977) surveyed incidents of victimization and then compared them with the official delinquent status of their cohort members. For both the whites and nonwhites in the period surveyed, they reported significant differences in being a victim of an assault by official delinquent status: 21 percent of the nondelinquent whites were victims, compared with 35 percent of the delinquents; and 13 percent of the nondelinquent nonwhites were victims, compared with 26 percent of the delinquents. For other types of incidents, robbery and extortion, they observed no significant difference by official delinquent status.

Table 13.10 presents the relationship between official arrest status and victimization within racial groups. By type of victimization, the data show that, in general, offenders in the follow-up sample had higher rates of victimization than did nonoffenders. For minor assaults during both the teenage and adult years the differences were in the direction expected. Although the proportion of victims

TABLE 13.10   Victims by Race and Official Arrest Status

Type of Offense and Age Period	Whites				Nonwhites			
	Nonoffender		Offender		Nonoffender		Offender	
	N	%	N	%	N	%	N	%
Simple assault								
<12	154	46.5	63	51.6	30	44.8	22	46.8
12–18***	115	34.7	63	51.6	20	29.9	22	46.8
>18***	62	15.9	21	32.8	5	8.5	13	23.4
Aggravated assault								
<18	35	10.6	14	11.5	12	17.9	9	19.1
>18***	12	3.2	13	15.7	4	6.8	16	29.1
<26	41	14.1	29	17.8	8	9.5	28	38.4
Assaultive crimes								
>18***	46	12.4	28	33.7	8	13.6	24	44.6
Robbery								
<12	72	21.7	27	22.1	24	35.8	14	29.8
12–18***	39	11.8	31	25.4	14	20.9	13	27.6
>18***	10	2.7	13	15.7	1	1.7	8	14.5
Theft								
<18	33	10.0	12	9.8	9	13.4	8	17.0
>18	27	7.3	9	10.8	11	18.6	14	25.4
Burglary								
<12	102	31.0	40	32.8	31	46.3	14	29.8
12–18	137	41.4	62	50.8	31	46.3	21	44.7
>18	255	68.9	54	65.1	31	52.5	32	58.2

***$p < .001$.

declined with adulthood, the difference in offender status was significant, with more than twice as many white and nonwhite offenders reporting incidents of victimization.

In the adult years, the chance of being a victim of an aggravated assault was more than three times as great if the respondents were offenders. When all incidents of assault were combined for the adult years, the difference was still highly significant: for the whites, 34 percent of the offenders were victims, compared with 12 percent of the nonoffenders; for the nonwhites the difference was even greater, with 45 percent of the offenders being victims, compared with 14 percent of the nonoffenders.

For both the teenage and adult years, robbery victimizations were highly related to official offender status. During the teenage years the proportional difference was stronger for the white offenders, who were twice as likely to report being victims, while for the nonwhites the difference between offenders and nonoffenders was only 7 percent. After age 18, however, the differences were dramatic for both races: The rate for the white offenders' being robbed in adulthood was nearly six times that for the nonoffenders, while for the nonwhites it was nearly eight times as great.

Although victims of theft were more likely to be offenders, especially if they were nonwhites, the proportional difference controlling for race did not reach the .05 level of significance. The probability of burglary was independent of offender characteristics.

Summary

Measures of delinquency and crime accounted for more of the probability of being a victim than did the social background variables previously identified. Although race as a control variable contributed substantially to much of the observed relationship, a life-style seemed to exist for the sample population in which victimization was a common event for those involved in committing crime. The existence of a "victim subculture," as Schafer suggested (see Wolfgang and Singer 1978), seemed to be supported if combined with the analytic framework provided by Wolfgang and Ferracuti (1982). The relationship, as repeatedly described, appeared specific to violent victimizations and not to the more typical property offenses. It may be that current surveys of victimization are measuring the degree to which respondents are offenders as well as victims; that is, the characteristics uncovered thus far indicate that victims of violence are also offenders.

14   An Empirical Study of Error in Reports of Crime and Delinquency

George S. Bridges

Four decades ago, surveys in which respondents reported their own involvement in crime revealed that many offenses escape official records; consequently, official statistics inaccurately portray the true number and types of offenses that occur (Murphy, Shirley, and Witmer 1946; Porterfield 1943; Robison 1936). More recently, self-report surveys have analyzed factors associated with criminal and delinquent behavior and found that delinquency is spread evenly across most social groups and that, except for serious offenses, race and socioeconomic position are poor predictors of admitted delinquency. Rebutting conventional "strain" or anomie theory of delinquent behavior, many researchers using self-report surveys have maintained that delinquency correlates with community organization within homogeneous racial and economic groups (Akers 1964; Clark and Wenninger 1962; Dentler and Monroe 1961; Erickson 1973; Hardt and Peterson 1968; Reiss and Rhodes 1961; Slocum and Stone 1963; Voss 1966). Current researchers suggest, however, that the difference between the findings of "self-report" studies and studies using "official" crime statistics observed in previous research are mostly illusory and may stem from differences in the domain of behavior measured by the different methods (Elliott and Ageton 1980; Hindelang, Hirschi, and Weis 1979; Thornberry and Farnworth 1982).

The widespread use of self-report surveys motivates this examination of measurement problems associated with the self-report method. One particularly serious problem involves errors survey respondents make in describing their offense activity. Unknown to the interviewer or researcher, some respondents may systematically overreport or inflate descriptions of their involvement in crime and others may underreport or conceal their involvement, thus distorting survey estimates of the extensiveness of crime. Further, if respondents err unevenly—that is, some respondents err more frequently and seriously than others—the errors may also confound statistical relationships between factors associated with participation in crime and self-reported measures of criminal behavior.

Because few previous self-report studies have examined this problem, there exists little empirical information on the types and effects of response errors in self-report surveys. This chapter describes the background and results of an empirical study that develops and applies a conceptual model of reported offenses to estimate those effects. The first section proposes a conceptual model of reported offenses for developing empirical estimates of the levels and effects of error. The second section reviews the treatment of response error in previous self-report studies with respect to the types, extensiveness, and correlates of error observed. The third section summarizes the study findings with respect to error in reports of offenses resulting in arrest. We use the average difference between reported and official measures of offenses to estimate the aggregate effects of response error on the amount and types of crimes reported, and we estimate effects of response errors on the association between reported and true levels of offense activity using a statistical model of self-reported and official measures of criminal behavior. The final section of this chapter offers recommendations for estimating and controlling the effects of response errors in future self-report studies and encourages development of more accurate descriptions of crime and delinquency in the general population.

A Model of Reported Offenses

Studies on measurement in surveys typically have viewed the response to a survey question in terms of the respondent's true value of the question and in terms of two general types of response error (Lord and Novick 1968; Magnusson 1967; Nunnally 1967). The first type is analogous to the "error involved when a measuring tape always gives a result which is two inches too long or ten percent too short" (Magnusson 1967, 64) and may be termed "response bias." In the present context, response bias corresponds to the error involved when respondents uniformly conceal or inflate descriptions of offense activity. The second type, termed "random response error," corresponds to the errors in responses that are orderless and that would offset one another over repeated administrations of the survey.

Figure 14.1 diagrams the relationship between reported offenses, true levels of offenses, response bias, and random response error using the symbols and notation of path models (Goldberger and Duncan 1973; Land 1969; Wright 1934). The elements in the figure enclosed in squares correspond to the unobserved elements of the model: true levels of offense activity (μ), response bias (β), and random response error (e). The circled element (x) corresponds to offense activity reported in the survey. The "paths" or arrows in the model correspond to the association between each unobserved factor and reported offense activity.

Overall, response errors may have three distorting effects on reported offenses. Aggregate estimates of crime, such as the average number of offenses reported by respondents, may be distorted if the average response bias is greater or less than zero. For example, estimates of total offenses committed will be artificially high if respondents uniformly overreport their involvement in crime. Similarly, estimates of total offenses will be artificially low if they underreport their involvement. The second effect involves the association between the reported and true nature of the offenses. The strength of the association, termed "validity," represents the overall accuracy of the survey measure (Lord and Novick 1968). The validity of the measure will be low if response bias is spread extensively among respondents. If respondents with long offense histories report very few offenses, for example, then the reported number of offenses will inaccurately represent the true levels of offense activity. The third effect of response

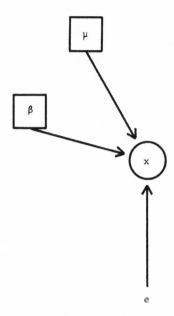

FIG. 14.1   Measurement model of self-reported crimes: x = observed response, μ = unobserved true score; β = unobserved response bias; e = random response error.

error involves the variation in responses occasioned by true scores and random errors. The proportion of variation in responses associated with true scores, termed "reliability," will be low if random response errors are extensive. Low reliability implies that measurement is imprecise. In the context of self-report surveys, it implies that no systematic pattern exists across respondents in the nature of reported offenses.

The effects of response errors on reported offenses may be estimated empirically using criterion measures of offense activity. For example, the average difference between self-reported arrests and officially recorded arrests—assuming the official measure has the same true value and no measure bias—is an accurate estimate of aggregate response bias (Bridges 1979). Estimates of the effects of response error on the validity and reliability of reported offenses may be approximated by using a statistical model with multiple measures of reported and official offenses. Such a model is diagramed in figure 14.2. The effects of response error on the validity and reliability of reported offenses may be estimated using the statistical methods developed by Jöreskog (1969, 1973).[1]

1. Methods for estimating such factors in multivariate models have developed in at least two literatures on the analysis of linear models. One method is commonly employed in econometrics to estimate the linkages or "paths" between the elements of models as well as the error variances (Duncan 1975; Goldberger and Duncan 1973). However, this method requires measures of additional variables that are uncorrelated with the errors in question and correlated with subjects' true scores. The additional variables, commonly termed "instrumental," permit analysis of the validity and reliability of measures subject to response biases and random errors.

An important property of instrumental variables is that they facilitate the estimation of statistical

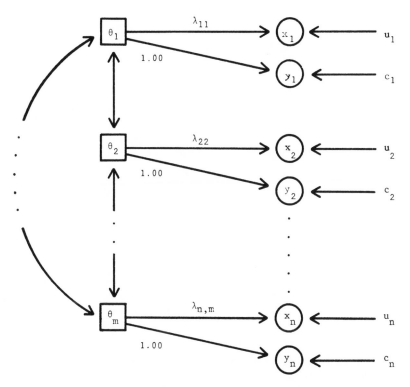

FIG. 14.2   Measurement model of self-reported and official crimes for multiple measures: θ_1, θ_2 . . . θ_m = unobserved true scores; λ_{11}, λ_{12} . . . λ_m = linear coefficients linking observed measures with true scores; x_1, x_2 . . . x_n = observed self-report and criterion measures; u_1, u_2 . . . u_n = composite random response errors and response biases; c_1, c_2 . . . c_n = errors in criterion measure.

Previous Research

Although there is little independent research on how response error affects reported levels of crime and delinquency, many self-report studies have examined aspects of the response error problem in conjunction with the analysis of reported offense activity. The studies may be organized into two areas corresponding to the types and effects of response error noted above: studies reporting

relationships between measured and unmeasured variables in multivariate models and aid in assessing variances of the unobserved variables. Accordingly, the method is useful in estimating the variation in survey responses attributed to subjects' true scores, response biases, and random response errors.

A second method for estimating the role of unobserved variables in multivariate models is found in the literature on factor analysis techniques. In general, that literature formulates responses across multiple measures as a composite of unobserved "common" factors, at least one factor that is specific to the item or variable in question, and a unique factor corresponding to random measurement or response error. Both methods—instrumental variables and factor analysis—are employed in models where there is information beyond that given in the models diagrammed in figures 14.1 and 14.2.

levels of random error and reliability, and studies reporting levels of response bias and validity.

Treatments of Random Errors and Reliability

Self-report studies commonly estimate reliability and levels of random error by comparing responses with highly correlated survey questions or by repeated administrations of the survey questionnaire.[2] Studies examining correlated survey questions about crime and delinquency have generally found that the magnitude of random error varies among the types of offenses reported in the surveys (Dentler and Monroe 1961; Erickson 1973; Farrington 1973; Hardt and Peterson-Hardt 1977; Hindelang 1971, 1972a; Hindelang and Weis 1972; Kulik, Stein, and Sarbin 1968; Nye and Short 1957; Scott 1959; Slocum and Stone 1963). Across all the studies, estimates of reliability—the proportion of variation in responses attributed to true scores—ranged from 62 percent to 96 percent (Bridges 1979). And while some researchers suggest that levels of reliability may vary systematically according to the age of respondents and the seriousness of offenses, there exists no analysis of that variation.

Studies examining repeated administrations of survey questions have found that random error occurred in relatively few responses, but the levels of random error varied significantly among respondents (Ball 1967; Belson 1968; Clark and Tifft 1966; Dentler and Monroe 1961; Farrington 1973; Kulik, Stein, and Sarbin 1968). For example, Belson (1968) and Clark and Tifft (1966) discovered that fewer than one-fifth of all responses were inconsistent between test administrations. Clark and Tifft added, however, that individual subjects could differ dramatically in reliability—where one subject reported 53 percent of his responses inconsistently, another reported just 3 percent inconsistently. None of the studies, however, established whether this variation in error was associated with the substance of items or with aspects of reported offenses.

Treatments of Response Bias and Validity

Although many techniques exist for estimating the extensiveness and effects of response bias, three general methods have been used most frequently in research on crime and delinquency. The first involves comparing the extensiveness of offenses reported by groups such as official delinquents and nondelinquents who are known to differ in levels of offense activity. This method infers the presence of response bias from the magnitude of the differences between groups. The second method involves survey response styles and the tendency of respondents to falsify responses or to respond to survey questions in a normative or acquiescent manner, estimating levels of response bias from the association between reported offenses and measures of particular response styles. Finally, a few studies have assessed bias by comparing self-reports and official records of

---

2. The object of using highly correlated survey questions or repeated administrations of the survey questionnaire is to ascertain whether respondents answer equivalent questions in the same way; inconsistent answers indicate random response error.

offenses. While some have examined how accurately respondents recalled offenses for which they were arrested or taken to court, others have looked at how accurately official criminality was predicted from reported crimes. In general, official records were used as estimates of respondents' true scores, and the differences between the official and reported offenses were taken as estimates of response error.

Studies examining the problem of bias with comparisons of reported offenses between groups of official delinquents and nondelinquents almost uniformly have observed that the former reported more offenses. As a result, the studies generally concluded that systematic bias was low and that survey responses were accurate estimates of true levels of delinquent involvement (Erickson and Empey 1963; Farrington 1973; Gould 1969; Hackler and Lautt 1969; Hardt and Peterson-Hardt 1977; Kulik, Stein, and Sarbin 1968; Williams and Gold 1972). Certainly, one consideration in evaluating this research is whether comparing reported offenses between official delinquents and nondelinquents accurately reflects the extensiveness of error. The method of comparison assumed that official delinquents actually committed more offenses than nondelinquents, but none of the studies established whether significant differences existed between the groups in delinquent behavior. Accordingly, applications of this method have provided no conclusive evidence on the extensiveness of bias.

Research examining response styles and reports of offense activity has made a greater contribution to knowledge on response bias. Nye and Short (1957) initially raised the problem of response styles in reports of crime and delinquency when they attempted to identify subjects with "overconforming" response patterns. Other studies explored the association between response styles and reported crimes more thoroughly. For example, Clark and Tifft (1966) and Farrington (1973) found that respondents' attitudes about the acceptability of delinquent behavior may influence their initial willingness or ability to discuss delinquent involvement. Wyner (1976) reached similar conclusions, finding that bias was smallest when the respondent perceived the question as one that it was desirable to answer accurately.

Although studies examining response styles have suggested that attitudes about offenses may influence reports of illegal activity, few have identified the response styles that may influence reports of different aspects of crime. Further, they have provided no uniform description of the extensiveness or nature of the influence. As a result, they have supplied relatively little evidence about the association between response bias, response styles, and the nature and extensiveness of reported offenses.

Finally, studies comparing reports of offenses with official records have suggested that levels of response bias are associated with subjects' official offense activity. Subjects with histories of many arrests and offenses uniformly have reported offenses less accurately than others (Ball 1967; Mandell and Amzell 1975; Petersilia 1977; Wyner 1976). Bias may also be associated with the seriousness of offenses for which subjects were arrested. Those with histories of arrests for serious offenses were more likely to underreport those offenses (Wyner 1976). This finding was consistent with the observation that error is associated with response styles and subjects' motivations for responding to particular types of questions regarding offense activity.

Two general issues regarding the nature and extensiveness of error require more thorough examination than previous studies have undertaken. The first is whether the magnitude of response bias and random error varies among measures of different aspects of crime. With the exception of Ball (1967), Hirschi (1969), and Petersilia (1977), studies have focused strictly on error in estimating the incidence of reported offenses. Because there are many aspects of offense activity, including recency, periodicity, and seriousness, it would be useful to examine whether levels of response error vary among those measures.

Equally important is whether variation exists in the effect response error has on the validity and reliability of self-reports of different aspects of crime. Because some aspects may be reported more accurately than others, it may be possible to identify the most accurate measures of offense activity and thereby suggest what measures may be most useful in subsequent research.

An Empirical Examination of Response Error

Because the follow-up study of the 1945 cohort collected both information on officially recorded arrests and respondents' *self-reports of their arrests,* issues of response error could be investigated with clearly specified criterion variables. The analysis compared the subjects' reported and official offense histories with respect to seven variables that were available in both the official and interview formats: total number of offenses resulting in arrest, age at first arrest, type of offense at first arrest, number of co-offenders at first arrest, age at last arrest, type of offense at last arrest, and number of co-offenders at last arrest.[3]

We estimated levels of response error using the arithmetic differences between reported offenses and official records. For purposes of the analysis, we assumed that the information obtained from the Philadelphia Police Department was subject to random measurement error.[4] As a result, the difference between the re-

---

3. Last arrest refers to the last arrest reported by the sample subjects during the interview at age 26. Official arrests occurring after age 26 were excluded from the analysis. The variable level of victimization (or type of offense) reflects the nature of the victim-offender relationship. The variable is scaled in the following manner: (0) no victims—juvenile status offenses; (1) mutual victims— adultery, statutory rape, and so on; (2) community victims/commercial victims—offenses against the public order or private business; and (3) personal victims—offenses against individuals.

4. A serious methodological criticism of measures of arrest that appears throughout the research and writing in criminology is that the incidence and types of crimes recorded officially reflect only the policies and screening practices of law enforcement agencies. Many writers argue that the volume of these offenses—particularly those attributed to juveniles—and the individual offenders and groups that are apprehended by the police evolve from law enforcement practices that are influenced in part by the demeanor and appearance of complainants and subjects as well as by the law enforcement and arrest policies of police departments. Bridges (1979) discussed the justification and implications of this assumption at length.

ported and official measures of arrests was a distorted estimate of response error, but the average of those differences across all respondents was an accurate estimate of aggregate response bias (Bridges 1979). By analyzing the effects of response error on the validity and reliability of reported offenses, we examined the variation among responses across all seven measures and estimated the variation in reported offenses associated with true scores and the association between reported and true levels of offense activity. We assessed the validity and reliability of each of the seven offense measures using the statistical techniques developed by Lawley and Maxwell (1963) and advanced by Jöreskog (1969, 1973).

The analysis of reported and official offenses indicated that respondents uniformly overstated the number of offenses resulting in arrest, their ages at the time of offenses, the seriousness of offenses, and the number of others arrested. Table 14.1 shows the mean levels and types of offense activity and indicates, for example, that while the average reported age at the initial offense was approximately 16.5, the average age reported for that offense in official records was 15.5. Perhaps most striking among the differences is that respondents reported one and a half times the officially recorded number of others arrested in the most recent offense.

Table 14.2 presents aggregate estimates of response bias ("raw bias") for each of the seven measures of offense activity. In absolute terms, reports of the most recent offenses resulting in arrest were most biased. Moreover, response bias in five of the seven measures was significantly greater than zero. To account for differences in bias resulting from the different values of each factor, we nor-

TABLE 14.1   Mean Levels of Reported and Official Offenses Resulting in Arrests

Measure	Reported	Official
First arrested offense		
Age	16.482	15.525
	(218)[a]	(198)
Level of victimization	2.592	2.518
	(218)	(85)
Number of others arrested	2.675	2.224
	(151)	(88)
Last arrested offense		
Age	20.278	19.542
	(126)	(120)
Level of victimization	2.278	1.852
	(128)	(81)
Number of others arrested	2.926	1.160
	(81)	(81)
Number of arrested offenses	1.373	1.279
	(558)	(566)

[a] Numbers in parentheses represent the number of observations on the variable in question.

TABLE 14.2   Aggregate Estimates of Raw and Normalized Response Bias in Reports of Arrests

Measure	Raw Bias	Normalized Bias
First arrest		
Age	616[†]	.185
	(151)[a]	
Level of victimization	.203	.134
	(69)	
Number of others arrested	.041	.015
	(49)	
Last arrest		
Age	.579*	.215
	(76)	
Level of victimization	1.070**	.740
	(74)	
Number of others arrested	1.094**	1.419
	(32)	
Number of arrests	.206*	.079
	(558)	

[a] Numbers in parentheses represent the number of observations on the variable in question.
*$p < .05$.
[†]$p < .025$.
**$p < .01$.

malized the estimates,[5] thus controlling for differences in variation between measures and providing comparable estimates of aggregate bias across measures. Analysis of normalized estimates indicated that they were proportional to the raw estimates and had a similar ordering with respect to size. Overall, aggregate response biases were positive, and the most biased of the self-report measures was the number of others arrested in the most recent offense. While levels of bias differed substantially among the measures of offense activity, bias in reports of recent offenses was generally greater than bias in reports of initial offenses.

To examine the variation in error among respondents, the study analyzed the association between aggregate estimates of bias and the respondents' true scores across all seven measures (see table 14.3). In general, bias was large and positive for low levels of each official measure and large and negative for high levels of the official measures. Thus response bias at the aggregate level was inversely related to the subjects' true scores. The significance of this finding is that aggregate response bias seemed to result from overreporting by subjects with the lowest true scores. Those with fewer arrests, earlier ages at first and last arrests, less serious offenses, and fewer co-offenders inflated their responses more than others. This does not necessarily imply that those having more arrests and official contacts with the police reported with any less bias. Indeed, those with the great-

5. Each estimate was divided by the standard deviation of the distribution of differences it was derived from.

TABLE 14.3   Aggregate Estimates of Raw and Normalized Response Bias in Reported Offenses by Official Offenses

Measure	First Arrest	Last Arrest
Age		
13	2.775***	
	(1.092)[a]	
14–15	1.500***	
	(.495)	
16–17	1.520	
	(.062)	
18+	−2.400	
	(−.789)	
17		2.047***
		(.761)
18–21		.808
		(.250)
22+		.689***
		(−.427)
Level of victimization		
0–1	1.909***	2.160***
	(2.200)	(5.790)
2–3	.200*	.000
	(.487)	(—)[b]
4–5	−.986***	−.353
	(−1.002)	(−.689)
Number of others arrested		
0	2.846***	2.350
	(1.745)	(.993)
1+	−1.055***	−1.00
	(−.566)	(−1.35)
Number of arrests		
0		.490***
		(.395)
1		.375***
		(.196)
2+		−.778***
		(−.159)

[a] Normalized estimates of response bias are in parentheses.
[b] The standard deviation of this distribution of errors is zero.
*$p < .05$.
***$p < .001$.

TABLE 14.4   Observed Zero-Order Correlations among Reported and Official Measures of Arrests

Variable[a]	Reported							Official						
	A1	V1	NO1	AL	VL	NOL	NA	A1	V1	NO1	AL	VL	NOL	NA
Reported														
A1	1.000													
V1	.109	1.000												
NO1	-.299	-.117	1.000											
AL	.279	-.086	-.120	1.000										
VL	-.364	-.004	.022	.180	1.000									
NOL	.079	-.123	.227	-.139	-.239	1.000								
NA	.348	.051	.133	.409	.225	-.156	1.000							
Official														
A1	.457	.052	-.030	.145	.015	.131	-.101	1.000						
V1	-.259	.038	-.112	-.505	.263	-.132	-.023	-.561	1.000					
NO1	-.332	.009	.431	-.494	-.002	-.169	-.032	-.518	.483	1.000				
AL	.161	.048	.005	.641	.065	-.216	.378	.298	-.286	-.205	1.000			
VL	-.036	.116	-.196	.136	.470	-.219	.139	-.135	.161	-.106	-.028	1.000		
NOL	-.058	-.009	-.144	-.053	.190	.109	-.009	-.152	.296	.034	-.262	.677	1.000	
NA	-.173	-.068	-.019	.282	.160	-.112	.603	-.327	.268	.203	.412	.287	.214	1.000

[a]The abbreviations used here are explained in figure 14.3.

$$x_{11} = \lambda_{11} \text{ (NA)} \qquad\qquad\qquad\qquad\qquad\qquad\qquad\qquad + u_{11}$$
$$x_{12} = 1.0 \text{ (NA)} \qquad\qquad\qquad\qquad\qquad\qquad\qquad\qquad\quad + u_{12}$$
$$x_{21} = \qquad\quad \lambda_{21} \text{ (A1)} \qquad\qquad\qquad\qquad\qquad\qquad\qquad + u_{21}$$
$$x_{22} = \qquad\quad 1.0 \text{ (A1)} \qquad\qquad\qquad\qquad\qquad\qquad\qquad + u_{22}$$
$$x_{31} = \qquad\qquad\qquad \lambda_{31} \text{ (V1)} \qquad\qquad\qquad\qquad\qquad\quad + u_{31}$$
$$x_{32} = \qquad\qquad\qquad 1.0 \text{ (V1)} \qquad\qquad\qquad\qquad\qquad\quad + u_{32}$$
$$x_{41} = \qquad\qquad\qquad\qquad \lambda_{41} \text{ (NO1)} \qquad\qquad\qquad\qquad + u_{41}$$
$$x_{42} = \qquad\qquad\qquad\qquad 1.0 \text{ (NO1)} \qquad\qquad\qquad\qquad + u_{42}$$
$$x_{51} = \qquad\qquad\qquad\qquad\qquad \lambda_{51} \text{ (AL)} \qquad\qquad\qquad + u_{51}$$
$$x_{52} = \qquad\qquad\qquad\qquad\qquad 1.0 \text{ (AL)} \qquad\qquad\qquad + u_{52}$$
$$x_{61} = \qquad\qquad\qquad\qquad\qquad\qquad \lambda_{61} \text{ (VL)} \qquad\quad + u_{61}$$
$$x_{62} = \qquad\qquad\qquad\qquad\qquad\qquad 1.0 \text{ (VL)} \qquad\quad + u_{62}$$
$$x_{71} = \qquad\qquad\qquad\qquad\qquad\qquad\qquad \lambda_{71} \text{ (NOL)} + u_{71}$$
$$x_{72} = \qquad\qquad\qquad\qquad\qquad\qquad\qquad 1.0 \text{ (NOL)} + u_{72}$$

FIG. 14.3   Algebraic specification of a general measurement model for reported and official offenses resulting in arrests: NA = true number of arrests; A1 = true age at first arrest; V1 = true level of victimization at first arrest; NO1 = true number of others arrested at first arrest; AL = true age at last arrest; VL = true level of victimization at last arrest; NOL = true number of others arrested at last arrest.

est offense activity underreported their offense histories with equally large biases. However, they represented a smaller proportion of the total sample than those who overreported and thereby contributed less to the aggregate levels of bias reported in tables 14.1 and 14.2.

The effects of response bias and random response error on the validity and reliability of the reports of offenses were estimated with the general measurement model diagramed in figure 14.2. The algebraic specification of the model is presented in figure 14.3. The estimation employs the correlations among the reported and official measures of offenses presented in table 14.4. As noted above, Jöreskog's (1973) method for analyzing statistical models with unmeasured variables let us estimate the associations between survey responses, true scores, and response errors.

Initial estimates of the reliability and validity of responses and thus the systematic effects of response error on reported offenses are exhibited in table 14.5. The estimates indicate that the proportion of variation in responses occasioned by random errors and response bias was large. Across all measures, no reliability coefficient exceeded .6, and only one was above .5. Clearly, reports of the time of the most recent offense had the highest reliability, while reports of the type of the initial offense had the lowest. Further, reports of most recent offenses were more reliable on two of the three measures of offense activity than were reports of initial offenses.

As noted above, the validity coefficients measured the association between the subjects' responses and their true scores. Table 14.5 indicates that the respondents reported ages at the most recent offense with the greatest accuracy. Since

Chapter Fourteen

many previous studies estimated the validity of reported offenses using direct correlations of reported and official offense activity, it is also instructive to examine how the measures of validity in table 14.5 differed from the direct correlations of reported and official offenses. Table 14.6 exhibits both sets of estimates and reveals significant discrepancies. The estimates "corrected" for the effects of response error and error in measures of official offenses were systematically lower than the direct correlations, and with the exception of age at the most recent offense, the corrected coefficients were roughly one-half the uncorrected co-

TABLE 14.5 Variances, Reliabilities, and Validities in Reports of Arrests

	Relative Slope $\lambda_{\chi,\mu}$	True Score Variance σ_μ^2	Error Variance σ_ε^2	Reliability Coefficient $\sigma_\varepsilon^2 \sigma_\chi^2$	Validity Coefficient $\rho_{\chi,\mu}$	Correlation of Error with True Scores $\rho_{\varepsilon,\mu}$
NA						
x_{11}	.604 (.04)[b]	1.000	.666 (.04)	.334	.323	−.031
x_{12}	1.000					
A1						
x_{21}	.564 (.04)	1.000	.768 (.05)	.232	.185	−.087
x_{22}	1.000					
V1						
x_{31}	.070 (.03)	1.000	.999 (.06)	.010	−.024	−.027
x_{32}	1.000					
NO1						
x_{41}	.349 (.04)	1.000	.855 (.04)	.145	.219	.086
x_{42}	1.000					
AL						
x_{51}	.678 (.04)	1.000	.483 (.04)	.517	.529	.060
x_{52}	1.000					
VL						
x_{61}	.437 (.04)	1.000	.792 (.04)	.208	.214	.016
x_{62}	1.000					
NOL						
x_{71}	−.207 (.04)	1.000	.951 (.06)	.049	−.059	−.014
x_{72}	1.000					

[a]The abbreviations used here are explained in figure 14.3.
[b]The numbers in parentheses represent standard errors of the estimates in question.

192

TABLE 14.6   Uncorrected and Corrected Validity Coefficients for Reports of Arrests

Variable	Uncorrected Coefficient	Corrected Coefficient
First arrest		
Age	.457	.246
Level of victimization	.038	−.024
Number of others arrested	.431	.212
Last arrest		
Age	.641	.529
Level of victimization	.471	.214
Number of others arrested	−.109	−.059
Number of arrests	.603	.323

efficients. Thus the relationship between reported and true levels of offense activity was not as strong as the direct correlations indicated.

In sum, response errors substantially distorted self-report measures of the incidence and nature of offenses. Most survey respondents overreported descriptions and thereby distorted aggregate measures of offense activity. Over the entire sample, responses about recent offenses were slightly more biased than responses about initial offenses. This finding does not necessarily imply that respondents reported temporally distant events with less bias than recent events. The finding may be in part an artifact of the relatively low number of respondents with multiple offense histories.[6]

Overall, the validity and reliability of the self-report measures were low. This finding implies that error in individual responses may substantially distort statistical relationships between self-report measures of offenses and other factors. Accordingly, the error may threaten the validity of inferences drawn from self-report surveys about the distribution of offenses in the general population.

Conclusion

The findings suggest that a thorough reexamination of the results of self-report studies is necessary, and they open to question the bases of empirical support. They also have implications for the direction of future research. Self-report studies of crime must examine more carefully the effects of errors on aggregate levels of reported offenses and on statistical relationships between predictors of crime and measures of offense activity. Experimental controls on errors incorporated into survey designs would help identify the effects.

Although the levels and effects of response error varied substantially among

---

6. We might expect that more recent events would be less difficult to recall than distant events and that responses on recent events would be less biased. Once we isolate subjects with multiple arrests, however, this relationship diminishes. For these subjects the differences in absolute normalized bias between responses on their first arrests were not dramatic and varied in magnitude from item to item.

aspects of offense activity, the sample respondents did not report any single aspect very accurately. To describe patterns and trends in offenses more accurately, future research should employ multiple indicators and measures of criminal behavior in the population.

Finally, there should be more extensive research on the links between concepts and measures of offense activity. Research should identify the problems of error in different measures of crime and ascertain how error affects empirical explanations of criminal behavior. Also, formal theories of crime should include "auxiliary theories" linking concepts to measures, thereby ensuring that empirical tests of theories assist our understanding of criminality and delinquency.

15   Summary and Conclusion

The 9,945 subjects of the 1945 Philadelphia birth cohort study were stratified into socioeconomic groupings based on Philadelphia residential census tracts. Of this population, a random sample of 975 subjects was chosen from educational and income groupings used to further develop the stratification scheme based on the SES classifications of the census tracts. As a result, this sample satisfactorily represented the entire birth cohort. The data for the study were derived from two sources: official police records and subject interviews. Official data collection occurred in two stages—at cohort ages 26 and 30, both utilizing Philadelphia Police Department records supplemented by FBI "rap sheets." The interview process was initiated through a variety of search and tracing procedures and yielded 567 responses (58.2 percent). Our inability to locate subjects, owing chiefly to age and mobility factors, accounted for 40.5 percent of the 408 noncompleted interviews, while subject and family refusals accounted for 24.7 percent.

Thus in *From Boy to Man, from Delinquency to Crime* we have traced the delinquent and criminal careers of the 1945 Philadelphia birth cohort until the members of that cohort were age 30, by which time very few were still active offenders and the age-specific rate of offensivity was rapidly approaching zero. For all practical purposes, this study has described the total criminal careers of the cohort members.

Of the 975-member sample, 47 percent had had an officially recorded arrest by age 30. As we found in *Delinquency in a Birth Cohort*, nonwhite and lower SES groups were more likely to be offenders. To examine the relationship of demographic background factors to offense type and seriousness, we classified the offenders into three groups: juvenile offenders, adult offenders, and persistent offenders whose offense histories extended over both periods. The offense careers of nonwhites were more likely to persist over both juvenile and adult years, whereas whites were more likely to finish their criminal behavior during the juvenile years.

Thus the prevalence of delinquent and criminal behavior in this cohort was 47 percent: nearly half the males were arrested at least once by age 30. Of these, 37 percent were arrested only during the juvenile years (here defined as before age 18), 24 percent were arrested only as adults, and 39 percent, classified as persistent offenders, were arrested both before and after age 18. The average number of offenses per offender was somewhat over two for both the juvenile and adult years and almost nine across both periods for the persistent violators, and the severity of the offenses placed adults (368.4) ahead of both juvenile (94.4) and persistent offenders (281.1). Analysis of persistent offenders by both juvenile and adult offenses yielded mean seriousness scores of 124 and 409, respectively. For noninjury offenses the average seriousness score was higher for persistent offenders, increasing by 4.3 percent, and the increment was 37.9 percent for injury offenses.

Persistent offenders were more likely to be drawn from socially disadvantaged groups and to demonstrate more extensive and serious offense careers. In fact, the social correlates of the follow-up sample's criminal involvement were similar to those observed in our earlier study of this group. Both race and socioeconomic status were significantly related to one's being listed in official records as an offender. By age 30, 70 percent of the nonwhites and 60 percent of the lower SES subjects, but only 38 percent of the whites and 36 percent of the higher SES subjects, had been arrested.

In accounting for adult criminality, however, the subject's delinquency status was even more important than these demographic characteristics. The data exhibited a strong concordance between the juvenile and adult years. Of the nondelinquents, 82 percent remained nonoffenders, and only 18 percent became offenders—3 percent of whom were classified as chronic—during the adult period. On the other hand, those juvenile offenders with extensive delinquency records were more likely to have extensive adult records. Indeed, 45 percent of the juvenile chronic offenders were also classified as chronic offenders during the adult years, though 22 percent of this group were not charged with any offenses during their adult years. When race and SES were held constant, juvenile delinquency status was the best predictor of adult criminality. The standardized regression coefficients produced when regressing the frequency of adult arrests on the frequency of juvenile arrest, race, and SES for offenders only indicated that juvenile arrests (.29) and race (.19) were the most significant variables accounting for adult arrests. Adult offense severity regressions for offenders only also indicated that seriousness of juvenile offenses (.29) and race (.19) were again the most significant variables. SES was not statistically significant in either model.

Even though there was consistency between juvenile status and adult status, the rate of desistance from criminal involvement during the adult years was high. The modal age for delinquency was 16, and following that peak the data reflected a sharp decline in criminal involvement. For example, whereas 12.0 percent of all offenses were committed by 16-year-olds, only 5.5 percent of the offenses were committed by 20-year-olds. However, the sharp peak in criminal behavior observed in the seventeenth year was not due to a small number of offenders who were exceedingly active in that period. Indeed, the aggregate mean number of offenses per year was remarkably constant during the entire study period, varying only from 1.2 to 1.8 arrests per year. Thus the rise in offensivity evident during these teenage years was due to an increasing number of offenders, each of whom tended to commit an "average" number of offenses in addition to the ongoing activity of the chronic violators. Thus, following the sharp drop in onset after age 16 there was a fairly steady decline from age 18 to age 22, with few subjects entering the criminal population after age 22. The relationship of age at onset to number of arrests indicated that the earlier an offender began his career, the more offenses he would commit. Those beginning careers at age 11 or 12 produced the highest average number of arrests per offender (ten) for any onset category. Analysis of age distribution of the sample indicated that 42.6 percent of all offenses were committed between ages 15 and 19; the average number of offenses committed at each age declined mildly with age after the mid-teens. However, seriousness of offense did not correspond to the modal age of onset and offense commission. For both index and nonindex crimes, the increase in offense seriousness corresponded to an increase in the offender's age for both whites and nonwhites; and at all ages the offense seriousness of nonwhites was slightly higher than that of whites.

While many consistencies were observed between the adult and juvenile periods, extending the observation period to age 30 also uncovered a number of important changes. Although adult offenses were significantly more serious than those committed by juveniles and the most serious offenses were committed by the persistent offenders during their adult years, these adult offenses tended to increase in seriousness as the adult careers developed. Unlike juvenile offenses, which did not become significantly more serious as the number of offenses increased, adult offenses, especially those involving injury, did become more harmful.

Even though juvenile and adult careers differed in the escalation of offense severity, the types of offenses charged to these two groups displayed considerable consistency. Thus the distributions of the types of offenses committed were very similar for the two time periods. Regardless of juvenile or adult status, most offenses were likely to be nonindex, followed by theft, injury, combinations of index offenses, and finally, damage offenses. Most important, during both the juvenile and the adult years, the offense careers could be modeled by a first-order Markov chain. Regardless of the type of offenses included in the analysis or the subgroup of offenders (juvenile, adult, or persistent offenders), the results indicated that the probability of committing a particular type of offense was dependent only upon the type of immediately preceding offense, not the person's offense history. As was the case during the juvenile years, there was little evidence of offense specialization during the adult years. Thus one of the most intriguing findings of *Delinquency in a Birth Cohort,* that offense careers can be modeled by a simple Markov process, was replicated when the analysis was extended to age 30. This finding obtained for juvenile offenses only, adult offenses only, and combined offenses that cut across the boundary of juvenile-adult status.

Our earlier findings in *Delinquency in a Birth Cohort* indicated that desistance probabilities (that is, the probability of not receiving another official recording of an offense) were replicated using survival-analysis techniques. The range of median survival times indicated a decrease in the percentage of offenders recidivating from the first to the third transition, while later transitions displayed uniformly similar percentages of recidivating. Estimation of the hazard rate indicated that the longer an individual was able to survive without committing an offense, the better were his chances of desisting from future criminal behavior. The hazard rates, the conditional proportion recidivating, and the cumulative proportions desisting all suggest that intervention programs should be focused on the first six months after an arrest, especially for the third through sixth arrests, since it is in this period that the heaviest concentration of delinquency exists.

To assess the reaction of the criminal justice system to criminal behavior, we reconstructed offense histories from arrest through release from prison using various sources, including Philadelphia police, court, and prison records. The dispositional outcomes of adult arrests were found to depend upon offense type and seriousness, quality of evidence, and individual arrest histories as well as two nonlegal factors—race and age.

It appears that individual decision-making criteria are more likely than formalized rules and processes to include racially discriminatory components. Thus, controlling for offense type and for prior record, the data indicated that early in the adjudication process, and also at the sentencing stage, whites fared better than nonwhites, who were more likely to be remanded for court action and to be incarcerated after conviction. The data did not indicate significant differences between the races at the court stage of adjudication: racial discrimination was more likely to occur in those parts of the system where visibility and formal rules were less apparent.

Further, to partially control offense seriousness, disposition of arrests was addressed by age for index offenses only. The probabilities of conviction and of incarceration given conviction were higher during the adult years than during the juvenile years, the highest rates being associated with the period between ages 18 and 21. While conviction and incarceration probabilities did not differ significantly for one-time and recidivist offenders, significantly more index arrests resulted in conviction (50 percent), indicating that the adjudication and incarceration processes for chronic offenders functioned from a *crime-control* rather than a legalistic perspective.

Delinquency in a Birth Cohort was based entirely on official records, and that portion of the follow-up study summarized up to now also concentrated on officially recorded behavior. In order to collect different, complementary data on the criminal careers of the subjects, we interviewed sample members as part of the follow-up study.

During the interviews subjects provided self-reports on their criminal involvement during both the juvenile and the adult years. As is often the case with comparisons between official and self-reported data, results from this study were somewhat confusing. For example, race and socioeconomic status were not significantly related to the frequency of self-reported delinquency; yet these characteristics were among the best predictors of the frequency of arrests. Based on these results, we would question the validity of one, if not both, of these measures. Yet other analyses yielded more consistent results. Race has been shown here to be significantly related to the seriousness of self-reported juvenile offenses; and Thornberry and Farnworth (1982) have noted that self-reported and official data on adult crime produce similar findings with respect to class and race when an effort is made to align the domains of criminality tapped by the alternative measures. Even though the official and self-reported data collected in the follow-up study did not always agree with one another, they did not present entirely contradictory pictures of criminal involvement.

This study examined potential race and SES differences in the seriousness of self-reported offenses and used the official dimension of delinquency to examine self-report offense data in context. No significant differences by race or SES were indicated on a global measure of self-reported delinquency. However, examination of the seriousness of self-reported offenses repeatedly indicated that race was a significant factor. In that sense the results reported in chapter 10 did not indicate discrepancies between official and self-reported offense measures. Nonwhites were significantly more likely to be delinquent overall and at each SES level and to be arrested, since they reported an appreciably higher number of violent and serious offenses. The data investigating the relationship between official delinquency status and self-reported measures indicated that the number of self-reported delinquent acts committed by officially recorded delinquents was significantly greater than the number reported by those sample members not labeled delinquent. These findings obtained across both race and SES levels. Nonetheless, even though delinquents reported a higher incidence of hidden delinquency than did official nondelinquents, high frequency or seriousness of offending was no guarantee of arrest status.

Official statistics underestimated the extent of delinquency. Official police data also indicated higher arrest rates for nonwhites, though indications of consistently higher levels of hidden delinquency were not found for this group, who reported higher levels of crimes against the person but lower rates of other offenses.

Thus the lack of validation checks for hidden delinquency and the difficulty of soliciting sensitive data hindered the resolution of the data validity issue as it pertained to the self-report versus official source question. This study indicates that multiple measures of delinquency should be obtained whenever possible and that the interpretation of single measures should be tempered by a realization of the inherent limitations of each type of data source.

The follow-up interviews also provided information about changes in social characteristics, life circumstances, and attitudes that the cohort sample reported experiencing as they matured. One purpose of collecting this information was to see if we could explain the desistance from criminal involvement observed in early adulthood. Results of this analysis were rather disappointing, however. Some life events—marriage, completing high school, and receiving vocational training in the military—were related to reduced criminal involvement. Other life transitions that theoretically should be related to desistance—for example, fatherhood, military service, extensive vocational training, and attendance at college—were not.

Boys who joined a gang were more delinquent than those who did not: those who belonged to a gang persisted in delinquent behavior almost three years longer than those who never joined. Although the time-series analyses indicated a higher probability of becoming an offender for gang members, the data did not support the hypothesis of a decrease in seriousness of offenses for nonwhite offenders after dissociation from a gang.

Overall, these data failed to provide a clear understanding of the extensive maturational reform that occurs in the late teens and early twenties. However, the examination of situational aspects and the issue of planning of criminal activities have important implications for crime-prevention policies. Evidence from previous studies has indicated that criminal behavior, especially juvenile delinquency, is not typified by extensive planning. In questioning 567 subjects directly on the amount of planning and indirectly on their motivations for committing crime, we found that only 17 percent devoted any time to planning their first offense, and only 21 percent of the sample of offenders devoted any time to planning their last offense, demonstrating that, in general, impulsivity characterized criminal behavior in all age groups. Impulsive offenses may result in criminal behavior of minimal or utmost seriousness, but planned crimes are not necessarily more serious. These findings suggest that the consequences of criminal behavior should be considered to a greater extent than intent or degree of planning in determining the punishment commensurate with the crime.

Crime and delinquency measures were more strongly related to being victimized than were social background measures. Although race contributed substantially to much of the observed relationship, the sample population seemed to have a life-style in which victimization was a common event for those committing crimes. In addition, for greater specificity, victimization variables were collapsed into five general categories: simple assault, aggravated assault, robbery, theft, and burglary. Three measures of social background were considered— SES, marital status, and employment status—to examine the relation between background characteristics and the probability of victimization. There appeared to be a modest relationship between social status and victimization, controlling for race. Married persons had a lower probability of being victims, while unemployed persons, as expected, experienced high victimization rates, with violence and theft being the most statistically significant. For both races, gang membership seemed to increase the likelihood of becoming a victim of violent offenses, though not of property offenses.

In general, then, the vast majority of offenses were rather spontaneous events and were not carefully planned; gang membership was strongly related to both the frequency and the seriousness of criminal involvement; and finally, being a victim of a crime was associated with higher rates of criminal involvement. Combined with the Markovian nature of the offense careers, these findings paint a rather interesting image of the offenders, especially the chronic, persistent offenders. They did not specialize and tended to commit a wide variety of acts over time. The interview data suggested that the offenders committed their offenses in a rather spontaneous, unplanned fashion, with the support of others, especially if they were gang members, and that they also often found themselves on the other side of the gun, in the role of victim. Their world appears to be characterized by almost random involvement in criminality, moving from one type of offense to another, without plan or design, being predator one day, prey the next. The extensiveness and randomness of the criminal activity suggest that it is a difficult world in which to intervene; however, we shall offer a few concluding remarks.

This is a descriptive study whose purpose was to estimate parameters for a variety of delinquency, criminality, and social background variables. It is neither an experimental study nor an attempt to test theories. To the extent that these data offer scholars, practitioners, and policymakers information useful for their various enterprises, it may be said that the work has served its purpose.

Nevertheless, we feel that certain policy-relevant implications can be seen in these data. The number of active offenders, not the offender rate alone, explained the disproportionate involvement of juveniles and young adults among the offender population, though more serious offenses were more likely to be committed during the adult years. Chronic offenders accounted for 74 percent of all arrests and 82 percent of all index arrests, although they represented only 15 percent of the total sample and 32 percent of the official offenders. By age 30 these chronic offenders averaged more than eleven total arrests and more than four index arrests each. Nonwhites were disproportionately more likely to be arrested and were responsible for a disporportionate number of arrests. Arrests for nonwhites were for more serious offenses as measured by proportion of arrests and by offense seriousness scores.

We must intervene to prevent and control the behavior of this group of societal predators. But we must also address the causative factors that produce such criminally troublesome population subgroups.

The probability of recidivism would be reduced, especially after the third offense, if some form of effective intervention was implemented rapidly (within six months of the event).

Delinquents who begin early tend to accumulate a lengthy career that carries over into the adult years. Further, these adult offenders tend to commit more serious crimes with repetition.

Thus societal resources for the criminal justice system should be concentrated on crime prevention during the juvenile years and most probably on crime control during the adult years. Of course the data are complex, and the offender type mix of chronic, serious and nonserious, and age characteristics argues against simplification. Nevertheless the data presented in this study do suggest that serious, violent criminality develops with age, and certain intervention points may be inferred from the data distributions.

For the prevention of juvenile delinquency we must emphasize the need for research into the causes of such behavior in contemporary society while we, by necessity, protect ourselves from the serious repeat offender through various control strategies.

These arrest data and the self-report data discussed earlier represent a profound theoretical and applied challenge to researchers and practitioners. Recent work and our continued studies strongly suggest that multidisciplinary, long-term, developmental studies must be carried further both theoretically and meth-odologically. But even beyond this orientation, a judgmental and critical analysis of our society and the ways its criminogenic forces operate must be examined as part of our exploration into the causes of early and sustained delinquency and criminality.

The work reported here is now being replicated with a large sample from a cohort of Philadelphia males and females born in 1958. Findings are now being developed from the interviews of that larger sample and will address in greater detail many of the issues raised by this research.

References

Akers, Ronald L. 1964. Socio-economic status and delinquent behavior: A retest. *Journal of Research in Crime and Delinquency* 1:38–46.

Alexander, Franz, and Hugo Staub. 1956. *The criminal, the judge and the public.* Glencoe, Ill.: Free Press.

Alissi, Albert S. 1970. Delinquent subcultures in neighborhood settings: A social system perspective. *Journal of Research in Crime and Delinquency* 7:46–57.

Amir, Menachem. 1971. *Patterns in forcible rape.* Chicago: University of Chicago Press.

Andrews, F. M., J. N. Morgan, J. A. Sonquist, and L. Klem. 1973. *Multiple classification analysis.* 2d ed. Ann Arbor: Institute for Social Research, University of Michigan.

Arnold, William R. 1966. Continuities in research: Scaling delinquent behavior. *Social Problems* 13:59–66.

Asch, Solomon E. 1955. Opinions and social pressure. *Scientific American* 193:31–35.

Bachman, Jerold G., Swayzer Green, and Ilona D. Wirtanen. 1977. *Dropping out—problem or symptom?* Youth in Transition, vol. 3. Ann Arbor: Institute for Social Research, University of Michigan.

Bachman, Jerold G., Patrick M. O'Malley, and Jerome Johnston. 1978. *Adolescence to adulthood: Change and stability in the lives of young men.* Youth in Transition, vol. 6. Ann Arbor: Institute for Social Research, University of Michigan.

Ball, John C. 1967. The reliability and validity of interview data obtained from fifty-nine narcotic drug addicts. *American Journal of Sociology* 72:650–54.

Belson, William A. 1968. The extent of stealing by London boys and some of its origins. *Advancement of Science* 25:171–84.

Biderman, Albert D. 1972. Notes on prevalence and incidence. Bureau of Social Science Research, Washington, D.C.

Biderman, Albert D., and Albert J. Reiss. 1967. On exploring the dark figure of crime. *Annals* 374:1–15.

Bishop, Joel P. 1856–58. *Commentaries on the criminal law.* Boston: Little, Brown.

Blankenburg, Erhard, and Johannes Feest. 1977. On the probability of a bank robber being sanctioned—inferring from known to unknown offenders: A secondary analysis of bank robbery data. *International Journal of Criminology and Penology* 5:113–27.

Bloch, Herbert A., and Arthur Neiderhoffer. 1958. *The gang: A study in adolescent behavior.* New York: Philosophical Library.

Blumstein, Alfred, and Jacqueline Cohen. 1979. Estimation of individual crime rates from arrest records. *Journal of Criminal Law and Criminology* 70:561–85.

Blumstein, Alfred, Jacqueline Cohen, and Daniel Nagin, eds. 1978. *Deterrence and incapacitation: Estimating the effects of criminal sanctions on crime rates.* Washington, D.C.: National Academy of Sciences.

Blumstein, Alfred, and Soumyo Moitra. 1980. The identification of "career criminals" from "chronic offenders" in a cohort. *Law and Policy Quarterly* 2:321–34.

Bogardus, E. S. 1943. Gangs of Mexican-American youth. *Sociology and Social Research* 28:55–66.

Boggs, Sarah L. 1965. Urban crime patterns. *American Sociological Review* 30:899–908.

Boland, Barbara, and James Q. Wilson, Jr. 1978. Age, crime, and punishment. *Public Interest* 51:22–34.

Bordua, David J. 1961. Delinquent subcultures: Sociological interpretations of gang delinquency. *Annals* 338:119–36.

———. 1962. Some comments on theories of group delinquency. *Sociological Inquiry* 32:245–60.

Braithwaite, John. 1981. The myth of social class and criminality reconsidered. *American Sociological Review* 46:36–57.

Briar, Scott, and Irving Piliavin. 1965. Delinquency, situational inducements and commitment to conformity. *Social Problems* 13:35–45.

Bridges, George S. 1979. Levels and effects of response error in self-reports of crime and delinquency. Ph.D. diss., University of Pennsylvania.

Cameron, Mary Owen. 1964. *The booster and the snitch.* New York: Free Press.

Cardarelli, Albert P. 1973. Socio-economic status and delinquency and adult criminality in a birth cohort. Ph.D. diss., University of Pennsylvania.

Cartwright, Desmond S., and Kenneth I. Howard. 1966. Multivariate analysis of gang delinquency: I. Ecologic influences. *Multivariate Behavioral Research* 1:321–71.

Cartwright, Desmond S., Kenneth I. Howard, and Nicholas A. Reuterman. 1970. Multivariate analysis of gang delinquency: II. Structural and dynamic properties of gangs. *Multivariate Behavioral Research* 5:303–23.

———. 1971. Multivariate analysis of gang delinquency: III. Age and physique of gangs and clubs. *Multivariate Behavioral Research* 6:75–90.

Cartwright, Desmond S., Barbara Tomson, and Hershel Schwartz, eds. 1975. *Gang delinquency.* Monterey, Calif.: Brooks-Cole.

Cartwright, Dorwin. 1959. Lewinian theory as a contemporary systematic framework. In *Psychology: A study of science,* ed. Sigmund Koch, 2:7–91. New York: McGraw-Hill.

Chambliss, William J. 1967. Type of deviance and the effectiveness of legal sanctions. *Wisconsin Law Review* 67:703–19.

Chambliss, William J., and Richard H. Nagasawa. 1969. On the validity of official statistics: A comparative study of white, black, and Japanese high school boys. *Journal of Research in Crime and Delinquency* 6:71–77.

Chelimsky, Eleanor, and Judith Dahmann. 1980. *Final report of the Career Criminal Program national evaluation: Case studies of four jurisdictions.* McLean, Va.: MITRE.

Clark, John P., and Larry L. Tifft. 1966. Polygraph and interview validation of self-reported deviant behavior. *American Sociological Review* 31:516–23.

Clark, John P., and Eugene P. Wenninger. 1962. Socio-economic class and area as correlates of illegal behavior among juveniles. *American Sociological Review* 27:826–34.

Cloward, Richard A., and Lloyd E. Ohlin. 1960. *Delinquency and opportunity.* New York: Free Press.

Cochran, William G. 1963. *Sampling techniques.* 2d ed. New York: Wiley.

Cohen, Albert K. 1955. *Delinquent boys: The culture of the gang.* Glencoe, Ill.: Free Press.

———. 1966. *Deviance and control.* Englewood Cliffs, N.J.: Prentice-Hall.

Cohen, Albert K., and James F. Short, Jr. 1958. Research in delinquent subcultures. *Journal of Social Issues* 14:20–37.

Cohen, Bernard. 1969. The delinquency of gangs and spontaneous groups. In *Delinquency: Selected studies,* ed. Thorsten Sellin and Marvin E. Wolfgang, 61–111. New York: Wiley.

Collins, James J., Jr. 1981. Crime control by incapacitation: Empirical ideo-political and bureaucratic views. Research Triangle Institute, Research Triangle, N.C.

Commonwealth v. Struphy. 1870. 108 Massachusetts 588, 590.

Conklin, John E. 1972. *Robbery and the criminal justice system.* Philadelphia: Lippincott.

Corsini, Raymond. 1949. Criminal psychology. In *Encyclopedia of criminology,* ed. V. C. Branham and S. B. Kutash, 108–15. New York: Philosophical Library.

Cressey, Donald R. 1957. The state of criminal statistics. *National Probation and Parole Association Journal* 3:230–41.

Deming, W. E. 1950. *Some theories of sampling.* New York: Wiley.

Dentler, Robert A., and Lawrence J. Monroe. 1961. Social correlates of early adolescent theft. *American Sociological Review* 26:733–43.

Deutsch, M., and M. E. Collins. 1951. *Interracial housing: A psychological evaluation of a social experiment.* New York: Russell.

Downes, D. M. 1966. *The delinquent solution.* New York: Free Press.

Duncan, Otis Dudley. 1975. *Introduction to structural equation models.* New York: Academic Press.

Einstadter, Werner J. 1969. The social organization of armed robbery. *Social Problems* 17:64–83.

Elliott, Delbert S., and Suzanne S. Ageton. 1980. Reconciling race and class differences in self-reported and official estimates of delinquency. *American Sociological Review* 45:95–110.

Elliott, Delbert S., and Harwin L. Voss. 1974. *Delinquency and dropout.* Lexington, Mass.: Lexington Books.

Empey, LaMar T., and Maynard L. Erickson. 1965. Hidden delinquency and social status. *Social Forces* 44:546–54.

Erez, Edna. 1979. Situational analysis of crime: Comparison of planned and impulsive offenses. Ph.D. diss., University of Pennsylvania.

Erez, Edna, and Simon Hakim. 1979. A geo-economic approach to the distribution of crimes in metropolitan areas. In *Perspectives in victimology,* ed. William H. Parsonage, 29–47. Beverly Hills, Calif.: Sage.

Erickson, Maynard L. 1972. The changing relationship between official and self-reported measures of delinquency: An exploratory-predictive study. *Journal of Criminal Law, Criminology and Police Science* 63:388–95.

———. 1973. Group violations, socioeconomic status and official delinquency. *Social Forces* 52:41–52.

Erickson, Maynard L., and LaMar T. Empey. 1963. Court records, undetected delinquency and decision-making. *Journal of Criminal Law, Criminology and Police Science* 54:456–69.

———. 1965. Class position, peers and delinquency. *Sociology and Social Research* 49:268–82.

Eysenck, Hans J. 1964. *Crime and personality.* Boston: Houghton Mifflin.

Fannin, Leon F., and Marshall B. Clinard. 1965. Differences in the conception of self as a male among lower and middle class delinquents. *Social Problems* 13:205–14.

Farrington, David P. 1973. Self-reports of deviant behavior: Predictive and stable? *Journal of Criminal Law and Criminology* 64:99–110.

Figlio, Robert M. 1975. The seriousness of offenses: An evaluation by offenders and non-offenders. *Journal of Criminal Law and Criminology* 66:189–200.

———. 1976. Biology and crime. Center for Studies in Criminology and Criminal Law, University of Pennsylvania.

Fuller, Carol. 1974. Weighting to adjust for survey nonresponse. *Public Opinion Quarterly* 38:239–46.

Gehan, Edmund A. 1975. Statistical methods for survival time studies. In *Cancer therapy: Prognostic factors and criteria of response,* ed. M. J. Stoquet. New York: Raven Press.

Gibbons, Don C. 1971. Observations on the study of crime causation. *American Journal of Sociology* 77:262–78.

Glaser, Daniel. 1972. *Adult crime and social policy.* Englewood Cliffs, N.J.: Prentice-Hall.

Glueck, Sheldon, and Eleanor Glueck. 1937. *Later criminal careers.* New York: Commonwealth Fund.

———. 1940. *Juvenile delinquents grown up.* New York: Commonwealth Fund.

Gobert, James J. 1977. Victim-precipitation. *Columbia Law Review* 77:512–53.

Gold, Martin. 1966. Undetected delinquent behavior. *Journal of Research in Crime and Delinquency* 3:27–46.

Gold, Martin, and David J. Reimer. 1975. Changing patterns of delinquent behavior among Americans thirteen through sixteen years old: 1967–1972. *Crime and Delinquency Literature* 7:483–517.

Goldberger, Arthur, and Otis D. Duncan, eds. 1973. *Structural equation models in the social sciences.* New York: Seminar Press.

Goodman, Leo. 1962. Statistical methods for analyzing processes of change. *American Journal of Sociology* 68:57–78.

———. 1978. *Analyzing qualitative/categorical data.* Cambridge, Mass.: Abt Books.

Gordon, Robert A., James F. Short, Jr., Desmond S. Cartwright, and Fred L. Strodtbeck. 1963. Values and gang delinquency: A study of street-corner groups. *American Journal of Sociology* 69:109–28.

Gould, Leroy C. 1969. Who defines delinquency: A comparison of self-reported and officially-reported indices of delinquency for three racial groups. *Social Problems* 16:325–36.

Greenwood, Peter W., Joan Petersilia, and Franklin E. Zimring. 1980. *Age, crime, and sanctions: The transition from juvenile to adult court.* Santa Monica, Calif.: Rand.

Hackler, James, and Melanie Lautt. 1969. Systematic bias in measuring self-reported delinquency. *Canadian Review of Sociology and Anthropology* 6:92–106.

Hagan, John. 1974. Extra-legal attributes and criminal sentencing: An assessment of a sociological viewpoint. *Law and Society Review* 8:357–83.

Halleck, Seymour. 1971. *Psychiatry and the dilemmas of crime.* Berkeley: University of California Press.

Hansen, Morris H., W. N. Hurwitz, and W. G. Madow. 1953. *Sample survey methods and theory.* Methods and Applications, vol. 1. New York: Wiley.

Hardt, Robert H., and George E. Bodine. 1965. *Development of self-report instruments in delinquency research.* Syracuse, N.Y.: Syracuse University Youth Development Center.

Hardt, Robert H., and Sandra J. Peterson. 1968. Neighborhood status and delinquent activity as indexed by police records and a self-report survey. *Criminologica* 6:37–47.

Hardt, Robert H., and Sandra Peterson-Hardt. 1977. On determining the quality of the delinquency self-report method. *Journal of Research in Crime and Delinquency* 14:247–61.

Hare, Robert D. 1970. *Psychopathy.* New York: Wiley.

Harris, D. B. 1948. The socialization of the delinquent. *Child Development* 19:143–53.

Hartshorne, H., and M. A. May. 1928. *Studies in the nature of character.* New York: Macmillan.

Heller, Nelson B., and J. Thomas McEwen. 1973. Applications of crime seriousness information in police departments. *Journal of Criminal Justice* 1:241–53.

Himber, C. 1941. *Meet the gang.* New York: Association Press.

Hindelang, Michael J. 1970. The commitment of delinquents to their misdeeds: Do delinquents drift? *Social Problems* 17:502–9.

———. 1971. Age, sex, and the versatility of delinquent involvements. *Social Problems* 18:522–35.

———. 1972a. The relationship of self-reported delinquency to scales of the CPI and MMPI. *Journal of Criminal Law, Criminology and Police Science* 63:75–81.

———. 1972b. Situational influences on the delinquent act. National Institute of Mental Health, Rockville, Md.

———. 1976. *Criminal victimization in eight American cities.* Cambridge, Mass.: Ballinger.

———. 1978. Race and involvement in common law personal crime. *American Sociological Review* 43:93–109.

Hindelang, Michael J., Michael R. Gottfredson, and James Garofalo. 1978. *Victims of personal crime.* Cambridge, Mass.: Ballinger.

Hindelang, Michael J., Travis Hirschi, and Joseph G. Weis. 1979. Correlates of delinquency: The illusion of discrepancy between self-report and official measures. *American Sociological Review* 44:995–1014.

———. 1981. *Measuring delinquency.* Beverly Hills, Calif.: Sage.

Hindelang, Michael J., and Joseph G. Weis. 1972. Personality and self-reported delinquency. *Criminology* 10:268–94.

Hirschi, Travis. 1969. *Causes of delinquency.* Berkeley: University of California Press.

Hirschi, Travis, and Michael J. Hindelang. 1977. Intelligence and delinquency—a revisionist review. *American Sociological Review* 42:571–87.

Homans, George C. 1961. *Social behavior: Its elementary forms.* Ed. Robert K. Merton. New York: Harcourt Brace Jovanovich.

Hood, Roger, and Richard Sparks. 1970. *Key issues in criminology.* New York: McGraw-Hill.

Jensen, G. F. 1976. Race, achievement, and delinquency—a further look at *Delinquency in a birth cohort. American Journal of Sociology* 82:379–87.

Johnston, Jerome, and Jerald G. Bachman. 1970. *Young men look at military service.* Youth in Transition, vol. 5. Ann Arbor: Survey Research Center, University of Michigan.

Jöreskog, K. G. 1969. A general approach to confirmatory maximum likelihood factor analysis. *Psychometrika* 34:183–202.

———. 1973. A general method for estimating a linear structural equation system. In *Structural equation models in the social sciences,* ed. Arthur S. Goldberger and Otis D. Duncan, 85–112. New York: Seminar Press.

Kahl, Joseph A., and James A. Davis. 1955. A comparison of indexes of socio-economic status. *American Sociological Review* 20:317–25.

Kaplan, Abraham. 1964. *The conduct of inquiry.* San Francisco: Chandler.

Kipnis, David. 1971. *Character structure and impulsiveness.* New York: Academic Press.

Kish, Leslie. 1965. *Survey sampling.* New York: Wiley.

Klein, Malcolm W. 1968. Impressions of juvenile gang members. *Adolescence* 3:53–78.

———. 1969. Gang cohesiveness, delinquency and a street-work program. *Journal of Research in Crime and Delinquency* 6:135–66.

Klein, Malcolm W., Susan Labin Rosensweig, and Ronald Bates. 1975. The ambiguous juvenile arrest. *Criminology* 13:78–89.

Kulik, James A., Kenneth B. Stein, and Theodore R. Sarbin. 1968. Disclosure of delinquent behavior under conditions of anonymity and non-anonymity. *Journal of Consulting and Clinical Psychology* 32:506–9.

LaFave, Wayne R. 1962. The police and nonenforcement of the law—part II. *Wisconsin Law Review* 113:179–239.

LaFave, Wayne R., and Austin W. Scott, Jr. 1972. *Handbook on criminal law.* Saint Paul, Minn.: West.

Land, Kenneth. 1969. Principles of path analysis. In *Sociological methodology 1969,* ed. Edgar F. Borgatta and George W. Bohrnstedt, 3–37. San Francisco: Jossey-Bass.

Lawley, D. N., and A. E. Maxwell. 1963. *Factor analysis as a statistical method.* London: Butterworths.

Lee, Elisa. 1980. *Statistical methods for survival data analysis.* Belmont, Calif.: Wadsworth.

Lemert, Edwin M. 1967. *Human deviance, social problems, and social control.* Englewood Cliffs, N.J.: Prentice-Hall.

Lewin, Kurt. 1951. *Field theory in social science.* Ed. Dorwin Cartwright. New York: Harper.

Lindesmith, Alfred R., and H. Warren Dunham. 1941. Some principles of criminal typology. *Social Forces* 19:307–14.

Lipton, Douglas, Robert Martinson, and Judith Wilks. 1975. *The effectiveness of correctional treatment: A survey of treatment evaluation studies.* New York: Praeger.

Lord, Frederic, and Melvin R. Novick. 1968. *Statistical theories of mental test scores.* Reading, Mass.: Addison-Wesley.

Luckenbill, David F. 1977. Criminal homicide as a situated transaction. *Social Problems* 25:176–86.

Lundman, Richard J., Richard Sykes, and John P. Clark. 1978. Police control of juveniles: A replication. *Journal of Research in Crime and Delinquency* 15:74–91.

McClintock, F. H. 1970. The dark figure. In *Collected studies in criminological research,* vol. 5. Report presented to the 6th European Conference of Directors of Criminological Research Institutes, 9–34. Strasbourg: Council of Europe.

McCord, William, and Joan McCord. 1959. *Origins of crime.* New York: Columbia University Press.

———. 1964. *The psychopath.* Princeton, N.J.: Van Nostrand.

McPheters, L. R., and W. E. Stronge, eds. 1976. *The economics of crime and law enforcement.* Springfield, Ill.: C. C. Thomas.

Magnusson, David F. 1967. *Test theory.* Reading, Mass.: Addison-Wesley.

Mandell, Lewis. 1974. When to weight: Determining nonresponse bias in survey data. *Public Opinion Quarterly* 38:247–52.

Mandell, Wallace, and Sili Amzel. 1975. Status of addicts treated under the NAPA program. Department of Mental Hygiene, School of Hygiene and Public Health, Johns Hopkins University.

Martinson, Robert. 1974. What works?—Questions and answers about prison reform. *Public Interest* 36:22–54.

Matza, David. 1964. *Delinquency and drift.* New York: Wiley.

Mayhew, Pat, R. V. G. Clarke, A. Sturman, and J. M. Hough. 1975. *Crime as opportunity.* Home Office Research Study no. 34. London: Her Majesty's Stationery Office.

Mednick, Sarnoff A., and Jan Volavka. 1980. Biology and crime. In *Crime and justice: An annual review of research,* vol. 2, ed. Norval Morris and Michael Tonry, 85–158. Chicago: University of Chicago Press.

Merton, Robert K. 1957. *Social theory and social structure.* Rev. ed. New York: Free Press.

Miller, Arthur. 1962. The bored and the violent. *Harper's Magazine* 225 (November):50–56.

Miller, George A., Eugene Galanter, and Karl H. Pribham. 1960. *Plans and the structure of behavior.* New York: Holt.

Miller, Walter B. 1958. Lower class culture as a generating milieu of gang delinquency. *Journal of Social Issues* 14:5–19.

———. 1966. Violent crimes in city gangs. *Annals* 364:96–112.

Mischel, W. 1968. *Personality and behavior.* New York: Wiley.

———. 1971. *Personality assessment.* New York: Holt, Rinehart and Winston.

Monahan, John. 1975. The prediction of deviance. In *Violence and criminal justice,* ed. Duncan Chappell and John Monahan, 15–31. Lexington, Mass.: Lexington Books.

Morris, Norval. 1974. *The future of imprisonment.* Chicago: University of Chicago Press.

Mukherjee, Satyanshu Kumar. 1971. A typological study of school status and delinquency. Ph.D. diss., University of Pennsylvania.

Murphy, Fred J., Mary M. Shirley, and Helen L. Witmer. 1946. The incidence of hidden delinquency. *American Journal of Orthopsychiatry* 16:866–96.

Nunnally, J. C. 1967. *Psychometric theory.* New York: McGraw-Hill.

Nye, F. Ivan. 1958. *Family relationships and delinquent behavior.* New York: Wiley.

Nye, F. Ivan, and James F. Short, Jr. 1957. Scaling delinquent behavior. *American Sociological Review* 22:326–31.

Nye, F. Ivan, James F. Short, Jr., and Virgil J. Olson. 1958. Socioeconomic status and delinquent behavior. *American Journal of Sociology* 63:381–89.

Packer, Herbert. 1962. Mens rea and the Supreme Court. *South Carolina Law Review* 1962:137.

———. 1964. Two models of the criminal process. *University of Pennsylvania Law Review* 113:1–68.

Parsons, Talcott. 1947. Certain primary sources and patterns of aggression in the social structure of the Western world. *Psychiatry* 10:167–81.

Perkins, Rollin M. 1969. *Criminal law.* 2d ed. Mineola, N.Y.: Foundation Press.

References

Petersilia, Joan. 1977. The validity of criminality data derived from personal interviews. Santa Monica, Calif.: Rand.

Petersilia, Joan, Peter Greenwood, and Marvin Lavin. 1978. *Criminal careers of habitual felons.* Washington, D.C.: U.S. Government Printing Office.

Peterson, Mark, Harriet Braiker, and Suzanne Polich. 1980. *Doing crime: A survey of California prison inmates.* Santa Monica, Calif.: Rand.

―――. 1981. *Who commits crimes: A survey of prison inmates.* Cambridge, Mass.: Oelgeschlager, Gunn and Hain.

Piliavin, Irving, and Scott Briar. 1964. Police encounters with juveniles. *American Journal of Sociology* 70:206–14.

Pittman, D., and C. Gordon. 1958. Criminal careers of the chronic police case inebriate. *Quarterly Journal of Studies on Alcohol* 19:255–68.

Pope, Carl E. 1975. Dimensions of burglary: An empirical examination of offense and offender characteristics. Ph.D. diss., State University of New York at Albany.

―――. 1976. The influence of social and legal factors on sentence dispositions: A preliminary analysis of offender-based transaction statistics. *Journal of Criminal Justice* 4:203–21.

Porterfield, Austin L. 1943. Delinquency and its outcome in court and college. *American Journal of Sociology* 49:199–208.

Radzinowicz, Leon, and Joan King. 1977. The growth of crime: An international perspective. In *Crime and justice,* vol. 1, ed. Leon Radzinowicz and Marvin E. Wolfgang, 3–24. 2d rev. ed. New York: Basic Books.

Reiss, Albert J., Jr. 1973. Surveys of self-reported delicts. Paper presented to the Symposium on Studies of Public Experience, Knowledge, and Opinion of Crime and Justice, Washington, D.C.

Reiss, Albert J., Jr., Otis D. Duncan, P. K. Hatt, and C. C. North. 1961. *Occupations and social status.* New York: Free Press.

Reiss, Albert J., Jr., and Albert L. Rhodes. 1961. The distribution of juvenile delinquency in the social class structure. *American Sociological Review* 26:720–32.

―――. 1963. Status deprivation and delinquent behavior. *Sociological Quarterly* 4:135–49.

Reppetto, Thomas A. 1976. Crime prevention and the displacement phenomenon. *Crime and Delinquency* 22:166–77.

Rheinstein, Max, ed. 1954. *Max Weber on law in economy and society.* Cambridge: Harvard University Press.

Riedel, Marc. 1975. Perceived circumstances, inferences of intent and judgments of offense seriousness. *Journal of Criminal Law and Criminology* 66:201–8.

Robin, Gerald D. 1964. Gang member delinquency: Its extent, sequence, and typology. *Journal of Criminal Law, Criminology, and Police Science* 55:59–69.

Robison, Sophia M. 1936. *Can delinquency be measured?* New York: Columbia University Press.

―――. 1966. A critical review of the Uniform Crime Reports. *Michigan Law Review* 64:1031–54.

Robison, Sophia M., N. Cohen, and M. Sachs. 1946. Autonomous groups, an unsolved problem in group loyalties and conflicts. *Journal of Educational Sociology* 20:154–62.

Roth, Jeffrey A. 1978. Prosecutor perceptions of crime seriousness. *Journal of Criminal Law and Criminology* 69:232–42.

Savitz, Leonard D., Michael Lalli, and L. Rosen. 1977. City life and delinquency: Victimization, fear of crime, and gang membership. Temple University, Department of Criminal Justice.

Schafer, Stephen. 1968. *The victim and his criminal.* New York: Random House.

Schrag, Clarence. 1962. Delinquency and opportunity: Analysis of a theory. *Sociology and Social Research* 46:167–75.

Schulhofer, Stephen J. 1974. Harm and punishment: A critique of emphasis on the results of conduct in the criminal law. *University of Pennsylvania Law Review* 122: 1497–1607.

Schwartz, Edward E. 1945. A community experiment in the measurement of juvenile delinquency. In *NPPA yearbook, 1945,* 157–81. New York: National Probation and Parole Association.

Scott, John Finley. 1959. Two dimensions of delinquent behavior. *American Sociological Review* 24:240–43.

Sebba, Leslie. 1980. Is mens rea a component of perceived offense seriousness? *Journal of Criminal Law and Criminology* 71:124–35.

Sechrest, Lee, Susan O. White, and Elizabeth Brown, eds. 1979. *The rehabilitation of criminal offenders: Problems and prospects.* Washington, D.C.: National Academy of Sciences.

Sellin, Thorsten. 1931. The basis of a crime index. *Journal of Criminal Law and Criminology* 22:335–56.

Sellin, Thorsten, and Marvin E. Wolfgang. 1978. *The measurement of delinquency.* Montclair, N.J.: Patterson Smith. Originally published 1964.

Shah, Saleem, and Loren H. Roth. 1974. Biological and psychophysiological factors in criminology. In *Handbook of criminology,* ed. Daniel Glaser, 101–73. Chicago: Rand-McNally.

Shannon, Lyle. 1977. Predicting adult criminal careers from juvenile careers: Progress report. Iowa Urban Community Research Center, Iowa City.

———. 1979. Changing trends in the relationships of juvenile delinquency to adult crime. Paper presented to the annual meeting of the Pacific Sociological Association, Anaheim, Calif., 4–7 April.

Shapiro, David. 1965. *Neurotic styles.* New York: Basic Books.

Shaw, Clifford R., and Henry D. McKay. 1942. *Juvenile delinquency and urban areas.* Chicago: University of Chicago Press.

Shinnar, Shlomo, and Reuel Shinnar. 1975. The effects of the criminal justice system on the control of crime: A quantitative approach. *Law and Society Review* 9: 581–611.

Short, James F., Jr., and F. Ivan Nye. 1958a. Extent of unrecorded juvenile delinquency. *Journal of Criminal Law, Criminology and Police Science* 49:296–302.

———. 1958b. Reported behavior as a criterion of deviant behavior. *Social Problems* 5:207–13.

Short, James F., Jr., Ramon Rivera, and H. Marshall. 1964. Adult-adolescent relations and gang delinquency. *Pacific Sociological Review* 7:59–65.

Short, James F., Jr., Ramon Rivera, and Ray A. Tennyson. 1965. Perceived opportunities, gang membership, and delinquency. *American Sociological Review* 30:56–67.

Short, James F., Jr., and Fred L. Strodtbeck. 1963. The response of gang leaders to status threats: An observation on group process and delinquent behavior. *American Journal of Sociology* 68:571–79.

References

————. 1965. *Group process and gang delinquency.* Chicago: University of Chicago Press.

Short, James F., Jr., Ray A. Tennyson, and Kenneth I. Howard. 1963. Behavior dimensions of gang delinquency. *American Sociological Review* 28:411–28.

Shover, Neal. 1973. The social organization of burglary. *Social Problems* 20:499–514.

Singer, Simon I. 1977. The effect of non-response on the birth cohort follow-up survey. Center for Studies in Criminology and Criminal Law, University of Pennsylvania.

Slocum, Walter L., and Carol L. Stone. 1963. Family culture patterns and delinquent-type behavior. *Journal of Marriage and Family Living* 25:202–8.

Smith, Anderson D. 1975. Aging and interference with memory. *Journal of Gerontology* 30:319–25.

Sonquist, J. A. 1970. *Multivariate model building.* Ann Arbor: Survey Research Center, University of Michigan.

Spaulding, C. B. 1948. Cliques, gangs, and networks. *Sociology and Social Research* 32:928–37.

Spergel, Irving A. 1961. An exploratory research in delinquent subcultures. *Social Service Review* 35:33–47.

Strodtbeck, Fred L., and James F. Short, Jr. 1964. Aleatory risks versus short-run hedonism in explanation of gang action. *Social Problems* 12:127–40.

Strodtbeck, Fred L., James F. Short, Jr., and E. Kolegar. 1962. The analysis of self-descriptions by members of delinquent gangs. *Sociological Quarterly* 3:331–56.

Sudman, Seymour, and Norman M. Bradburn. 1974. *Response effects in surveys.* Chicago: Aldine.

Sutherland, Edwin H., and Donald R. Cressey. 1974. *Criminology.* 9th ed. Philadelphia: Lippincott.

Sykes, Gresham M. 1972. The future of criminality. *American Behavioral Scientist* 15:402–19.

Terry, Robert M. 1967a. Discrimination in the handling of juvenile offenders by social-control agencies. *Journal of Research in Crime and Delinquency* 4:218–30.

————. 1967b. The screening of juvenile offenders. *Journal of Criminal Law, Criminology and Police Science* 58:173–81.

Thornberry, Terence P. 1973. Race, socioeconomic status, and sentencing in the juvenile justice system. *Journal of Criminal Law and Criminology* 64:90–98.

————. 1979. Sentencing disparities in the juvenile justice system. *Journal of Criminal Law and Criminology* 70:164–71.

Thornberry, Terence P., and Margaret Farnworth. 1982. Social correlates of criminal involvement: Further evidence on the relationship between social status and criminal behavior. *American Sociological Review* 47:505–18.

Thornberry, Terence P., and Robert M. Figlio. 1974. Victimization and criminal behavior in a birth cohort. In *Images of crime: Offenders and victims,* ed. Terence P. Thornberry and Edward Sagarin, 102–12. New York: Praeger.

Thrasher, Frederic M. 1927. *The gang: A study of 1,313 gangs in Chicago.* Chicago: University of Chicago Press.

Tittle, Charles R., Wayne J. Villemez, and Douglas A. Smith. 1978. The myth of social class and criminality: An empirical assessment of the empirical evidence. *American Sociological Review* 43:643–56.

Tracy, Paul E., Jr. 1978. An analysis of the incidence and seriousness of self-reported delinquency and crime. Ph.D. diss., University of Pennsylvania.

Tuma, Nancy Brandon, and Michael T. Hannan. 1978. Approaches in the censoring problem in analysis of event histories. In *Sociological methodology 1979,* ed. Karl Schuessler, 209–40. San Francisco: Jossey-Bass.

Turner, Stanley. 1969. Delinquency and distance. In *Delinquency: Selected studies,* ed. Thorsten Sellin and Marvin E. Wolfgang, 11–26. New York: Wiley.

———. 1978. Introduction to *The measurement of delinquency,* by Thorsten Sellin and Marvin E. Wolfgang, v–xxi. Montclair, N.J.: Patterson Smith.

U.S. Bureau of the Census. 1970a. *Household surveys of crime, second pretest (Baltimore, Maryland).* Washington, D.C.: U.S. Government Printing Office.

———. 1970b. *Victim recall pretest (Washington, D.C.).* Washington, D.C.: U.S. Government Printing Office.

U.S. Department of Justice. Federal Bureau of Investigation. 1983. *Crime in the United States, 1982.* Washington, D.C.: U.S. Government Printing Office.

U.S. Department of Justice. Law Enforcement Assistance Administration. 1972. *The San Jose methods test of known crime victims.* Washington, D.C.: U.S. Government Printing Office.

U.S. National Commission on the Causes and Prevention of Violence. 1967. *Crimes of violence,* vols. 11–13. Washington, D.C.: U.S. Government Printing Office.

van den Haag, Ernest. 1975. *Punishing criminals.* New York: Basic Books.

Vaz, Edmund W. 1966. Self-reported juvenile delinquency and socio-economic status. *Canadian Journal of Corrections* 8:20–27.

von Hirsch, Andrew. 1976. *Doing justice: The choice of punishments.* New York: Hill and Wang.

Voss, Harwin L. 1966. Socio-economic status and reported delinquent behavior. *Social Forces* 13:314–24.

Walberg, Herbert J. 1972. Urban schooling and delinquency: Toward an integrative theory. *American Educational Research Journal* 9:285–300.

Wallerstein, James A., and Clement J. Wyle. 1947. Our law-abiding law-breakers. *Probation* 25:107–18.

Williams, Jay R., and Martin Gold. 1972. From delinquent behavior to official delinquency. *Social Problems* 20:209–29.

Winslow, Robert H. 1967. Anomie and its alternatives: A self-report study of delinquency. *Sociological Quarterly* 8:468–80.

Wolfgang, Marvin E. 1975. *Patterns in criminal homicide.* Montclair, N.J.: Patterson Smith. Originally published 1958.

———. 1963. Uniform Crime Reports: A critical appraisal. *University of Pennsylvania Law Review* 3:708–38.

———. 1967. International criminal statistics: A proposal. *Journal of Criminal Law, Criminology and Police Science* 58:65–69.

Wolfgang, Marvin E., and Franco Ferracuti. 1982. *The subculture of violence.* Beverly Hills, Calif.: Sage. Originally published 1967.

Wolfgang, Marvin E., Robert M. Figlio, and Thorsten Sellin. 1972. *Delinquency in a birth cohort.* Chicago: University of Chicago Press.

Wolfgang, Marvin E., and Simon I. Singer. 1978. Victim categories of crime. *Journal of Criminal Law and Criminology* 69:379–94.

Work, Charles. 1974. Proposed career criminal impact program of the United States Department of Justice. Memorandum to the Honorable William B. Saxbe, Attorney General, U.S. Department of Justice.

References

Wright, Sewall. 1934. The method of path coefficients. *Annals of Mathematical Statistics* 5:161–215.

Wyner, Gordon E. 1976. Sources of response error in self-reports of behavior. Ph.D. diss., University of Pennsylvania.

Yablonsky, Lewis. 1959. The delinquent gang as a near-group. *Social Problems* 7: 108–17.

———. 1970. *The violent gang*. Rev. ed. Baltimore: Penguin.

Zimring, Franklin E., and Gordon J. Hawkins. 1973. *Deterrence: The legal threat in crime control*. Chicago: University of Chicago Press.

Index

Index

Index